A LIFE WORTHY OF THE GOSPEL

A Life Worthy of the Gospel

Studies in the Macedonian Epistles

Edited by Jason S. Longstreth

Florida College Annual Lectures
February 2023

FLORIDA COLLEGE
PRESS

Contents

Foreword

Given their prominence in the Macedonian Epistles, it is appropriate to offer both greetings and thanks in a forward to a lecture book on Philippians, 1 & 2 Thessalonians. I'm thankful for the work of the authors and editors who made possible this book, and may God bless you, dear reader, to progress in Christian faith through the truth and insights contained herein.

The Macedonian Epistles are, like all of God's Scriptures, both sublimely beautiful and profoundly practical for both individual Christians and the communal life of the church. These divinely inspired writings illustrate and encourage "a manner of life worthy of the gospel." I'm hopeful that the lectureship's focus on this Pauline theme in Philippians 1.27 will unite us in a striving to share the gospel and to live with the Christlike purity and humility to which God calls his people.

Much of these ancient letters to Macedonian churches has a dual focus: both future cosmic events of divine judgment and the smaller-scale human lifestyles of Christians in Paul's day—and in ours, by application. I pray that the insights and instructions of this FC lecture book will impact your lives in ways both profound and precise, in your worldview and your daily disciplines. May the Lord's grace and peace be with you all and may all this book be to God's glory.

Dr. John B. Weaver
President
Florida College

Preface

Beginning in the second verse of Paul's first letter to the Thessalonians, he wrote, "We give thanks to God always for all of you, making mention of you in our prayers; constantly bearing in mind your work of faith and labor of love and steadfastness of hope in our Lord Jesus Christ in the presence of our God and Father, knowing, brethren beloved by God, His choice of you;" (1 Thess 1.2–4). In many ways, this sets the tone for the entire epistle. Paul went on to say that the Thessalonians had imitated the Lord and became examples to all the believers in Macedonia and Achaia. In like fashion, Paul praised the Philippians for their participation in the gospel and the way in which they were partakers of grace with him. Nevertheless, the Thessalonians were encouraged to excel still more, and Paul prayed for the Philippians that their "love may abound still more and more in real knowledge and all discernment" (Phil 1.9). They were doing well, but they could do more. In fact, all three of Paul's letters to the Macedonian churches (1 & 2 Thessalonians and Philippians) contain exhortations for the Christians to live their lives in such a way that they would demonstrate the worthiness of the gospel. This should also be the goal for each one of us.

The 2023 Florida College Lectureship is focused on *A Life Worthy of the Gospel* and is based on studies in the Macedonian epistles. Our evening lectures are designed to help us examine the priority, distinctiveness, and fullness of the gospel. The day lectures explore various aspects of these themes. On Tuesday, we will focus on the gospel by considering the topics of our thoughts, preaching, prayers, and daily life. On Wednesday, our fellowship in the gospel will be explored through the lens of humility, unity, relationships, and correction. On Thursday, our attention will turn to joy, contentment, comfort, and hope as we turn our attention to the fruit of the gospel. I know each of these lectures will challenge you to be even more devoted to a life of service, in keeping with the gospel call.

This year has been filled with many changes at Florida College, including the movement of several members of the Biblical Studies Department into new roles at the college. You are all aware that John Weaver moved from his position as Academic Dean to the President of Florida College. As a result, Tom Hamilton was moved from his position as the Chair of the Biblical Studies Department to the Provost and Academic Dean of the college. Therefore, I have found myself fulfilling a new role as the Chair of the Biblical Studies Department. Thankfully, I am blessed with a department filled with godly men who are extremely talented and are devoted to their task of studying and teaching God's Word. They have already proven to be invaluable in the planning and production of this year's lectureship. I want to thank my colleagues in the Biblical Studies Department: Will Dilbeck, Tom Hamilton, Ray Madrigal, David McClister, Doy Moyer, Jared Saltz, Shane Scott, Nathan Ward, and John Weaver. I am honored to serve as their Chair.

I am also thrilled that we can continue the tradition of the Florida College Lectures. For many years, these lectures have been provided as a way to encourage and strengthen our students, alumni, and friends. We are so thankful for so many of you who have supported us in our mission to educate young people by firmly grounding them in God's Word as they learn more about God's world. We could not continue in this mission were it not for the sacrifices of time, money, and effort that have been given over the years. This lectureship is just one token of our appreciation. Thank you.

I also want to thank the men who have volunteered their time and effort in preparing and presenting these lectures. Often, these men do not regularly produce manuscripts such as the ones they were requested to provide for this lectureship. However, they have done an excellent job. I know you will appreciate what they have produced. I also want to thank those individuals who have been involved in a special way in publishing this lecture book. The work of editing the manuscripts can be a tedious and time-consuming task. This year, three of our English majors agreed to help us in this effort. I am so thankful for the contributions of Gracie Sanchez, Rachel Wellington, and Audra Witherington in editing the lecture book. In addition, Nathan Ward has also once again provided his services in preparing this volume for publishing and Carrie Black, the Manager of the Florida College Bookstore, oversaw the publication of the work.

As a result of this lecture program, I pray that each one of us will be reminded of how much the Lord has done for us and that we will be motivated to live a life worthy of the Gospel of Jesus Christ.

Jason S. Longstreth
Chair, Department of Biblical Studies
Florida College

Part One

The Evening Lectures

Only Live Worthy of the Gospel
The Priority of the Gospel

Todd Chandler

This past September the world watched the funeral for Queen Elizabeth II. There was great pomp and ritual, and if you observed even a little you likely heard explanations of why the proceedings were appropriate for the context. The locations, music, the royal family wardrobes, and the guest list all reflected the majesty of Her Highness. The meaning of British royalty defined what was proper for anyone and anything connected to the ceremony. One's behavior, attire, and company had to be congruent with the reverence inherent in the one honored in the ceremony. To fall short of that honor would have been impertinence, impudence or even malice. It would have revealed a person to be openly opposed to the royal family or ignorant of who they were dealing with. To hit the mark right meant you gave what was worthy.

This lectureship focuses on the Macedonian epistles, Philippians and 1 and 2 Thessalonians. Acts 16 records Paul's Macedonian call and how Paul, Silas, Timothy, and Luke crossed the Aegean Sea and established the church at Philippi and then Thessalonica. The gospel met fierce opposition in both cities—Paul and Silas were arrested and beaten in Philippi, and both made a night get-away from Thessalonica due to mob violence. However, the churches they left behind survived and continued to grow. Though written at least a few years apart—1 and 2 Thessalonians around the early 50s and Philippians in the mid 50s to early 60s—the Macedonian letters share some common themes.[1] This study focuses on a theme that appears in all three letters—living worthy of the gospel. It requires that we take careful stock of what we understand the gospel to be, to consider its core substance and weight, and allow that to define what is proper for day to day living. This lesson takes a high altitude look at that theme and the primacy it holds in Paul's instruction to saints. This series will help us all hit the mark and live worthy.

Let Your Conduct Be Worthy

Philippians 1.27 begins with an interesting phrase, "Only let your conduct be worthy of the gospel of Christ." Without getting technical (I do not teach Greek) we will gain helpful insight with a look at Paul's word choice here. We think of conduct as general behavior, but this term is more precise, and it matters that Paul uses it with the Philippians. It is a word specific to behavior that fits citizens of someplace.[2] That is relevant because Philippi was a Roman colony, so the Philippians were Roman citizens. Rome gave privileges to its citizens and had expectations of certain behaviors from them, because they were Romans. There was a way Romans did things, and all citizens did them that way. We see the importance of citizenship to the people of Philippi in their complaints to city leaders about Paul; "and they teach customs which are not lawful for us, being Romans, to receive or observe" (Acts 16: 21).[3] They were proud of their status as Roman citizens. In choosing this word, Paul calls Saints to know who they are as citizens of Jesus' kingdom and

---

[1] L. Morris, *1 & 2 Thessalonians*. The Tyndale New Testament Commentaries 13. (Grand Rapids: William B. Eerdman's Publishing Company, 1984) 21; R. Martin, *Philippians*. The Tyndale New Testament Commentaries 11. (Grand Rapids: William B. Eerdman's Publishing Company, 1987) 37.

[2] R. Martin, *Philippians*. The Tyndale New Testament Commentaries 11. (Grand Rapids: William B. Eerdman's Publishing Company, 1987) 86.

[3] All Bible quotes are from the New King James Version.

to consider the practical applications for a citizen. There is a way citizens of Christ's kingdom walk, a distinct gait to their steps, and all citizens are to walk that way (cf. Phil 3.20; Eph. 2.19–22; 4.1ff; Col 3.1–3; 1 Pet 2.10–12).

It is important to note that Paul applies the word to a specific standard when he writes, "be worthy of the gospel of Christ." Let us establish up front that Paul is not teaching that Saints must live so well as to earn their worth. The gospel is clear that no amount of obedience, nobility, and courage today can atone for yesterday's rebellion, shame, and timidity. Only God's grace does that, and nobody can be worthy of grace. He does not in this verse contradict what he says of himself in Philippians 3.9, "and be found in him, not having my own righteousness, which is from the law, but that which is through faith in Christ, the righteousness which is from God by faith." Paul's consistent message across his writings is that our faith moves us to yield to the reign of Jesus, and such faith—which leads us to be obedient, noble, and courageous—is accounted to us for righteousness (Rom 4.5).

"Worthy" is a translation of *axios*, which means suitably, in a manner worthy of something, or of the weight of another thing.[4] Picture an ancient merchant in the Philippi market standing next to a balance scale. There are two items on the scale, one on each side, and their weight is exactly balanced. In this passage, the gospel with all its substance or weight is on one side of the scale and my life is on the other. The two should be balanced. That is, the substance of my life should reflect that of the gospel. We see an example of this image, and a use of the same word, in Romans 16.2 when Paul spoke about Phoebe and instructed, "that you may receive her in a manner worthy of the saints, and assist her in whatever business she has need of you." Their treatment of Phoebe was to be congruent with how

---

[4]Vine, W. "Worthy, Worthily—Vine's Expository Dictionary of New Testament Words." Blue Letter Bible. Last Modified 24 Jun, 1996. https://www.blueletterbible.org/search/dictionary/viewtopic.cfm.

saints treat saints, knowing what it means to be a saint. Paul implies that there is a knowable, understandable standard of behavior that Christians are to learn, and such understanding begins with a proper appreciation of the core substance of what a saint is. John uses the same word when he writes, "Beloved, you do faithfully whatever you do for the brethren and for strangers, who have borne witness of your love before the church. If you send them forward on their journey in a manner worthy of God, you will do well" (3 John 5–6). Treatment of others was measured by who God is, because they are *God's*. It is clear that John is not talking about people earning their worth, but rather the expectation that his readers should have a proper understanding of who God is and let that guide their behavior. Other versions of this word and its core idea are scattered in Paul's other letters. For example, "I, therefore, the prisoner of the Lord, beseech you to walk worthy of the calling with which you were called" (Eph 4.1), and also, "that you may walk worthy of the Lord, fully pleasing him, being fruitful in every good work and increasing in the knowledge of God" (Col 1.10).

Paul uses the same word in 1 Thessalonians. He speaks first of their reputation and example and then describes his own conduct. Largely using himself as an example, the same way he used Timothy and Epaphroditus in Philippians chapter 2 to illustrate the same point, he gives the charge, "that you would walk worthy of God who calls you into his own Kingdom and glory" (1 Thes 2.12). In 2 Thessalonians he says the same idea with words that share etymology with *axios*: "that you may be counted worthy of the kingdom of God," and later, "therefore we also pray always for you that our God would count you worthy of this calling" (2 Thes 1.5, 11). There are dozens of applications to draw from that charge, but the point here is to make clear the meaning of Paul's instruction to "walk worthy of the gospel"—the substance of the life of a Christian is to equal the weight and substance of the gospel.

The Gospel

The natural next step is to consider the substance of the gospel, and though an exhaustive study requires more space than we have here, we get a sufficient idea from a review of the Macedonian epistles. Just what is the weight of the gospel? It is, in a word, Jesus. As Paul preached in Philippi, a demonic girl correctly identified the core of the message when she declared, "These men are the servants of the Most High God, who proclaim the way of salvation" (Acts 16.17). In Thessalonica, Paul, "…reasoned with them from the scriptures, explaining and demonstrating that the Christ had to suffer and rise again from the dead, and saying, 'This Jesus whom I preach to you is the Christ'" (Acts 17.2b-3). Paul wrote that the gospel made both his life and death meaningful; "Christ will be magnified in my body whether by life or by death" (Phil 1.20). In Philippians 2 Paul gives a golden picture of the gospel as he describes the heart of Jesus and what He did for us because of it: Jesus is God who chose to became an obedient slave with the aim to be executed by His own creation; God exalted Him with a name above all names and to a place in which all will bow to Him and declare His exaltation as the Lord (Phil 2.5–11).

The gospel is the message of the victory of Jesus and the reconciliation of all things to God, things in heaven and things on earth, through the blood of His cross (Col 1.20). When I hear the gospel, I see Jesus, my sin and the death I have because of it, and I see the salvation He gives to me—and all of that displays the overwhelming glory of God (Phil 2.11). There is weight to that message that needs to lift my spirit in comfort and consolation and impress on me the magnitude of the gospel.

We see more about the gospel as we read that it is the word of life (Phil 2.16) and shows us the righteousness that comes through faith in Christ rather than through law-keeping (Phil 3.9). That message is necessary if I am to have any hope at all, for it tells me my redemption depends on His goodness, not my own. When I learn that message, surely I will value the significance of the gospel above all else—for what else matters if it is not true—and see it as the incredible expression of God's nature and love, a love that makes redemption reachable even for me. It is reachable because it is through the gospel that I come to know Jesus and the power of His resurrection and learn that I, too, can attain to the resurrection of the dead (Phil 3.10–11). Do not quickly pass by and miss that point—the gospel is about knowing *Jesus*, not simply knowing about Him; "… that I may know Him…." The gospel reveals a person, not merely an account. Further, it teaches me of my citizenship in heaven, to anticipate the transformation of my lowly body to be conformed to His glorious body, and to obtain the peace that passes understanding (Phil 3.20, 21; 4.7).

In the Thessalonian epistles we are blessed with knowledge of what to expect when Jesus returns. For example, we know the destiny of the dead in Christ, that God will bring with Jesus those who sleep in Him (1 Thes 4.14). The gospel dresses us with faith, love and salvation and gives us comfort, knowing that God did not appoint us to wrath but to salvation (1 Thes 5.8–9). The aim of the gospel is, "the obtaining of the glory of our Lord Jesus Christ" (2 Thes 2.14)—not an appeal to an appetite for personal glory, but to a desire to lose my life so Jesus, who is my life (Col. 3.4), is glorified through my walk. I obtain the glory of Jesus in my life because I no longer live, but Christ lives in me.

Does that brief review leave you wanting to express something, needing to pray thanksgiving and awe? Even a glimpse of the gospel can be overwhelming because it shows us Jesus—the width, length, depth, and height of His person and nature—and He is magnificent. About twenty years ago I was in Colombia with my dad meeting with brethren. One day at a picnic a 14 or 15-year-old boy asked me, "What do you think of Jesus Christ?" I never had been asked that question and as I considered how to reply the boy offered his own answer. "He is beautiful, yes?" I was mulling some sort of historical or informative response, but that boy hit squarely the substance of the gospel. The weight of the gospel which my life is to meet is the truth that Jesus is beautiful. He is the Son of God, declared to be so by His resurrection (Rom 1.4), and He is the Savior. Certainly, we can understand why Paul exclaimed:

> Oh, the depth of the riches both of the wisdom and knowledge of God! How unsearchable are His judgments and His ways past finding out! 'For who has known the mind of the LORD? Or who has become His counselor?' 'Or who has first given to Him And it shall be repaid to him?' For of Him and through Him and to Him are all things, to whom be glory forever. Amen. (Rom 11.33–36)

The weight of the gospel is also enhanced by its nature of being true. We cannot overvalue what it means to know truth. Paul exhorted, "therefore, whatever things are true... think on these things." (Phil 4.8). Satan is the ruler of this world (John 12.31; 14.30) and as the father of lies (John 8.44) the world is his massive megaphone of falsehood. In the cacophony of deceit, we desperately need truth. There is no value in a peace or contentment that comes from ignorance of my spiritual condition, nor in following a message that tells me I am free while I am shackled to a treachery that tells me I am someone different than God made me in body or spirit. Only loss is to be had in the arguments and high things that act to build up strongholds in my mind which are against the knowledge of Christ (2 Cor. 10.5–6).

The gospel is truth, so my life is to be congruent with truth. The Thessalonians modeled this in their reception of the gospel; "when you received the word of God which you heard from us you welcomed it not as the word of men, but as it is in truth, the word of God, which also effectively works in you who believe" (1 Thes 2.13). When truth works effectively in a hearer, that person's life is worthy of truth. John illustrates the opposite when he writes, "He who says, 'I know Him', and does not keep His commandments is a liar, and the truth is not in him... He who says he is in the light, and hates his brother, is in darkness until now" (1 John 2.4, 9). We see both the worthy and unworthy life when John states, "They are of the world. Therefore they speak as of the world, and the world hears them. We are of God. He who knows God hears us, he who is not of God does not hear us. By this we know the spirit of truth and the spirit of error" (1 John 4.5).

Living truthfully is not abstract but practical and is measured by concrete actions. Paul gives another example of this principle when he contrasts two groups of teachers in Philippians 1.15–18. Some preached the truth falsely—they spoke truth about Jesus but with a devious, disingenuous motive—so their lives were unworthy of the gospel they taught. Their actions were discordant with the gospel they preached. In contrast, other teachers were true both in the information they taught and their motives for teaching.

This charge, to live worthy of the gospel, is a tall order, but not one from which we can turn. God gives us the responsibility because He gives us the ability to meet it. Inherent in the exhortation is the need for me to look at it square in eye and see it clearly, and that is an additional element of what Paul calls us to do.

Only

The introductory phrase to Philippians 1.27 is vital to living worthy of the gospel. Paul prefaces the charge with a key word, "Only." Where the New King James translates the Greek with a single word, Barclay uses eight, "One thing you must see to whatever happens."[5] It is a single word which communicates something similar to those statements we hear from preachers sometimes, "If you don't get anything else, get this." Paul gives a singularity of focus to the charge to walk worthy of the gospel; it is priority. This is not simply a technicality of a word study to note quickly and then move along to other

---

[5] W. Barclay, *The Letters to the Philippians, Colossians, and Thessalonians.* The Daily Study Bible Series Revised Edition. (Louisville, KY: The Westminster Press, 1975) 29.

more worthwhile passages. The charge to walk worthy is priority for a reason and it is wise to consider it.

In the Philippian letter Paul regularly emphasizes a singularity of focus and it is always about Jesus. In Philippians 1.12–16 he interprets his entire prison experience by its relation to the gospel: the progress of the gospel because of his imprisonment (v.12), the reason he was in prison (v.13b), the effects on the courage of others (v.14), and how it revealed the real motives of others who preach (v.15–16). In 2.16 He measures the long-term value of his work by the Philippian's fidelity to the word of life.[6] Chapter 3 includes an extensive expression of the priority the gospel had in Paul's own life, and he summarizes it in a rich statement of unqualified commitment:

> But what things were gain to me, these I have counted loss for Christ. Yet indeed I also count all things loss for the excellence of the knowledge of Christ Jesus my Lord, for whom I have suffered the loss of all things, and count them as rubbish, that I may gain Christ and be found in Him, not having my own righteousness, which is from the law, but that which is through faith in Christ, the righteousness which is from God by faith; that I may know Him and the power of His resurrection, and the fellowship of His sufferings, being conformed to His death, if, by any means, I may attain to the resurrection from the dead. (Phil 3.7–11)

What a remarkable declaration! Perhaps you share my wonder at the work Paul did for the gospel, work which was unique even among apostles (1 Cor 15.10). His ability to endure betrayal by brethren, hardships of travel, the emotional load of working with so many churches, constant intellectual battles with enemies of the gospel, the loss of any sort of typical financial stability, foregoing a wife and family, ever present threats of physical persecution, unjust imprisonments and legal actions, physical exhaustion and discom-

---

[6]Notably, Jesus said His own words are life; "It is the Spirit who gives life, the flesh profits nothing. The words that I speak to you are spirit, and they are life." (John 6.63). To be loyal to the word of life is to be loyal to Jesus.

fort, the forfeiture of professional respect or title—it is incredible! Some of those sacrifices were part of life in the first century, but the majority were due to his deliberate choice to fully accept the reign of Jesus in his life without challenge. I learn from Paul that his commitment to Christ produced an equal devotion to Christ's gospel, for the two are inseparable, and all else that ensued because of that choice he accepted as part of the commitment.

Importantly, God calls us to prioritize the gospel because He prioritizes it. God initiated the gospel, planned it, carried it out, and revealed it. It truly is God's gospel; "But even after we had suffered before and were spitefully treated at Philippi, as you know, we were bold in our God to speak to you the gospel of God in much conflict" (1 Thes 2.2; cf. v.8,9). In addition, the gospel accomplishes God's work. Paul expressed gratitude for his sharing in the gospel with the Philippians and for the work God was doing through them: "being confident of this very thing, that He who has begun a good work in you will complete it until the day of Jesus Christ" (Phil 1.6). Further, Paul explains that it is God who works in Christians both to will and to do for his good pleasure (Phil 2.12–13).

It seems to me that Paul prioritized the gospel to a degree that was and is unusual. It filled him so completely that every other thing in his life was "loss." We should not overstate the case, for we know Paul had his own struggles and asked God to remove at least some hardships (2 Cor. 12.7–10), but his absolute all-in commitment to the gospel seems almost extreme. Perhaps you know what I mean. If Paul worked at my local church today, would I consider him a bit fanatical? Would I look at the way the gospel consumed him and conclude that he is out of balance? Would people call him a "try-hard"? It is possible to be overly righteous (Ecclesiastes 7.16) and get to the point that I pursue something other than Christ, but that is not what we see in Paul. Instead, we see the model of the exhortation (Phil 1.27; 1 Thes 2.12) and that the gospel is to be the dominant influence of every detail and every moment of my life. In fact, Paul uses himself as an example (1 Thes 2.2–12) and praises the Thessalonians for a similar mindset (1 Thes 1.6–10). Such commitment is extreme, it is radical, and our enemy will work to help us rationalize that something less will be acceptable to the radical Lord who left heaven, became an obedient God and gave Himself for slaughter by His own creation, to redeem the slaughterers. May God help us not dilute what the Spirit teaches on this matter.

The Word

It is important to consider one more characteristic which gives substance to the gospel and clarity to its priority. The gospel is a word, and that is significant. It is, "the word of life" (Phil 2.16; 1 Thes 1.8), the "word of God" (1 Thes 2.13) and "the word of the Lord" (1 Thes 4.15; 2 Thes 3.1). Word is the dominant agency God used to exercise his power in history. Only the incarnation of Christ surpasses the power of God's action through words. God created the universe with his word. Jesus is the Word (John 1.1) and he rides to victory wielding a sword in his mouth and his name is called "The Word of God" (Rev 19.11–13). Consider just some of what God's word does: it is the source of life (Matt 4.4), is our firm foundation (Matt 7.24), makes us free (John 8.31), judges us (John 12.48), is God's power to save (1 Cor 1.18; Rm. 1.16), is how Jesus washes us (Eph 5.25–26), upholds all things (Heb 1.3), discerns hearts (Heb 4.12), is how we are born again (1 Pet 1.23), and provides growth once we are reborn (1 Pet 2.2).

It is no wonder the enemy is the father of lies. He opposes God and so works to thwart the work of God's true word, and nothing opposes truth like a lie. Jesus came to overcome him and the world he rules (John 12.31; 16.33), and to give us that victory (1 John 5.4–5). His gospel is the word that saves us from the world because it shows us Jesus. What is at stake—my salvation and the need to live a life that meets God's purpose for me—requires that the gospel have primacy in my life. God acts on and through me with His word, so it must be my preeminent focus, the one thing by which all other elements of life are weighed, judged, evaluated, and guided.

The deceiver will offer endless alternative measures by which I may evaluate the worth of what I offer to God. Philosophies, self-help books, and my own good intentions are popular replacements. I easily may confuse normal behavior, this is, what is common, for an acceptable walk. A related trap is to justify my walk by the majority opinion of other Christians—if most saints I see make a certain choice, then it must be acceptable—a false and unscriptural strategy. Each of those measures fail because they are not the one God gives to us. Nothing can replace the gospel. Learn it, hear it, meditate on it, pray over it, give up everything necessary for it and only it and when the implications of truth seem to extreme, difficult, or unusual it may well be that you and I finally are beginning to see truths of Jesus to which we have been blind.

Conclusion

Paul charges us with a singular task—as we walk, prioritize the gospel above all else. A life worthy of the gospel is not something to consider once we get through the truly important matters of being a disciple; it is the "only" thing. Singular though it is, the breadth and depth of the task will take a lifetime of work: "Not that I have already attained, or am already perfected, but I press on... Brethren, I do not count myself to have apprehended, but one thing I do..." (Phil 3.12–13). It takes growth and I will learn what things are worthy of the gospel as I learn to approve what is excellent (Phil 1.9–11). There are things I approve today that I will learn I must put away, and other things will rise to consume my time and resources which today get little of either. After all, Paul said this all-for-the gospel mindset requires maturity of mind (Phil 3.15) and that requires time and a whole lot of work. It demands that I see the unseen, a perspective that can be difficult to grasp and to sustain, and our enemy throws distractions of every sort before our eyes to cloud our vision. At the same time, God's word shines through it all and when I see it, I will live my life differently—which is exactly what God intends. Anything less is impertinent, impudent, or possibly even malicious. May the Father grant us the wisdom and character to make the gospel visible in the practical reality of our walk.

Our Citizenship is in Heaven
The Distinctiveness of the Gospel

Terry Francis

My son claims one of the first songs he remembers singing is, "I'm Proud to Be an American." The popular Lee Greenwood song has replaced "God Bless America" and "America the Beautiful" as the most popular patriotic song behind the National Anthem. For many, the lyrics of the song are an accurate representation of a core belief we hold as Americans. If we lost every possession, at least we are still citizens of the United States of America. No one can take away our citizenship.

The citizenship we Americans treasure provides the perfect background to understand Paul's letter to the Philippians. The residents of Philippi were just as proud of their citizenship as we are of ours. If you had asked a Philippian to identify himself in some way, chances are good he would have proudly proclaimed, "I'm a Roman citizen!"

Paul challenges them to push their Roman citizenship to the side for a better citizenship: "Our citizenship is in heaven" (Phil 3.20). This declaration of new citizenship was more than just a new identity. It was a call to live a completely new life; a distinctive life providing a stark contrast to the culture and community around them.

The Roman Colony of Philippi
Philippi was "a leading city of the district of Macedonia and a Roman colony" (Acts 16.12). In 42 BC the battle of Philippi marked

the end of the war between the supporters of Julius Caesar, Marc Antony and Octavian, and his assassins, Brutus and Cassius.[1] Following the battle of Actium in 31 BC, the city of Philippi was established as a Roman colony. Under Roman rule, the designation "colony" was used to grant land to retiring veterans who had gained or retained their Roman citizenship.[2] Philippi had a large contingency of veterans from both the battle of Philippi and the battle of Actium. No doubt the city was overflowing with appreciation for the veterans who had proudly fought to protect and promote the Empire. Philippi would have been a city who proudly expressed her nationalism and patriotism.

As a Roman colony, the city was an extension of the city of Rome. This was unlike other parts of the Roman Empire. Additionally, it received the *ius Italicum* which provided the city the same status as if it had been located in Italy itself.[3] This granted the residents of Philippi Italian citizenship in addition to their Roman citizenship which resulted in the exemption of any taxes for their land.[4] It was living on Italian soil even though they were residing in Macedonia. The city was governed by Roman law and the Philippian people considered themselves first and foremost as Roman citizens. Witherington writes, "… that the city was legally set up and run as if it were a miniature of Rome, following Roman laws and customs. Latin was the language of jurisprudence in this town, and its officials followed Roman protocols and customs."[5]

---

[1] D. deSilva, *An Introduction to the New Testament: Contexts, Methods & Ministry Formation, Second* Edition (Downers Grove, IL: IVP Academic: An Imprint of InterVarsity Press, 2018), 565.

[2] W. A. Heidel, "Colony," in Geoffrey W. Bromiley, ed., *The International Standard Bible Encyclopedia, Revised* (Wm. B. Eerdmans, 1979–1988), 729.

[3] Ibid.

[4] B. Witherington III, *Paul's Letter to the Philippians: A Socio-Rhetorical Commentary* (Grand Rapids, MI; Cambridge, U.K.: William B. Eerdmans Company, 2011), 5.

[5] Ibid.

In Acts 16, as Paul and Silas worked in Philippi during the second missionary journey, Paul casts out the spirit of divination from the slave girl after her continual annoyance (vv. 16–18). Recognizing the loss of their income, the owners of the slave girl drag Paul and Silas to the magistrates at the marketplace. Notice the wording of their complaint: "These men are Jews, and they are disturbing our city. They advocate customs that are not lawful for us as Romans to accept or practice." (Acts 16.20–21). They considered themselves to be "Romans" rather than Macedonians or Philippians. Upon being released and asked to leave quietly, Paul announces his own Roman citizenship forcing the magistrates to publicly acknowledge their rush to judgment (Acts 16.25–40). A Roman citizen was guaranteed a proper trial and was exempt from scourging.[6] Certainly even from Paul's short time in the city, Philippi's pride as a Roman colony and the importance they placed on Roman citizenship are evident.

But why is the colonization of Philippi important to understanding Paul's letter to Philippi? The residents of Philippi took great pride in their Roman citizenship. They were true patriots. Living in Philippi was like living in Rome itself. Unlike other cities within the Empire who were allowed to maintain much of their identity and cultural practices, the residents in Philippi considered themselves to be Romans. They viewed their lives as if they were living within the city walls of Rome. This included not only the laws and legal practices of Rome but also the very culture of Rome, including the religious culture of Rome.

My good friend, Edwin Crozier, once said this about the residents of Philippi:

> Understand, this was the town that was proud to be Roman, where they wouldn't forget the men who died to make them a Roman colony. If they had to, no doubt, many of them would gladly stand

---

[6] G. L. Borchert, "Philippi," ed. Geoffrey W. Bromiley, *The International Standard Bible Encyclopedia, Revised* (Wm. B. Eerdmans, 1979–1988), 836.

up next to you and defend her still today. There ain't no doubt they loved that land. God bless Rome and Philippi.[7]

The Religious Culture of Philippi

Imperial cult worship had a strong presence in Philippi. Inscriptions have been uncovered referring to priests serving the deified leaders Julius, Augustus, and Claudius.[8] Roman Emperors were viewed as gods largely because they were responsible for providing and maintaining what men typically sought from their gods: peace, justice, protection, relief from hardship, etc. Since the Emperor provided what typically was received from gods, it seemed only appropriate for the people to worship them and treat them as divine beings. In addition to Imperial worship, the city of Philippi contained temples and practices associated with the traditional Greek gods such as Zeus, Apollo, Dionysus, and Artemis. By the second century AD there is evidence of other gods being imported from the East including Isis from Egypt and the Phrygian goddess Cybele.[9] The city had a considerable cultic and pagan culture. It is difficult to establish how dominant the cult of Emperor worship might have been in the first century as compared to other religious influences, but there is little doubt it was a large part of the religious fabric of the city.

What seems to be absent from the religious culture of Philippi is a strong Jewish presence. Paul's typical custom was to visit the local synagogue upon his arrival in a city as he did upon arriving in Thessalonica (Acts 17.1). In Philippi, Paul goes to the "place of prayer" which is located by the river outside of the city itself (Acts 16.13). Far from the strong Jewish presence we see in other cities, their presence in Philippi seems limited to a small contingency of women. Unlike

---

[7] E. Crozier, *Philippians: Worthy of Christ's Gospel*, presented to the Livingston Ave Church of Christ (Lutz, FL), March 13, 2022.

[8] deSilva, *An Introduction to the New Testament: Contexts, Methods & Ministry Formation*, 567.

[9] deSilva, *An Introduction to the New Testament: Contexts, Methods & Ministry Formation*, 568.

cities such as Thessalonica with an established synagogue and presence of worshippers of Jehovah, Philippi presents a unique religious background for the early church.

In addition to the challenges of serving Christ in this culture, there appears to be opponents from within the church itself. Those who preach "out of envy" (Phil 1.15–18), the Judaizing missionaries referred to as "dogs" (Phil 3.2), and Christians who live "as enemies of the cross" (Phil 3.18–19) are all presented in opposition to the growth and success of the gospel in Philippi. The Christians at Philippi faced opposition from within and without as they attempted to grow in the favor of King Jesus.

"Just one thing: As citizens of heaven, live your life worthy of the gospel of Christ." The Christian Standard Bible renders its translation of Philippians 1.27 with the above words. It is quite different from many of the translations which are often more like the English Standard Version: "Only let your manner of life be worthy of the gospel of Christ." This "manner of life" concept is used by Paul in three other places (Eph 4.1; Col 1.10; 1 Thes 2.12). In each of those texts, Paul uses a Greek word which simply means "walk." Here in Philippians 1.27, Paul uses a different word which carries a different meaning. The verb here can refer to the conversation or conduct of a person or to live as a good citizen—a nuance often overlooked by many of the translations that are commonly used. The word "citizenship" in Philippians 3.20 shares a similar root word to the word translated "let your manner of life be" here in 1.27. Paul appears to be making a play on words here connecting these two texts by the idea of citizenship. The idea of citizenship provides a kind of bookends to the message of becoming more like Jesus. While some commentators push back at this idea, Fee boldly asserts, "The verb thus means (literally) to "live as citizens."[10] In

---

[10] G. Fee, *Paul's Letter to the Philippians*, The New International Commentary on the New Testament (Grand Rapids, MI: Wm.B. Eerdmans Publishing Co., 1995), 162.

any event, the Philippian brethren would not have glossed over this word choice by Paul. In a city of people raised to see Roman citizenship as one of their most treasured possessions, Paul instructs them to "live like good citizens."

But what citizenship is Paul referring to—the Roman citizenship they have treasured since birth, or this new citizenship being introduced by Paul? Paul seems to erase any possible confusion when he simply states, "But our citizenship is in heaven, and from it we await a Savior, the Lord Jesus Christ" (Phil 3.20). Paul is telling this group of Roman citizens, "live a life worthy of your actual citizenship, your true citizenship… your citizenship in heaven."

Placing this new citizenship against the background of the colonization of Philippi gives us a more accurate understanding of Paul's point. At question here is more than just being loyal subjects of a king. It is more than even determining if you serve King Jesus or Caesar. Paul is presenting the church itself as a colony of the kingdom of heaven on earth with Christ as its ruler. Of this idea Bockmuehl writes:

> Against the colonial preoccupation with the coveted citizenship of Rome, Paul interposes a counter-citizenship whose capital and seat of power are not earthly but heavenly, whose guarantor is not Nero but Christ. Philippi may be a colony enjoying the personal imperial patronage of Lord Caesar, but the church at Philippi is a personal colony of Christ the Lord above all.[11]

The claim of heavenly citizenship is much deeper than simply worshipping with other Christians every Sunday. It is deeper than wearing the name Christian. It is a complete change of perspective and loyalty. It is a change in identity. No longer should these Philippians passionately respond to questions of identity with proud claims of Roman citizenship. They are now citizens of a spiritual kingdom serving an executed, yet resurrected, King sitting on a heav-

---

[11] M. Bockmuehl, *The Epistle to the Philippians*, Black's New Testament Commentary (London: Continuum, 1997), 98.

enly throne. As Wright points out, "the whole business of being a Christian is about living by the belief that Jesus is already the true Lord of the World."[12]

In Thessalonica, as the Jewish opponents attack the brethren there and bring them out to an angry mob, notice the accusation: "These men who have turned the world upside down have come here also, and Jason has received them, and they are all acting against the decrees of Caesar, saying that there is another king, Jesus" (Acts 17.6–7). These men don't serve Caesar. They serve another king named Jesus. Paul and Silas were constantly declaring that Jesus was already sitting on the throne and reigning as King.

This new citizenship is not an explicit judgement against their Roman citizenship. As Witherington states, "Paul does not say that it is a bad thing or evil or to be rejected, but simply that there is a greater and higher citizenship that the Philippians ought to focus on."[13] The good news about Jesus isn't just a message of redemption and salvation. It is a message of transformation for those who accept it and submit to the King. The believer is no longer walking in darkness because he now walks in the light (Eph 5.8–14). The once dead sinner, following the path of the crucified and resurrected King, becomes a living believer (Col 2.13). The citizen of the worldly domain of darkness becomes a citizen of the kingdom of God's beloved Son (Col 1.13). With this change of citizenship, Paul tells the Philippian brethren of several things that must and will occur. It is important to consider these statements of Paul in the context of a Roman colony made up largely of former soldiers.

First, living as a citizen of heaven demands the behavior of a heavenly citizen. Paul's focus in Philippians 1.27 is a citizenship

---

[12] T. Wright, *Paul for Everyone: The Prison Letters: Ephesians, Philippians, Colossians, and Philemon* (London: Society for Promoting Christian Knowledge, 2004), 95.

[13] Witherington III, *Paul's Letter to the Philippians: A Socio-Rhetorical Commentary*, 102.

being worthy of allegiance to King Jesus. Bockmuel rewords Paul's statement this way: "You *are* citizens of heaven; therefore live accordingly, in a manner that is worthy of your king."[14] Believers are expected to exhibit a marked change in their behavior and practices. One simply does not put on Christ and continue to act the same way he or she did prior to their obedience. On this, Wright comments:

> That is why it's all the more important that Christian behaviour in the public sphere should be beyond reproach. The Philippians' public behaviour, as he says, must match up to the gospel. They must not acquire a reputation for being uncivil, boorish or rude. They must be known as honest, reliable, good neighbours, even if people are accusing or attacking them.[15]

In both Philippi and Thessalonica, Paul had seen lives which had been transformed and brought in line with the gospel. Paul was thankful for the good work of salvation begun in the Philippian brethren from the beginning (Phil 1.6). Similarly, the Thessalonians accepted the word of God which immediately began working in them as believers (1 Thes 2.13–14). In his second letter to the church in Thessalonica, Paul boasted of their faith and behavior describing them as "worthy of the kingdom of God" (2 Thess1.4–5). The brethren in Macedonia had been set apart from the culture and world they grew up in as subjects of King Jesus—as citizens of heaven.

Their behavior change was, no doubt, noticeable. One does not simply push aside the practices of Roman citizenship which would have included the Imperial cult worship without being noticed. If the believers in Thessalonica were openly labeled as serving King Jesus instead of Caesar, we can be certain the same is true of the believ-

---

[14] Bockmuehl, *The Epistle to the Philippians*, Black's New Testament Commentary, 98.

[15] Wright, *Paul for Everyone: The Prison Letters: Ephesians, Philippians, Colossians, and Philemon*, 95.

ers in Philippi. Suddenly neighbors would recognize these individuals no longer participated in the cultic practices of their former life.

Warren Wiersbe comments, "The most important weapon against the enemy is not a stirring sermon or a powerful book; it is the consistent life of believers."[16] One of the more glaring differences for this group of former soldiers was a change in the way they respond to others. The veteran trained to fight and kill would no longer lift up his sword in conflict. In contrast, following the example of his King the former soldier now responds with humility and compassion for others (Phil 2.1–11). Imagine the drastic change of a former soldier who has sheathed his sword and picked up a cross of sacrifice and service to others.

These people were different now. Those differences fostered division among friends, family, and neighbors.

Second, living as a citizen of heaven will result in suffering like a citizen. As the believers became more distinctly divided from the world around them, they would be treated differently. After all, they are in a sense traitors. That was exactly the sentiment of the accusation mentioned earlier from Acts 17.7, "They are all acting against the decrees of Caesar, saying that there is another King Jesus." If they serve King Jesus, they are not serving Caesar. In a city filled with veteran soldiers, this betrayal would not be ignored. At the very least, relationships had to change.

Paul warns the brethren any believer who fully surrenders and follows Jesus will suffer. They will face opponents to their faith (Phil 1.28). They will suffer for His sake (Phil 1.29). Paul compares their imminent suffering to the suffering they have witnessed in Paul's own life, both during his time in Philippi and during his imprisonment as he writes to them (Phil 1.30). As to the depth of suffering and opposition Paul faced during his second journey in Philippi, he described it to the Thessalonians as being "shamefully treated" (1

---

[16] W. Wiersbe, *The Bible Exposition Commentary*, vol. 2 (Wheaton, IL: Victor Books, 1996), 71.

Thess 2.2). This shameful treatment included an unlawful arrest, an unmerciful beating with rods, and an unjust imprisonment.

Surprisingly, in Philippians Paul describes this suffering as a gift, or something that is "granted to you" (Phil 1.29). Further, the sufferings of the saints are not portrayed in these letters as possibilities. Instead, they are presented as certainties. If you live like a citizen of heaven, you will suffer like the King suffered (1 Thes 2.14–15). There is a stark contrast of the two citizenships presented here by Paul. A Roman citizenship guaranteed fair trials protecting the individual from unjust accusations as well as prohibiting scourging. Paul's experience in Philippi, however, demonstrates heavenly citizenship guarantees unjust treatment and the possibility of beatings or worse, even if you were also a Roman citizen.

In Acts 16, Paul has the opportunity to exercise his Roman citizenship in order to avoid suffering as he later does in Jerusalem (Acts 22.25). As he is being dragged before the magistrates of Philippi, Paul would have been justified in proclaiming his Roman citizenship which would have demanded a fair trial while simultaneously prohibiting the beating and jailing from the crowd (vv. 20–24). A simple mention of his Roman citizenship would have prevented all of the suffering. But Paul chose to be silent and willingly suffered for the kingdom and his heavenly citizenship.

Third, living as a citizen of heaven includes life in a colony of believers. Philippi was a colony with a large contingent of veterans. These former soldiers had settled in Macedonia surrounded by many alongside whom they had fought with in war. They gained a community and land by settling in Philippi. Rome gained a military outpost filled with a band of reserve soldiers who would have been willing to serve the emperor when necessary.

When Paul connects the faith of these believers to this new citizenship, he also connects the church to the concept of a colony. Fee describes the connection: "As Philippi was a colony of Rome in Macedonia, so the church was a 'colony of heaven' in Philippi, whose members were to live as its citizens in Philippi."[17] Philippi served as a military outpost for Rome; the church should operate as a military outpost for heaven. Christians are to rise each morning putting on the armor of God ready to fight the good fight against the "cosmic powers over this present darkness" (Eph 6.10–20). These former soldiers no longer fight against enemies of the Roman Empire. They now find themselves fighting against forces of evil.

Sometimes, the forces of evil would be the forces of the Roman Empire. As Christians, some of these former soldiers and their families now serve this new King Jesus above the emperor. They no longer practice the cultic worship of Caesar. How strange it must have been for their fellow former soldiers to see these Christians switch allegiances. To retired soldiers, that might even be seen as betraying the emperor. They now find themselves on opposites sides of the battlefront.

The words "standing firm in the one spirit, with one mind striving side by side for the faith of the gospel" can be interpreted as a team of athletes or a group of soldiers (Phil 1.27). Based on the history of Philippi and the strong military background, it seems more appropriate to see this as a military image of soldiers locking their shields, standing their ground firmly, and refusing to break ranks regardless of suffering, attack, or persecution.[18] The Roman Legionnaires would use their shields in the battle formation called the *testudo,* or tortoise. Locking shields on all sides and even above the formation provided maximum protection from the enemy's archers. The veterans in the church at Philippi would be familiar with these types of formations and Paul's words would certainly bring them to mind.

Under King Jesus, the believer finds new enemies and experiences new suffering, but also in Christ, the believer finds a new fellow-

---

[17] Fee, *Paul's Letter to the Philippians,* The New International Commentary on the New Testament , 162.

[18] Witherington III, *Paul's Letter to the Philippians: A Socio-Rhetorical Commentary,* 103.

ship, a new family, a new battalion willing to face persecution and suffering "side by side" (Phil 1.27). In Christ, these veterans find themselves locking arms and shield side by side with new soldiers who march under the royal banner of the cross. While they had lost the relationships with their former fellow soldiers, they find themselves blessed with a new army of believers who share the same mind, purpose, and mission.

Fourth, living as a citizen of heaven includes the reward of citizenship. At first glance of what this change demands, one might ask, "Why would anyone give up their Roman citizenship for this citizenship?" After all this change would include guaranteed suffering and a loss of relationships. Why is it worth it to these believers?

These believers gladly choose this new citizenship because of blessings of the kingdom of heaven. First and foremost this begins with the resurrection: "But our citizenship is in heaven, and from it we await a Savior, the Lord Jesus Christ, who will transform our lowly body to be like his glorious body, by the power that enables him even to subject all things to himself" (Phil 3.20–21). Those who submit to serving Jesus as their King are promised salvation and transformation. One day these believers will be glorified with a new body like His and live with the King for eternity. The coming judgment provides more than the glorification of the believer. It also promises justice in the end. Paul says when Jesus is revealed from heaven, He will come with flaming fire to avenge those who have suffered as His disciples. After all, it is "just to repay with affliction those who afflict" believers (2 Thes 1.5–9).

Revelation provides an amazing story filled with images of war and victory. The greatest lesson from the apocalyptic book can be simply stated, "God always wins." Within the apocalyptic story, there are two definite sides: good and evil. The good side includes God, the Lamb of God, and all those who have the Son and the Father's name on their foreheads (Rev 14.1–5). The evil side includes the dragon, the two beasts, and those who wear the mark of the beasts (Rev 13).

The resulting judgment provides complete devastation for those who practice evil but life beyond compare for those who align themselves with God (Rev 20–22). Two things are clear from this great story. First, you must choose sides. You cannot be on both sides of the conflict. Any failure to fully choose to serve God will place you squarely on the side of evil. Jesus Himself explains, "Whoever is not with me is against me" (Matt 12.30). Second, only those aligned with God are victorious. Evil always loses. God always wins.

These former soldiers through their faith now understand they faced a much greater battle than the earthly ones they had formerly fought. The spiritual battle of good and evil rages on every day and every soldier must choose which army they will march with. In the end, the decision each person faces ultimately mirrors the choice made in Genesis 3: will you choose the tree of life? Or will you choose the tree of death? For the believer in Philippi, treasuring Roman citizenship over a citizenship in heaven would be equal to joining Adam and Eve in their choice of the wrong tree. Choosing to live as citizens of heaven would result in eternal life.

Are we citizens of heaven?

The choice to live as a distinctive citizen of heaven not only applies to the people of Philippi—it is a choice all believers must make. When the world looks at each one of us, do they see someone who is distinct? Do they see someone who has been changed? Do they see someone who is different? Do our churches provide the fellowship of a heavenly colony we see portrayed here in Philippians?

Consider for a moment our churches. Do churches today look like a military outpost or a social gathering? Certainly, Christians should be friends and enjoy the company of one another. But the church is also a band of suffering soldiers who stand side by side. The fellowship of this spiritual army provides a place to share burdens (Gal 6.1–5), a place to confess sins (Jam 5.16), and a place to be stimulated and encouraged (Heb 10.24–25). To be clear, our assemblies should look like a collection of battle-worn soldiers coming together to be recharged before they step back on the battlefield.

Even when we are battered and bruised from the fight, we hide it from our fellow soldiers. When was the last time you asked someone to carry your burden? When was the last time you confessed to a brother? When was the last time you simply went to a brother in tears needing to be loved and reminded that you're not alone? Too many of us are terrified of sharing our struggles and confessing our sins. The result is a collection of believers who come together to worship God three hours a week and then return to the battlefield alone ready to be defeated once again.

When we compare ourselves to Paul's description of heavenly citizens, do we look like they did? Do we suffer for our faith? Do we fight daily against the forces of evil? Are we focused on the eternal reward or immediate gratification? Are we distinctive from the non-Christians we interact with daily? Or, are we blending into the world around us?

Is it possible we aren't acting like these heavenly citizens because our heavenly citizenship isn't our most treasured citizenship? Like the Philippians, we pride ourselves in being citizens of a dominant world super-power. From an early age we are taught we should be "proud to be an American where at least I know I'm free." We justify the value we place on our American citizenship by weaving our faith and patriotism together making it difficult to establish where one begins and the other ends. Look no further than the inclusion of patriotic songs like "America the Beautiful" which according to hymnary.org is included in 487 different hymnals or "My Country, 'Tis of Thee" which is included in 1,873 hymnals. And yes, they occur in many of "our hymnals," not just "their hymnals." After all, we are a "Christian nation," we are "one nation under God," and we proclaim with our currency "in God we trust."

As Americans, our nationalism and pride are quite similar to what is seen in the Roman Empire. While we may not deify our presidents (although that is debatable), we do believe our nation can provide the deliverance and salvation the world needs. As Douthat points out many Americans "regard the United States… as a New Israel, a holy nation, a people set apart."[19] Just as Israel brought about the Messiah who would change the world, some are even convinced "American democracy can actually fulfill God's purpose on earth—whether by building the New Jerusalem at home, or by spreading the blessings of liberty to every race and people overseas."[20]

This concept of America being the social and political savior of the world pulls us deeper into our citizenship and the "God-given rights" it carries. If we can simply elect the right people, the entire world could be different. To be clear, both sides of the political spectrum in our country are convinced this is true. The left believes the world needs to be saved from antiquated beliefs and an oppressive sense of morality. For the left, the key to saving the world is tearing down definitions and standards that have "oppressed" humanity for centuries while promoting a post-modern worldview where you can be anything you want without consequence—even to the point of sexual identity. The right believes the world needs to be saved from post-modern thinking and the immoral efforts of the left. The left is a threat to traditional roles, definitions, and the ability to serve God.

This is most recognized during the election of the POTUS every four years. Our politics has become a sort of gospel for many today because the good news about our platform, our party, and our candidate is that he, or she, can literally change the world. People on both sides passionately believe in their candidate and what they offer. Believers regularly share the good news of their political candidates (regardless of which side of the aisle they are on) with far greater passion or energy than they will share the good news about Jesus Christ. I have yet to hear someone say, "I just don't know if I can tell some-

---

[19] R. Douthat, *Bad Religion; How We Became a Nation of Heretics*, (New York: Free Press, 2012). 249.

[20] Ibid, 254.

one about my political party because I may not say it the right way." But mention talking about Jesus and suddenly, like Moses, we are "slow of speech and tongue" (Exo 4.10). While Paul makes it clear heavenly citizens will suffer, we have become convinced suffering can be avoided if we keep the wrong people from having power. This approach provides a stark contrast to Paul's own choice in Acts 16 to willingly suffer in the name of Christ rather than use his citizenship as protection (vv. 25–40).

All of this results in a country locked in an ongoing power struggle between two sides entrenched in the belief their platform, policies, and political party are the key to creating a better life. Our country is locked in an intellectual and philosophical civil war with both sides convinced it is not just about the country, but the entire planet. Our freedom, our faith, and the very fiber of our nation are at risk which demands we take up our political swords and defeat the other side because this is how Jesus will save the world. A simple scroll through social media shows just how polarized we are today. Brother attacks brother… not over what is actually said but over the fear of what is not said. In this battle, if you fail to agree with our side you must automatically be an ally of their side which makes you my enemy. Swords are drawn and the duel ensues until one person, or both, crawl away wounded and defeated.

Brethren, is it time we put down our sword and pick up our cross? Jesus said the meek shall inherit the earth—not the rebels, protestors, and warriors (Matt 5.5). Servants of the King are humble, merciful, compassionate peacemakers who love their enemies (Matt 5.3, 7, 9, 43–48). Citizens of heaven look out for the interests of others regardless of whether they agree or not (Phil 2.1–11). More importantly, Christians are so engrossed with the civil conflict and using their political swords that we have forgotten we have the sword of the Spirit that is able to provide salvation for everyone (Eph 6.17; Rom 1.16). That is how we can know we have treasured the wrong citizenship. When we put our confidence in our politics to change the course of the world more than the gospel of Jesus Christ, we are living more as American citizens than heavenly citizens.

The world needs changing. It needs saving. That is not done through our earthly citizenship. It will not happen through military means, political positioning, or congressional conquest. If we want to truly save the world, we will do so one soul at a time with the gospel of King Jesus. Jesus didn't say, "Go therefore and make capitalists, republics, and democracies out of all nations." He said, "Go therefore and make disciples" (Matt 28.19). Changing the culture and the world around us isn't just a noble cause, it is our mission as heavenly citizens. We cannot and will not fulfill our mission if we serve America more than we serve King Jesus.

To be clear, it is not sinful to be American. It is not sinful to be thankful or even proud you are an American. It is not sinful to be involved in politics. Rather, we must understand we have a greater citizenship. We are expected to live in a way worthy not of the Declaration of Independence but of the gospel.

The question is, at what point has our patriotism become our god? At what point has our political affiliation not only become our passion but even our savior? At what point have we become so enamored with our American citizenship that we no longer serve King Jesus? Jesus said, "No one can serve two masters" (Matt 6.24). As a young person growing up in Sunday School classes, I was taught idolatry was still a real concern. We needed to look out for greed, fame, pleasure, recreation, work, etc. because they could become idols who could lead us away from the Lord. As an adult, I am afraid we forget about the idolatry of national pride, political affiliation, and patriotism.

The vision of Daniel 2 features four sections representing four separate dominant world empires. The statue is destroyed by a stone that was not cut with hands (vv. 34–35). Daniel explains this important part of the vision:

And in the days of those kings the God of heaven will set up a kingdom that shall never be destroyed, nor shall the kingdom be left to another people. It shall break in pieces all these kingdoms and bring them to an end, and it shall stand forever, just as you saw that a stone was cut from a mountain by no human hand, and that it broke in pieces the iron, the bronze, the clay, the silver, and the gold. A great God has made known to the king what shall be after this. The dream is certain, and its interpretation sure. (Dan 2.44–45)

This vision provides two vital truths to consider. First, no human empire will stand forever. That includes the United States. Second, the kingdom of heaven will reign supreme forever. Today Jesus sits on the throne ruling over heaven and earth (Matt 18.18). As citizens, or subjects, of the King we must put him on the throne of our lives. Who among us could be charged with "saying there is another king, Jesus?" (Acts 17.7). Not only do our neighbors not understand we serve a different king, but for most of us they aren't even aware of where we are on Sunday mornings. If we can place signs in our yards and stickers on our cars promoting a candidate but we still haven't told our neighbors we are servants of Jesus, who is our real master? Who is our King?

I am glad I am an American where I have freedoms to worship and teach the good news about Jesus. But I must admit I am more glad to be a Christian who is free from sin. I won't forget the King who died to give that gift to me. I'll gladly stand up next to you and defend His kingdom today because there ain't no doubt I love the King. May God bless our work as heavenly citizens on earth.

Bibliography

Bockmuehl, Markus. *The Epistle to the Philippians,* Black's New Testament Commentary. London: Continuum, 1997.

Borchert, G. L. "Philippi," ed. Geoffrey W. Bromiley, *The International Standard Bible Encyclopedia, Revised.* Wm. B. Eerdmans, 1979–1988.

Crozier, Edwin. *Philippians: Worthy of Christ's Gospel.* Presented to the Livingston Ave Church of Christ (Lutz, FL), March 13, 2022.

deSilva, David. A. *An Introduction to the New Testament: Contexts, Methods & Ministry Formation, Second Edition.* Downers Grove, IL: IVP Academic: An Imprint of InterVarsity Press, 2018.

Douthat, Ross. *Bad Religion: How We Became a Nation of Heretics.* New York: Free Press, 2012.

Fee, Gordon D. *Paul's Letter to the Philippians*, The New International Commentary on the New Testament. Grand Rapids, MI: Wm.B. Eerdmans Publishing Co., 1995.

Heidel, W. A. "Colony," in Geoffrey W. Bromiley, ed., *The International Standard Bible Encyclopedia, Revised.* Wm. B. Eerdmans, 1979–1988.

Wiersbe, Warren W. *The Bible Exposition Commentary*, vol. 2. Wheaton, IL: Victor Books, 1996.

Witherington III, Ben. *Paul's Letter to the Philippians: A Socio-Rhetorical Commentary.* Grand Rapids, MI; Cambridge, U.K.: William B. Eerdmans Company, 2011.

Wright, Tom. *Paul for Everyone: The Prison Letters: Ephesians, Philippians, Colossians, and Philemon.* London: Society for Promoting Christian Knowledge, 2004.

Excel Still More
The Fullness of the Gospel

Andy Cantrell

Have you ever achieved an agonizing goal you set for yourself, a project you sacrificed and strove for with all your being, changes you made that consumed your time and energy and exhausted every emotional resource, a season in which you grew in profound ways and finally felt as if you'd arrived at a destination worthy to be celebrated—only to have someone come along and say that you needed to do better, you should do more, you ought to be further along? Did you find such feedback disheartening and frustrating, or encouraging and inspiring? The answer to that question likely depends on three factors: what we believe about our capacity and capability; our level of desire and ambition; and, thirdly, our work ethic and energy level. How we receive information regarding personal growth has much to do with whether we see ourselves the way God see us, and whether we're willing to submit to His encouragement toward desire and diligence.

The above scenario is clearly seen in Paul's letters to the Macedonian churches. When he wrote to the saints in both Philippi and Thessalonica, he urged them often to "abound" or "excel still more"[1] in areas of life they painstakingly had already made great strides in. Notice both his praise and prescription in the following examples:

---

[1] The *perisseuo* word family is unusually dense in the Macedonian letters (Phil 1.9, 14, 26; 4.12, 18; 1 Thes 2.17, 3.10, 12; 4.1, 10; 5.13).

And this I pray, that your love may abound still more and more in real knowledge and all discernment, so that you may approve the things that are excellent, in order to be sincere and blameless until the day of Christ. (Phil 1.9)[2]

Finally then, brethren, we request and exhort you in the Lord Jesus, that as you received from us instruction as to how you ought to walk and please God (just as you actually do walk) that you excel still more. (1 Thes 4.1)

Now as to the love of the brethren, you have no need for anyone to write to you, for you yourselves are taught by God to love one another; for indeed you do practice it toward all the brethren who are in all Macedonia. But we urge you, brethren, to excel still more. (1 Thes 4.9, 10)

There is something both excruciating and exhilarating in such passages of Scripture. For those of us who have already allowed God to refine us in profound ways, we may remember all the pain involved with such growth and crave a reprieve. The reality that there is still more to come may solicit a range of challenging emotions—from fear to fatigue. As Jesus said, "For the gate is small, and the way is narrow that leads to life, and there are few who find it." (Matt 7.14). Learning to embrace and celebrate the painstaking journey of perfecting holiness and love is necessary to running the race of life with joy and energy.

It's important to notice what these passages specifically encourage us to "excel still more" in. Some read this phrase as a mandate to pursue all sorts of endeavors that the Holy Spirit didn't intend as he inspired Paul's writing. While it's valuable for Christians to do everything "heartily, as to the Lord" (Col 3.23), there are certain pursuits singled out in these letters as deserving greater priority and attention. When we look closely at the context of these exhortations, there are two great

---

[2] Unless noted otherwise, all quotations of scripture are from the 1995 update to the NASB.

pursuits encouraged: sanctification (1 Thes 4.1–8) and love (Phil 1.9; 1 Thes 4.9–12). It makes perfect sense that sanctification and love are the two qualities in which Christians are encouraged to abound, considering how God prophetically defined the citizens of Zion.

> A highway will be there, a roadway,
> And it will be called the Highway of Holiness.
> The unclean will not travel on it,
> But it will be for him who walks that way,
> And fools will not wander on it.
> No lion will be there,
> Nor will any vicious beast go up on it;
> These will not be found there.
> But the redeemed will walk there, (Isa 35.8–9)

Holiness and peace were always to be the mark of God's people. The Hebrew writer alludes to the Zion prophecies from Isaiah 34–35 in Hebrews 12, "Pursue peace with all men, and the sanctification without which no one will see the Lord." (Heb 12.14). Divine love and sanctification are not destinations we reach in this life. Rather, we are to constantly pursue deeper levels of "perfecting holiness in the fear of God" (2 Cor 7.1) while learning to "walk in love, as Christ also loved us" (Eph 5.2).

It is a high calling to "excel still more" in sanctification and love, as these are two of the most agonizing changes that God accomplishes in us through the years. Think of your own life for a moment. Do you remember the suffering and sacrifices you made in just the first steps of pursuing sanctification in your walk with Christ? It is not the suffering of persecution that Peter writes of in 1 Peter 4.1–3, but the suffering of sanctification. No longer fulfilling the "lusts of men" (vs. 2) or living for the "desires of the Gentiles" (vs. 3) is an extraordinarily painful kind of suffering in those who intend to live the "rest of the time in the flesh…for the will of God" (vs. 2). What about your pursuit of genuine love? How difficult was it to learn to sincerely, fervently, and from the heart, love (1 Pet 1.22) even the first few people closest to you in your life? The characteristics of love listed in 1 Corinthians 13.4–8 are some of the most challenging and costly changes we will ever pursue. Herein lies the great burden of excelling still more. How well we remember the triumph of successfully tackling that one persistent sin, or learning to genuinely love that seemingly unlovable person. But those wins are simply milestones, not the destination. Not even close. There remains yet another sinful deed to put to death, another attitude to bring into submission, another thought to take captive, another Christian to learn to love, another unbeliever, another enemy. We have before us a race to run that constantly demands that we "excel still more." Is it any wonder some give up? That some reach a mile marker and stay put, or relegate their pursuits of excellence to worldly matters and satisfy their conscience by claiming such pursuits are in the name of the Lord?

Is it even possible to abound and excel to the level of holiness and love that God's Word sets as a standard? When Jesus spoke of love in His well-known mountain sermon, He said, "you are to be perfect, as your heavenly Father is perfect" (Matt 5.48). When the Hebrew writer spoke of God's formative discipline in our lives, he wrote, "He disciplines us for our good, so that we may share His holiness" (Heb 12.10). God has been clear about our potential and capacity. Such transcendent thoughts are stirred by the promises contained in God's Word. Christ *can* truly be "formed in you" (Gal 4.19). We *can* grow in maturity to the "measure of the stature of the fullness of Christ" (Eph 4.13). We *can* achieve "this attitude in yourselves, which was also in Christ Jesus" (Phil 2.5). We *are currently* "being renewed to a true knowledge according to the image of the One who created" us (Col 3.10). As painful as that process might be, there simply is nothing more valuable than knowing with certainty that we "may become partakers of the divine nature" (1 Pet 1.4). We must believe these truths with all our hearts if we ever hope to "excel still more" in sanctification and love.

Paul was confident in God's ability to cause the Christians in both Philippi and Thessalonica to abound and move toward perfection in love and holiness. "For I am confident of this very thing, that He who began a good work in you will perfect it until the day of Christ Jesus." (Phil 1.7). "And may the Lord cause you to increase and abound in love for one another, and for all people, just as we also do for you; so that He may establish your hearts without blame in holiness before our God and Father at the coming of our Lord Jesus with all His saints." (1 Thes 3.11–13). This confidence was fueled not only by what Paul knew about God, but by what he knew about the Christians in these places.

The Philippians had already proven their love in profound ways. They had participated with Paul in the gospel by sending gifts to provide for his needs more than once (Phil 1.5; 4.15–16). They had sent Epaphroditus to be their messenger and minister to Paul (Phil 2.25). Even the longing and distress Epaphroditus felt is evidence of the deep bonds the Philippian saints had developed for one another (Phil 2.26). Paul praises them for such things, but also calls them to greater levels of love and maturity. The succinct prayer he offers for them in 1.9–11 is both rich and profound. Godly love can only abound in "real knowledge and discernment" (vs. 9). We live in a world filled with people who claim that love is their greatest virtue, but so often it is a love uninformed by godly wisdom and void of the character of God. For us to grow in genuine love, we must intimately know the God who is love and understand more and more what He believes is best for those made in His image. This leads to the next part of the prayer, "that you may approve the things that are excellent" (vs. 10). The world often defines love through approval, accompanied by an attitude of, "if you love me, you must support and approve of whatever path I choose to take, however I choose to identify myself, and whatever life I decide to live." God's profound love is vastly superior. He teaches us to love people in a way that acknowledges their true essence and potential, as those made in the image of God. To truly excel in love, we must approve the things that are excellent. The goal of this prayer is for people to be "sincere and blameless" (vs. 10) and be "filled with the fruit of righteousness" "to the glory and praise of God." (vs. 11). In order for these qualities to be realized in our own lives and the lives of those around us, we must have a love that abounds in the discernment and excellence God provides.

Likewise, the Thessalonian disciples had already displayed incredible levels of sanctification and love. Paul thanked God always, constantly remembering their "work of faith and labor of love and steadfastness of hope" (1 Thes 1.2–3). Words like work, labor, and steadfastness remind us that there is nothing easy about developing and nurturing faith, love, and hope in our lives. A few verses later, Paul describes the report he'd received concerning the Thessalonians from other believers around Macedonia. Notice how this report in verses 9 and 10 parallels the description Paul uses in verse 3. Their "work of faith" (1.3) was manifested in "how they turned to God from idols" (1.9). Their "labor of love" (1.3) was evidenced by the fact that they had decided to "serve a living and true God" (1.9). Their "steadfastness of hope" (1.3) was demonstrated in their willingness to "wait for His Son from heaven" (1.9). Each of these descriptions carries with them incredible implications of sacrifice and struggle. Imagine living your entire life in a culture of idolatry, only to one day come to a faith in Jesus that undermines and exposes countless investments of time, energy, and resources. This would be overwhelming, and turning from such things would require genuine faith, a newfound trust and vast amounts of work that could be wearying beyond measure. Learning to "serve a living God" day in and day out is laborious on every level. Only love can fuel such labor. Those who attempt to serve God out of obligation, guilt, or fear will almost always lag in diligence. Love is the only motive that will eventually cast out fear (1 John 4.18) and make the labor of service "not burdensome" (1 John 5.3). Finally, these disciples, in "steadfastness of hope," were to "wait for the Son." Waiting is one of the most challenging aspects in our walk with the

Lord. "Hope deferred makes the heart sick, but desire fulfilled is a tree of life." (Prov 13.12). There was so much to celebrate and admire in how the Thessalonians had changed and grown. And yet, it was to these same Christians that Paul would say, "excel still more."

Why is there such a concentration of the exhortation to "abound" and "excel" in the Macedonian letters? While not exclusive to these letters, the theme is noticeably prominent. Among many valid explanations, one captures my attention. Paul had a relationship with the Macedonians because God had providentially urged *him* to "excel still more." Paul was only asking the Macedonians to follow in the footsteps in which the Holy Spirit had already guided him. Luke records the event:

> They passed through the Phrygian and Galatian region, having been forbidden by the Holy Spirit to speak the word in Asia; and after they came to Mysia, they were trying to go into Bithynia, and the Spirit of Jesus did not permit them; and passing by Mysia, they came down to Troas. A vision appeared to Paul in the night: a man of Macedonia was standing and appealing to him, and saying, 'Come over to Macedonia and help us.' When he had seen the vision, immediately we sought to go into Macedonia, concluding that God had called us to preach the gospel to them. (Acts 16.6–10)

Until this moment, Paul had spent months during his first missionary journey developing relationships and learning to deeply love the Christians throughout Asia Minor. What a tremendous achievement this labor of love had been for him! While Paul might have expected God to say, "well done, good and faithful servant," and allowed him to spend the rest of his days in a now-familiar place, the Lord did not permit Paul to speak in those regions. The Spirit led him further west to the Hellespont. The Macedonian call could rightly be referred to as one of the many moments in Paul's life where God challenged him to "excel still more." There were people in Europe who Paul needed to love.

This is all very similar to what Paul wrote to the Thessalonians. "Now as to the love of the brethren, you have no need for anyone to write to you, for you yourselves are taught by God to love one another; for indeed you do practice it toward all the brethren who are in all Macedonia. But we urge you, brethren, to excel still more" (1 Thes 4.9–10). Notice the superlatives in verse 10: "All" the brethren in "all" Macedonia. That's incredible to contemplate. How many of us struggle to love "all" the people in our own family? If we do wrestle our hearts to that point, how many of us can honestly say we love "all" the brethren in our own congregation, let alone our city, state, or region? The Thessalonian Christians had grown to a place many of us have yet to achieve—not simply to feel love for all the brethren around them, but to "practice" it (vs. 9). And yet, "excel still more" is the exhortation they are given. In what way were they to understand this exhortation? Were they to abound in the purity of love? Depth of love? Scope of love? I would suggest all of these are true, but since the verse seems to be about the geographic range of their love, scope is worth exploring.

To excel still more in love, we must continue to grow our sphere of affection. Perhaps, like Paul in Acts 16, you have had seasons in your life when God providentially took you out of your comfort zone. The people you were content loving and serving were no longer in your life, and you found yourself surrounded by unfamiliar faces, people you had no history with, strangers who were culturally uncomfortable to you. How did you respond? I'm ashamed to admit I've often tended toward reclusion and reticence. My Lord deserves better from me. Some have never experienced such moments. Perhaps you've always been surrounded by family and friends and have grown comfortable with the circle of people you love and serve. We do not have to wait for God to change our circumstances. We can choose to abound more and more. For those of us who have learned to deeply love a child we brought into the world, it's time to lift our eyes and see the many children who need to feel such love in their own lives. For those of us who have successfully learned the names and stories of the Christians who sit in our quadrant of the church building, it's time to start sitting somewhere new. For those of us who have finally understood what *philadelphia* (1 Thes 4.9) means in our lives, it's time to "pursue *philoxenia*" (Rom 12.13). Listen closely to Paul's prayer for the Thessalonians. "And may the Lord cause you to increase and abound in love for one another, and for all people" (1 Thes 3.12). There is no limit to the bounds of God's love—nor should there be to His children's.

The repeated exhortation to "excel still more" will not let us forget the fullness of the gospel. Failing to present the gospel in its fullness is a mistake I've made at times when presenting the Good News of Jesus to others, and I fear it's more prevalent than we care to admit. The Good News concerning salvation is not only what we can be saved *from*, but what we are saved *for*. The gospel is not simply good news about being saved from our past, but all the wonders of our future. It is not just being forgiven for being unholy, but actually being made holy. It is not merely that we are pardoned for being unloving, but that we become lovers. The washing that sanctified something or someone being made holy was only the beginning of its service (Exod 40.9–13). When the prophets who foretold of the grace that would come to us (1 Pet 1.10) painted pictures of our salvation, they wouldn't merely speak of what God would do *for* us, but what He would do *with* us.

Take Isaiah 61 as an example. The first three verses of that great prophecy speak of the incredible things our Messiah would do *for* us. "Bring good news to the afflicted" (vs. 1). "Bind up the broken hearted" (vs.1). "Proclaim liberty to captives, and freedom to prisoners" (vs.1). "To comfort all who mourn" (vs. 2). And blessing upon blessing, to make us the "oaks of righteousness, the planting of the Lord, that He may be glorified" (vs.3). However, that is just the beginning of the Good News in this passage. Verses 4–11 describe what God promised to do *with* us and *through* us. These people who had been rebuilt, raised up, and repaired by Jesus would be the ones privileged to "rebuild the ancient ruins," "raise up the former devastations," and "repair the ruined cities" (vs. 4). Isaiah prophesied that we would be "called the priests of the Lord" and "be spoken of as ministers of our God" (vs. 6). What an extraordinary blessing to serve God on behalf of men and men on behalf of God! "Everlasting joy" (vs. 7) is promised to those of us who "will be known among the nations" because we "are the offspring whom the Lord has blessed" (vs. 9). We are given "garments of salvation" (vs. 10) and made to be God's garden in which He causes "righteousness and praise to spring up before all the nations" (vs.11).

The Gospel of our Savior should never be diminished to a presentation of God taking care of our messy pasts. It should always include the exhilarating truth that God can and will make us abound more and more to be genuine children of our Father. Sharing His holiness. Loving as He loves. The exhortations to "excel still more" in the Macedonian letters should never cause us to feel weary or anxious, but to "rejoice always" (1 Thes 5.16) in a God who knows what He is capable of accomplishing in and through us.

"Now may the God of peace Himself sanctify you entirely; and may your spirit and soul and body be preserved complete, without blame at the coming of our Lord Jesus Christ. Faithful is He who calls you, and He also will bring it to pass." (1 Thes 5.23–24)

Part Two

The Day Lectures

Think on These Things
An Attitude That is Worthy of the Gospel

Collin Stringer

We live in a time when feelings often take precedence over facts. If we present to our neighbors what we believe to be verifiable moral truth, they will likely prefer to live by *their* "truth" derived from what they feel in their hearts. Most who live in this world with us stubbornly reject absolute truth. Our unanchored society is drifting into deeper darkness, falling into a degenerate state as they leave the higher ground of their Creator's truth and light. In July of this year, a survey from Gallup revealed that a record-low 20% of Americans believe the Bible is the literal word of God.

Since the majority of our culture ignores the eternal truth we find in our God, we are hearing lies every day from every corner. When thoughts arise from the hearts of flawed, ungodly humans, we can expect them to be diverse, illogical, and conflicting. The ones spouting their varied ideas might not see how unreasonable they are—if they even care about reasonable discussions and arguments. Thinking of Paul's custom to enter synagogues and reason with his Jewish brothers from the Scriptures, how successful would he be today with this strategy? We know from experience that this approach will not persuade an audience as successfully as it would have just a few decades ago. It is hard to reason with someone who does not recognize an unchanging standard and prefers to go with what is trending.

As we struggle to keep our footing on this shaky ground, we hear our gracious God calling us to live a life "worthy of the gospel of Christ" as we are "standing firm in one spirit, with one mind striving together for the faith of the gospel" (Phil 1.27).[1] Living in a din of deceptive half-truths and outright lies, let's eagerly join fellow soldiers of the cross who strive together to defend the faith of the gospel and stand firm in the truth. Our noble efforts will succeed when we recognize excellent virtues and "think on these things."

Our aim is to live up to the high calling of the gospel. To reach this goal, our minds must think as our Lord thinks. When "we have the mind of Christ" (2 Cor 2.16), we will love His truth and be eager to live by His truth as we do all "to the glory and praise of God" (Phil 1.11). Yes, we live in troubled times, but in the steps of our Lord, we will rise above our dark world.

When the church at Philippi was troubled by error, Paul presented the remedy: "Have this attitude in yourselves which was also in Christ Jesus" (2.5). Some in this church preached divisive sermons. Others exalted fleshly validation over the supreme value of knowing Christ. A few sisters were at odds with one another. How do saints overcome such doctrinal division? They look to our Savior! Like good sheep, they carefully follow our Shepherd. Then, with their eyes fixed on Him, they will develop His admirable attitude and become "of the same mind, maintaining the same love, united in spirit, intent on one purpose" (2.2).

Seeking to have our Lord's mind is a lofty ambition. We press on, though, to think as He thinks. In the Macedonian epistles, we can find helpful instructions that will lead us to His higher thoughts. God gives us a perfect example to follow and some admirable virtues to develop.

A Sincere Humility—Found in Christ

Those who have humble hearts are well-equipped to develop the mind of Christ. We see this truth when Paul fleshes out the challenge

---

[1] New American Standard Bible (1995) is used throughout.

to have the attitude of Christ in us. When he completes the sentence that begins in Philippians 2.5, he brings us to the humbling of the Son of God. Jesus made a remarkable sacrifice by leaving His perfect home. He did not grasp the glory while thinking only of Himself, but instead, He emptied Himself by taking on a human body to live on earth as a bondservant. He went even lower in His fleshly existence, humbling Himself to the point of death on a cross.

We aim to "do nothing from selfishness or empty conceit, but with humility of mind regard one another as more important" than ourselves (Phil 2.3). The admirable example of Jesus is before us. "The highest example of such a self-forgetful regard for the interest of others is now portrayed, viz. the condescension of Christ in His incarnation."[2] Our Lord sacrificed so much and descended so low in order to "look out for … the interests of others" (Phil 2.4). He did not give up His deity for us. However, He gave Himself up as a sacrifice for all who are lost in sin.

If we are going to think as Jesus thinks, we must sacrifice what is important to us. We have to push aside high thoughts of ourselves, our knowledge, and our abilities. We cannot tenaciously and proudly hold on to our watertight conclusions based on human reasoning. Humble servants in the Lord's kingdom bow before Him with open hearts, ready to receive His higher truth that we find in His infallible word. When we join Mary at His feet, we are in that better place where His words are shaping all our thoughts. In the revealing light of His words, we must let go of any conclusions that oppose the truth found in Him (Eph 4.21).

Pride is our enemy. We might be tempted to think, "After studying this for so long, I feel like I have the right answer," or, "There's really no other way to see this," or even, "They're all so wrong; I'm the only one who has the truth on this issue." Let's remember, though, that our feelings are not reliable guides for those searching for truth.

---

[2] J. Muller, *The Epistles of Paul To The Philippians And To Philemon*. NICNT. (Grand Rapids: Eerdmans, 1955) 77.

It is a prideful heart that refuses to listen to other students of the word and chooses to take an overconfident stand on his beliefs.

So, how do we defeat this pride, and where do we find sincere humility? We agree with Paul as he points us to Christ's "death on a cross." Pride will spring up and flourish everywhere—except at the cross. When we come to Calvary and gaze upon that great act of atonement, His sacrifice humbles us. Our pride is squashed when we come to that hill, linger with eager eyes, and see what our selfish sins have done to our Savior.

As we walk away from the One who redeemed and reconciled us, we know we can trust Him to guide us to the truth. We do not follow our fallible hearts now; we follow our all-wise Lord. We do not rely on human wisdom; the spirit of Jesus Christ guides us. With humility, we seek His ways that tower above the ways of men. Striving for the faith of the gospel, our confidence is in the revealed truth we find when we open our Bibles and fill our minds with His words.

A Focused Mind—Centered in Peace

Our awesome Creator has given us minds with astounding abilities that we take for granted. As I write these words and you read them, our brains are busily processing information at incredible speeds. According to the Laboratory of Neuro Imaging at the University of Southern California, the average brain generates 48.6 thoughts per minute, which is 70,000 thoughts per day. There are 86 billion neurons in the brain, and they are constantly at work, sending electrical impulses that transmit information to other areas of the brain.

Since our multi-tasking minds can be heading in various directions, perhaps toward anxiety or other sins, our God says, "Set your mind on things above" (Col 3.2) and "dwell on these things" (Phil 4.8). He is calling us to a narrow focus that shuts out the worldliness and centers on the holiness. What a challenge it is to corral our thoughts in this way! In Christ, however, we find our example. When He was troubled by pride-filled disciples who argued over which of them was the greatest, He set His face to go to Jerusalem, where He would give Himself up for our salvation. With important things to consider, He chose to center His mind on His mission.

If we hear troubling news about world events, worries will likely fill our minds. Whenever we absorb social media, listen to music, or watch shows and movies, "the world forces of this darkness" (Eph 6.12) are actively trying to lead us into sinful thoughts. Our greatest mental challenge might be keeping our minds away from our selfish pursuits.

In this fight for the purity of your mind, your Lord has given you an effective weapon: prayer (Phil 4.6). What a wonderful privilege you have when you use your mind to address your holy Father. In this time of communion with Him, your mind is set on things above. You will joyfully praise your God, desperately seek His help, and eagerly thank Him as you let your requests be made known to Him. Knowing that His ears are open to your prayers and that He is in control, His peace will "guard your hearts and minds in Christ Jesus" (Phil 4.7). This incomprehensible peace will surround your mind and keep the evil thoughts out. You must make good choices, however, as you do your part in keeping your mind pure. Think carefully about the potential worldly influences that could enter your mind through screen time, car radio moments, and movie viewings. Are you seeing and hearing things marked by "excellence" (*arete*) and "worthy of praise" (Phil 4.8)?

We have specific virtues to focus on. God wants our minds to ponder what is true, honorable, right, pure, lovely, and of good repute. Those who obey this command to "think on these things" will raise their thoughts to the moral high ground. Their minds will soar above the darkness and deceit of the world, and they will be fed by what is true and right by God's eternal standard. Songs on pop radio stations often celebrate and encourage the indulgence of fleshly desires, and our minds could be replaying the words, even though we despise them. When we listen to songs with clean lyrics, however, our thoughts will dwell on what is pure, and they will be pleasing residents in our hearts. If spending copious amounts of time on social media is moving your thoughts toward harmful comparisons, realize that time in God's word will help you see yourself as your Creator sees you. If you think you are not good enough, pretty enough, or rich enough, then listen to Him and be encouraged by His estimation of you.

An interesting study was recently done with 259 college students from the United Kingdom and Japan who were isolated in rooms with no objects to interact with. They were asked to predict how much they would enjoy their time in this isolation with no phones or books, only accompanied by their own thoughts. Researchers discovered that these young people enjoyed this time significantly more than they anticipated.[3] They did not realize that sitting alone without distracting devices can be richly rewarding! As we consider this result, could it be that we all would benefit greatly from quiet, undistracted time with our Lord? When large, demanding crowds came to Jesus with their needs, "He Himself often withdrew into the wilderness to pray" (Luke 5.16). In His steps, seeking to have His attitude in us, we need time to be alone with our Lord and with our thoughts. In these faith-building moments, we can be focused on Him, fixated on truth, and filled with peace.

An Abounding Love—Expressed in Knowledge

Consider again the incarnation of our Lord Jesus. He descended to this lower realm to do the work His Father had given Him to do (John 17.5). He came to us, though, with a willing heart that "emptied Himself" and "humbled Himself" for those struggling in sin. His fateful choice clearly demonstrates what love is. He fully understood the helpless state we were in, and He actively sought to save us and bring us home. He also had a complete knowledge

---

[3] Winerman, Lea. "Put down devices, let your mind wander, study suggests." July 28, 2022. www.apa.org/news/press/releases/2022//07thoughts-mind-wander.

of the excruciating pain He would endure in order to open a way for us into His holy presence. His love for us truly abounded as He gave Himself up for us.

If the mind of Christ is going to emerge in you, you must remain in His steps and love as He loved. God's desire for you is that "your love may abound still more and more in real knowledge and all discernment" (Phil 1.9). Living a life worthy of the gospel necessitates a daily choice to love everyone. Our love for others will reach our families, lift up the church, and overflow into the broken lives of those in the world. Our neighbors who are struggling outside of Christ need to be loved and taught.

We often come up short in expressing our love, but Jesus shows us the way. His love abounded in knowledge as He redeemed us with a full understanding of what was in view. He knew the state of those He came to rescue, He understood what they needed to hear, and He fully comprehended the necessary steps. He told the sinners near Him that He loved them—but He also told them that they were sick and needed to repent.

Likewise, we need to express our love in "real knowledge." This phrase points us to a knowledge that is maturing, even as our love abounds. It is good when our hearts move us to serve others with warm, emotional love. This love, however, should be well-informed with the eternal truth that is needed to bring others to Christ. To love as Christ loved, we must think about the lost as He did. When our minds dwell on what is true and right, we will share undiluted truth with sinners that help them see the right way to go. We can also help them see the superb benefits of directing our lives by the restrictive truth of our God. Those who champion inclusiveness will likely resist this narrow way, but with a smart approach to them, we can help them find their way out of the darkness of deception and perversion they are in. It is an informed love that will open their eyes to the light of the gospel.

A Strong Unity—Developed in Fellowship

One of the blessings of being in a church is the opportunity to fellowship with those who share the same worldview. In many ways, brothers and sisters in Christ will be "standing firm in one spirit, with one mind striving together" in their communities. Being unified in the same purpose and same salvation encourages us toward a strong, mutual faith. Isn't it great to be with those who see things the way we see them? When we seek to set our minds on things above, common sense tells us to seek the company of others who also seek to have such minds.

Paul knew, however, that the Christians in Philippi were not living in harmony as saints should (4.2). His joy would be completed only if they would be "of the same mind, maintaining the same love, united in spirit, intent on one purpose" (2.2). They needed to build a strong unity through the growth of a common mind, but they did not see things the same way. A shared mind is elusive when our varied and different beliefs divide us.

When we look at the twelve apostles, we see men who differed greatly in regard to their personalities and their perspectives. In the world, they would not have bonded as they did in Christ. Living with Jesus for three years, they developed His mind. At times, their thinking was definitely flawed, but they were unified because Jesus believed in them, recruited each one for His team, and showed them how to live in peace with others.

In our churches, we can and must agree on the basic truth of salvation and the matters of common service. We are in agreement regarding being born again, shared worship actions, and the use of our funds. With issues outside these matters, however, we can disagree and still enjoy fellowship. This means that we challenge ourselves to think about the different views our sisters and brothers present. It is inevitable that they will be "bringing some strange things to our ears" (Acts 17.20). In Christ, however, we will work together in a strong unity. We will maintain an encouraging fellowship of Christians bound by love, and this will prove to everyone that we are learning from the same Lord. If the twelve could overcome their differences, so can we—if we spend time with Jesus as they did.

So, as you strive toward a common understanding with others, you will need "discernment so that you may approve the things that are excellent, in order to be sincere and blameless" (Phil 1.9,10). We noted earlier in this text that love should abound in knowledge. It should also abound in discernment. "Love must be intelligent and morally discerning, however, if it would be truly *agape*."[4] We learn here that love does not accept everything a sister in Christ says. Or if I love my brother, I should listen to his views with a discerning mind. If I detect error in their words, I can express my love for them by leading them to the truth we find when our Bibles are open. Studying together, we also open our minds, and we reexamine our beloved beliefs.

Paul encourages the church in Thessalonica, "Do not quench the Spirit; do not despise prophetic utterances. But examine everything carefully; hold fast to that which is good; abstain from every form of evil" (1 Thes 5.19–22). When prophets spoke in this church, the congregation should have listened to these Spirit-guided men. They should not have treated the prophet's words with contempt. If, however, one claimed to be a prophet but was not truly appointed by God, he would speak truth mixed with error. What the saints greatly needed was a discerning spirit. They needed to think carefully on the words they heard, hold firmly to what aligns with divine revelation, and reject the evil ideas that might appear to be truth.

Minds filled with the Lord's wisdom are equipped for this crucial mental feat. The apostle John, who absorbed the words of Jesus into his heart, writes, "Beloved, do not believe every spirit, but test the spirits to see whether they are from God" (1 John 4.1). This testing requires us to be so familiar with words from God that we recognize any

---

[4] H. Kent, Jr., *Philippians*. EBC. (Grand Rapids: Zondervan, 1978) 108.

words that are not from Him. We listen intently. We test the words. We aim for agreement. Then, we remain in fellowship when we share the unifying mind of our Lord Jesus. "It is part of the process of living out the Christian life that constantly the servant of the Lord is called upon to discriminate between the base and the true, and to fashion his conduct accordingly."[5] As we compare, contrast, and distinguish the words we hear, we will "approve the things that are excellent."

An Outward Look—Realized in Obedience

When Jesus chose to rest at Jacob's well, He was tired and thirsty (John 4). He could have drawn some water for Himself and sat in peace as He recuperated. When the Samaritan woman arrived, however, His thoughts turned toward this struggling, lonely woman. Instead of looking inward and satisfying His own needs, He gazed into the woman's soul to see what she longed for. Unlike other Jewish men, He spoke gently to her. Fully aware of her troubled past, He strengthened her with hope, turning her heart toward living water, true worship, and the present Messiah. He enlivened her spirit to go into her city and share the news about the Christ. The obedient Son of God was beautifully accomplishing the work His Father had sent Him to do.

Here is the attitude we should have in ourselves. Looking away from our "personal interests" and doing "nothing from selfishness," we look into the lives of others to see their needs. We leave self-centered activities. We break away from the screens when they distract us from our pursuit of excellence. We limit time for our hobbies. These wise choices are necessary, as they free our minds to look outward toward those the Lord brings into our lives. We look over the directory, think about brethren who are hurting, and we "give preference" to them as we serve them (Rom 12.10). If we look into the world and think deeply about those who are floundering in the darkness, we will be "snatching them out of the fire" (Jude 23). As we interact

---

[5] L. Morris, *The First And Second Epistles To The Thessalonians.* NICNT. (Grand Rapids: Eerdmans, 1959) 177.

with those who have made bad choices in their lives, we approach them with a "gentle spirit" that stirs hope and points them to a better life. In those times when we are alone with no devices to distract us, our minds will wander into the lives of others, where we will see the Lord opening doors for us to serve in His steps.

A life lived worthy of the gospel will be reaching out to others and looking out for their interests. When we center our minds on our Savior, His encouraging example will dominate our thoughts. Throughout each day, our "outward" thoughts will be replaying in our minds, and we will be moved to take steps toward those in need. Henry David Thoreau wrote, "As a single footstep will not make a path on the earth, so a single thought will not make a pathway in the mind. To make a deep physical path, we walk again and again. To make a deep mental path, we must think over and over the kind of thoughts we wish to dominate our lives." The Lord will certainly be pleased when our "mental path" leads us into an unselfish life that is filled with sacrificial service.

The apostle Paul is a worthy example, too. He writes, "The things you have learned and received and heard and seen in me, practice these things, and the God of peace will be with you" (Phil 4.9). The virtues he commended in verse 8 could be seen in his Christ-centered life. He was able to say, "Be imitators of me, just as I am of Christ" (1 Cor 11.1). If we are in the steps of Paul, who was in the steps of Christ, we will be right where we should be. Paul's selfless example should inspire us. When his mind turned to his fleshly kinsmen who had stubbornly rejected their Messiah, his heart was filled with "great sorrow and unceasing grief" (Rom 9.2). This is the heart of His Lord, who wanted to gather the residents of Jerusalem under His wings—but they were not willing to come to Him (Matt 23.37). When our minds settle upon our loved ones who are outside of Christ, shouldn't we think of them as Paul did? Shouldn't our steps follow our thoughts and walk into their lives with the life-changing truth they need to hear?

Overcoming selfishness is no easy task. When Paul wrote to the saints in Rome, he spoke of the dramatic transformation that is needed to move us into the will of God. "And do not be conformed to this world, but be transformed by the renewing of your mind, so that you may prove what the will of God is, that which is good and acceptable and perfect" (Rom 12.2). If we are to become more thoughtful of others, it will require a change from within. "There must be a radical change in the inner man for one to live rightly in this evil age, 'by the renewing of your mind.'"[6] Where is the power that will affect this radical change? It is in God's words!

Our inner person will "be renewed day by day" (2 Cor 4.16) when our minds are dwelling on His transforming truth daily. Time in the Bible each day will change us into humble, loving, and obedient servants who glorify God with our Christ-like minds.

[6] A. Robertson, *Word Pictures in the New Testament, Volume IV.* (Grand Rapids: Baker Book House, 1931) 402–3.

Not the Word of Men, but the Word of God

Preaching that is Worthy of the Gospel

Mark Reeves

All scripture indeed is profitable (2 Tim 3.16–17), but with so relatively little doctrine in 1 Thessalonians, some of us might be tempted to wonder wherein lies its profitability. What little is mentioned (chapters 4–5) was, in fact, a repeat of what Paul had already taught these Christians orally.[1] Frankly, this epistle is mostly a reminder of *Paul's work of preaching* among these Christians (chapters 1–3).[2] So why was so much devoted to this reminder? Could there be any practical purpose in it for us today?

Our present task in this lecture is to study the text of 1 Thessalonians 2.1–16—which recounts Paul's preaching in this city—and then try to answer these two questions. In the process, we hope to learn something about preaching that is worthy of the gospel.

The Macedonian letters (Philippians, 1–2 Thessalonians) use the expression "worthy of ..." a number of times. Paul, for example, spoke

---

[1] Consider, e.g., "as you received from us *instruction* ..." (2 Thes 4.1), "you know what commandments we gave you" (4.2), "you have no need of anything to be written to you. For you yourselves know full well ..." (5.1–2), et. al.

[2] Like 2 Corinthians, the five chapters of 1 Thessalonians "reveal so much of Paul's mind and heart ... and show the depth of his feeling for the Christians in Thessalonica," K. Barker, *Expositor's Bible Commentary (Abridged Edition: New Testament)* (Grand Rapids, MI: Zondervan Publishing House, 1994) 843.

of the Philippian Christians conducting themselves "in a manner worthy of the gospel" (Phil 1.27) and the Colossian brethren walking "in a manner worthy of the Lord" (Col 1.10). Some three times he employs it with the Thessalonian church: walking "in a manner worthy of the God who calls you" (1 Thes 2.12), being considered "worthy of the kingdom of God" (2 Thes 1.5), and that God would count them "worthy of [their] calling" (2 Thes 1.11). Whether it be the *Lord God* Himself, or the *gospel* through which He calls men into His *kingdom*, all of these elements exude lofty value. At the heart of the gospel, for example, is a redemption price paid for man higher than silver or gold, indeed the precious blood of Christ (1 Pet 1.18–19). Thus, it stands to reason that the *preaching* of the gospel should measure up. Indeed, Paul's manner of preaching in Thessalonica was on this high plane.

Now to some background from Luke's inspired account in Acts 16.16—17.15. Just prior to coming to Thessalonica, the apostle Paul had successfully preached the gospel in Philippi to Lydia and the other women by that riverside outside the city gate, but he had also been unjustly beaten and cast into prison. Given the proximity of Philippi, news of this mistreatment may well have preceded Paul in Thessalonica.[3] At any rate, God provided his release from prison with an earthquake, but not without producing other conversions—that of the Philippian jailer himself and his household. Given their serious error in having beaten Paul without trial, the Philippian magistrates were more than willing to comply with the release (Acts 16.35–39). Passing through Amphipolis and Apollonia, Paul and his traveling companions then came to Thessalonica (Acts 17.1). After several weeks of reasoning from the Scriptures with the Jews in the local synagogue, fruit began to be born. However, the majority of the converts were, surprisingly, not from among the Jews (only "some" were persuaded, 17.4). Rather, they were from among the "God-fearing Greeks" (17.4). What followed was another round of persecution by

---

[3] Cf. "as you know" in 1 Thessalonians 2.2.

the Jewish majority in Thessalonica so that the brethren immediately sent Paul and Silas away by night to Berea. When Thessalonian Jews came there as well to harass Paul, he moved on to Athens.

The Proposition

In brief, Paul's proposition in our text is that he and those with him had behaved themselves without blame in bringing the gospel to Thessalonica (1 Thes 1.5; 2.10). Furthermore, the gospel had not come to the Thessalonians in vain (2.1; 2.13): they became imitators of Jesus and the apostles in suffering, became examples to others (1.6–7; 2.14), sounded forth the word to all Macedonia and Achaia (1.8), and made the astonishing turn from idols to serve a living God (1.9). All of this, Paul says, was tangible evidence of how that message currently "performs its work[4] in" the Thessalonians (2.13). Therefore, what they had been taught *must be the truth!* The Thessalonians can be assured that they are firmly established on a divine message (2.13). The present need then is, not only for them to continue in it, but to *abound* (3.12) or *excel* in it still more (4.1, 10).

Related to this is the idea that when facing persecution, "it is easy to be overwhelmed and discouraged and to distort the facts, even of recent history."[5] The Thessalonians would be tempted to focus only on the negative aspects of their suffering. So, Paul will keep things straight by reminding them of the powerfully *positive* things that had happened, that they not be overwhelmed by their distress.

Some commentators[6] see an apologetic effort here by Paul against critics in Thessalonica. He could be responding to real accusations or

---

[4] Greek present tense emphasizing *continuous* action.

[5] D. Mangum, Ed., *Lexham Context Commentary: New Testament*, Lexham Context Commentary (Bellingham, WA: Lexham Press, 2020).

[6] E.g., W. Hendriksen and S. Kistemaker, *Exposition of I-II Thessalonians*, New Testament Commentary (Grand Rapids: Baker Book House, 1953–2001) 59–60. R. Lenski, *The Interpretation of St. Paul's Epistles to the Colossians, to the Thessalonians, to Timothy, to Titus and to Philemon* (Columbus, OH: Lutheran Book Concern, 1937) 237.

simply anticipating charges that might be leveled.[7] Such adversaries were probably accusing Paul and his companions of being deluded individuals who, as religious charlatans, were selfishly out "to make money or build personal reputations"[8] at the expense of the Thessalonians. Apparently many religious and philosophical teachers traveled around the Roman world of that time trying to get what they could out of their audiences.[9] Paul's defense here is a reminder of the above-board nature of his recent work in Thessalonica. If it didn't silence the critics, it could at least encourage and strengthen the Thessalonian brethren against them.

Finally, it is hard not to think that the Holy Spirit moved Paul to write about the character of his work in this city as a *model to be imitated* by future preachers of all times and places. In conjunction with his letters to Timothy and Titus, these New Testament texts will provide a wonderful "manual" to be followed by anyone today desiring to preach in a manner worthy of the gospel of Jesus Christ.

The Text[10]

In our text of 1 Thessalonians 2.1–16 we first of all observe that Paul elaborates on something he briefly introduced in 1.5, namely, that the gospel had come to the Thessalonians powerfully and that they knew full well "what kind of men we proved to be among you for your sake." He will remind them that his arrival in Thessalonica with the gospel was "not in vain" (2.1), literally, empty, without

---

[7] Crossway Bibles, *The ESV Study Bible*. (Wheaton, IL: Crossway Bibles, 2008) 2306.

[8] T. Constable, "1 Thessalonians," *The Bible Knowledge Commentary: An Exposition of the Scriptures*. Ed. J. F. Walvoord and R. B. Zuck. (Wheaton, IL: Victor Books, 1985) 2.694.

[9] I. H. Marshall. "1 Thessalonians." In *New Bible Commentary: 21st Century Edition*, edited by D. A. Carson, R. T. France, J. A. Motyer, and G. J. Wenham, 4th ed. (Leicester, England; Downers Grove, IL: Inter-Varsity Press, 1994) 1279. Barker, *Expositor's Bible Commentary*, 852.

[10] Unless otherwise noted, all quotations are from the *New American Standard Bible: 1995 Update*. (La Habra, CA: The Lockman Foundation, 1995).

content.[11] It was not empty of results, substance, or character,[12] all of which will encourage the Thessalonians in the validity of the message and their continued practice of it.

The Circumstances of the Message

Paul will also remind the Thessalonians of the difficult circumstances in which the church was started there—difficult for Paul and his preaching companions, as well as for the Thessalonians. These started even before Paul arrived in Thessalonica. The reference to suffering and being "mistreated in Philippi" (2.2) is based on the events of Acts 16.19ff. which we briefly summarized in our introduction. The Greek word for "mistreated"[13] brings out the insolent, insulting treatment that Paul and Silas received there when they were dragged into the marketplace, falsely accused, publicly stripped of their outer clothing, beaten with rods, and then thrown into prison. All of this, as Paul pointed out to the jailer, had happened to them unlawfully given their Roman citizenship (Acts 16.36–37). Yet, Paul *did not unduly press the matter.* He only requested that the magistrates come personally and set them free. He and Silas largely took the brunt of the outrage, and men of that caliber are not cheats; they are "not engaged in empty work."[14]

Arriving in Thessalonica, things were not easier. They spoke the gospel of God "amid much opposition" (2.2). Here Paul used the Greek *agón* which originally referred to "the place where the Greeks assembled for the Olympic and Pythian games" and then came to re-

---

[11] Greek *kenos,* "without result, without effect," J. Louw and E. Nida. *Greek-English Lexicon of the New Testament: Based on Semantic Domains* (New York: United Bible Societies, 1996) 1.783.

[12] Crossway Bibles, *The ESV Study Bible,* 2306.

[13] Greek hybrízo, "to treat in an insolent or spiteful manner, mistreat, scoff at, insult," W. Arndt, F. Danker, W. Bauer, and F. Gingrich. *A Greek-English Lexicon of the New Testament and Other Early Christian Literature.* 3rd ed. (Chicago: University of Chicago Press, 2000) 1022. Henceforth, BDAG.

[14] Lenski, *The Interpretation of St. Paul's Epistles,* 239.

fer to the "contest of athletes."[15] Our English word "agony" descends from it. Here it is used of "a struggle against opposition."[16] The amazing thing in all this is that, from Philippi to Thessalonica, Paul only got bolder in his preaching! This was not a common response to opposition! In the boldness of Paul, the Thessalonians observed a "separation of the men from the boys." This was preaching that was worthy of the gospel.

The Motives Behind the Message

Beginning at verse 3, Paul addresses the *motivations* that lay behind his preaching and he starts with the negative aspect: "our exhortation does not come from error…" Most modern English versions translate with the word "error."[17] The primary meaning of the Greek word *pláne* is "roaming, wandering,"[18] from which comes our English word "planet."[19] Paul employs a figurative extension of the meaning: "wandering from the path of truth" thus, "error, delusion … to which one is subject."[20] Paul may be saying quite simply that his message was one of truth, not error,[21] or that he spoke "out of concern for truth (as opposed to 'misguidance')."[22] The translation "deceit"

---

[15] W. Vine, M. Unger, and W. White Jr. *Vine's Complete Expository Dictionary of Old and New Testament Words* (Nashville, TN: T. Nelson, 1996) 2.121.

[16] BDAG 17. The KJV translates with "contention." Any "contention," of course, involved not Paul with the believers, but the unbelieving Jews with Paul (Acts 17.1–5; 1 Thes 2.1416). The real idea here is that of Paul *contending, struggling* against opposition.

[17] NASB95, NKJV, ASV, ESV, RSV, NIV84, HCSB.

[18] BDAG 822. Commenting on the same word in Romans 1.27, Zerwick (460) says it comes from *plandomai*, wander, and indicates "a going astray, perversion."

[19] Vine, *Vine's Complete Expository Dictionary of Old and New Testament Words*, 2.151.

[20] BDAG 822.

[21] Lenski, *The Interpretation of St. Paul's Epistles*, 241. Constable, "1 Thessalonians," 2.694.

[22] R. Gundry, *Commentary on the New Testament: Verse-by-Verse Explanations with a Literal Translation* (Peabody, MA: Hendrickson Publishers, 2010) 814.

of the KJV[23] will better be expressed in the third Greek term to follow. Secondly, Paul's message was not motivated by "impurity"[24] or "uncleanness."[25] That is, it did not come from "impure motives"[26] or "mixed motives, insincerity."[27] Thirdly, Paul says their preaching included *no* "deceit"[28] or "guile."[29] There was no "trickery"[30] employed. The Greek word properly means a "bait" and here refers to "deceit … by subterfuge."[31] In summary, Paul did not employ "a faulty message, impure motives, or dubious methods."[32]

In verses 4–6 Paul continues reviewing what motives lay behind their preaching when he contrasts a desire to please God with an attempt to please men. Negatively, they had preached, "not as pleasing men." For example, they didn't use words of flattery (v. 5). They didn't seek glory from men by asserting their apostolic authority (v. 6).[33] They didn't use a "cloak of ("for" NKJV) covetousness" (ASV, KJV), that is, a cover or "pretext for greed" (v. 5 NASB95).[34] The New

---

[23] Also NRSV, New Living Translation (NLT).

[24] NASB95, ESV, HCSB.

[25] KJV, NKJV, ASV, RSV.

[26] NRSV, NIV84, NLT.

[27] Zerwick, *A Grammatical Analysis of the Greek New Testament,* 614. "Of impure motives" (BDAG 34).

[28] NASB95, NKJV; cp. "any attempt to deceive" (ESV) or "intent to deceive" (HCSB).

[29] KJV, ASV, RSV.

[30] NRSV; cf. "nor are we trying to trick you" (NIV84).

[31] Zerwick, *A Grammatical Analysis of the Greek New Testament,* 614.

[32] Crossway Bibles, *The ESV Study Bible,* 2306.

[33] The Greek word *báros* translated "burdensome" by the KJV literally means "weight, burden." However, here it is used figuratively in the way we might say, "throw one's weight around," and means "claim of importance" (BDAG 167). In this context it will be the idea of "wield authority, insist on one's importance" (Ibid.), "[claim] authority as apostles" (ASV), or "[make] demands as apostles" (ESV).

[34] Comp. "nor did we put on a mask to cover up greed" (NIV84, TNIV); "or had greedy motives" (HCSB). The Greek word behind *pretext* is *próphasis,* "falsely alleged motive, pretext, ostensible reason, excuse" (BDAG 889). The Greek word for *greed* is *pleonexsía,* from *pleon,* "more," and *echo,* "to have." Here it means "graspingness, selfish greed" (Zerwick 609). Note how our words "plenary" and "plenty" come

Living Translation extrapolates, "we were not pretending to be your friends just to get your money!"

Positively, Paul says they *were* motivated by a desire to please God (v. 4). They had a keen sense of having been "approved by God,"[35] with an awareness of having passed the test. The Greek word is *dokimázo*, "to put the test, hence approve," here translated "we have been adjudged fit."[36] Approved for what, we might ask? To be entrusted ("put in trust," KJV) with the gospel (v. 4). Paul reveals a tremendous inward sense of responsibility that no swindler would have borne. Paul knew that God examines (NASB95), tests (ESV), tries (KJV), or proves (ASV) the heart (v. 4).[37] Paul was conscious of always being watched from above: "God is witness" (v. 5). The Thessalonians were not first-hand witnesses to God's commissioning of Paul, and they couldn't read Paul's heart, but they certainly did know that Paul hadn't spoken in a way just to please them ("as you know," v. 5). That much they could be sure of.

Two Figures: Nursing Mother and Firm Father

In verses 7–12 Paul uses two figures to describe his manner of preaching in Thessalonica, a manner that truly brought out the relational nature of the gospel. The first figure was, "we proved to be gentle ... as a nursing mother" (v. 7). Here is a step beyond the idea of not asserting their authority in the previous verse. The Greek word

---

from this Greek word *pleon*.

[35] "approved" (NASB95, NKJV, ASV, ESV, RSV, NRSV, NIV84, HCSB); "allowed" (KJV). The English "allow" as used in the KJV is not "to permit," but "4. to approve, justify, sanction" as going back to the Latin, *allocare*, "to admit as approved" (N. Webster, *Webster's New Universal Unabridged Dictionary.* Second ed. New York: Simon & Schuster, 1983).

[36] Zerwick, *A Grammatical Analysis of the Greek New Testament*, 614. Barker comments, "after calling Paul on the Damascus road, God subjected him to necessary rigors in order to demonstrate his capability for his assigned task. Having thus prepared him, he committed to him the Gospel message to proclaim among Gentiles" (Barker, *Expositor's Bible Commentary Abridged*, 852).

[37] The same verb, *dokimázo*, is used twice in the same verse 4: "we have been approved," and "examines."

translated *nurse* is from *trophós*, in turn from *trépho*, "feed," meaning "nursing mother."[38] It portrayed the nurture, the fostering, the shelter, the comfort and tenderness of a nursing mother with her child. It also portrayed the love, "having so fond an affection for you" (v. 8). As a nursing mother, Paul and Silas didn't want something *from* these people, they rather wanted to *impart* something, namely, the gospel of God and their own lives[39] (v. 8)! Paul was ready to give to them of his ability, energy, and time, as the next verse will demonstrate. We might compare 2 Corinthians 12.14, "for I do not seek what is yours, but you," in which context Paul thinks of himself as a "parent" saving up for his "children," the Corinthian Christians. Here in 1 Thessalonians 2, we observe that Paul could give of himself to them "because you had become very dear to us" (v. 8).

"For you recall" (v. 9) introduces an illustration of *how* Paul and his companions were willing to impart their own lives to the Thessalonians. "For you recall, brethren, our labor and hardship, *how* working night and day so as not to be a burden to any of you, we proclaimed to you the gospel of God" (2.9). Paul and his companions did secular work to support themselves while preaching the gospel to the Thessalonians. In his second letter to them (3.7ff.), Paul makes the same point saying they hadn't eaten anyone's bread without paying for it. Did they make tents for a living as in Corinth (Acts 18.3)? Whatever the secular work, it was "so as not to be a burden to any of you." Paul had the right to get his "living from the gospel" and argues for it in 1 Corinthians 9.1–14. On some occasions he accepted these wages (2 Cor 11.8; Phil 4.15); on others he didn't use this right (1 Cor 9.12,15ff.), such as here in Thessalonica, but not because he didn't have the right (2 Thes 3.9). Why on one occasion and not another? As always, it was all for the gospel's sake (1 Cor 9.23). When he accepted wages, it was

---

[38] Zerwick, *A Grammatical Analysis of the Greek New Testament*, 615.

[39] NASB95 footnote: "Or souls" and so in KJV, ASV, LEB; "selves" (ESV, RSV, NRSV); Gk. *psyché*.

from an already established congregation, like Philippi, after he had moved on to help others (Phil. 4.15–16). When he refused wages, it was from a congregation with which he was presently working, still establishing it, and so as not to burden them. In this vein it is parallel with verse 6 and the apostolic authority that he there refuses to exercise. Both were rights that Paul was willing to give up when the occasion warranted it. This was preaching that is worthy of the gospel.

There was a second figure: "exhorting ... as a father" (v. 11). Together we observe mother *and* father—a balance with the "gentleness" of verse 7. Paul and Silas had come with some substance, with more than just a warm feeling toward these brethren. As a father they were "exhorting" the Thessalonians (v. 11). The Greek word is *parakaléo*. Its basic meaning is to "call to one's side, summon." The purpose for the summons can range from "appeal to, urge, or exhort" to "request, implore" to "comfort, encourage, cheer up."[40] If a distinction is to be made with the next word, then *parakaléo* here probably carries the meaning "exhort," that is, to urge one to *do* what he *knows* to be right. They were also "encouraging" the Thessalonians. The Greek word is *paramuthéomai*, "console, cheer up."[41] It's the idea of picking someone up when he is down, of lifting spirits. It is used of the Jews who were consoling Mary and Martha in the death of their brother Lazarus (Jn. 11.19, 31), and later on in 1 Thessalonians 5.14 Paul uses this Greek term for encouraging the fainthearted. As a father would his own children, they were "imploring" the Thessalonians (v. 11). The Greek word is *martyromai*, which in some contexts means "testify," in the sense of "bear witness." Here it probably means "to urge something as a matter of great importance, *affirm, insist, implore*."[42]

---

[40] BDAG, 764–65.

[41] BDAG, 769. "comforted" (KJV).

[42] BDAG, 619. KJV has "charged." Ephesians 4.17 demonstrates how it is used as a strong statement or command, "So this I say, and affirm together with the Lord..."

With the statement, "you are witnesses" in verse 10, we are reminded that Paul is not just "tooting his own horn." The real test of one's character is to let others critique it. Paul can't bluff here—the whole letter will be a failure if this wasn't true. The Thessalonians themselves could verify (or disavow!) what Paul was claiming regarding his behavior: "devoutly and uprightly and blamelessly." Devoutly (*hosíos*) means, "pertaining to a manner pleasing to God."[43] Uprightly (*dikaíos*) could also be translated "correctly, justly."[44] Blamelessly (*amémtos*) means "without blame, innocent, guiltless."[45]

Not only were the Thessalonians witnesses; Paul adds, "and so is God." Man, of course, is fallible and often renders faulty judgement. So even if the Thessalonians had failed to see properly, Paul is not afraid to say, "God knows."

Now, what was the objective of Paul's sterling character? Why the careful work among the Thessalonians? Why go to such lengths? He explains in verse 12, "so that you would walk in a manner worthy of the God …" It was not merely to impress their *emotions*, but to affect the way they would *live*. "The God who calls you," speaks of something special for the Thessalonians. They were not forced to obey the gospel. They had been extended an invitation, a call. A "call" implies that preparations had been made, that this was something worthwhile. "Into His own kingdom and glory" begins to speak to the *value*, to the *worth* of that call.

Verses 13–16 round out this section with Paul's expression of thanks for the way the Thessalonians received the gospel as a message from God, and how it immediately began to work in them producing their willingness to endure persecution. He sounds like the mother and father figure explaining things to his children and comforting them. Just as the initial churches in Judea had suffered

---

[43] BDAG, 728.

[44] BDAG, 250.

[45] Louw and Nida, *Greek-English Lexicon of the New Testament: Based on Semantic Domains* (New York: United Bible Societies, 1996) 1.776.

persecution (2.14; cf. Acts 8.1ff.), the Thessalonians recently were going through the same. In both cases, unbelieving Jews were the instigators. "But don't worry," Paul says in essence, "you're not alone in your trial—you are in good company including us, the prophets, and Jesus himself (2 Thes 2.15)! Furthermore, God will punish the persecutors accordingly (2 Thes 2.16)."

Some Applications

Preaching that is worthy of the gospel will first of all proclaim "the word of God" (1 Thes 2.13). It will not proffer "the word of men" (2.13), "flattering[46] speech" (2.5), or that which pleases men (2.4). Remember, God examines our hearts and knows if our preaching is limited only to topics that make people feel good (2.4–5), or if in fact we are willing to preach "the whole counsel of God" (Acts 20.27, KJV, ESV). Worthy preaching, rather than draw attention to the speaker (2.6), as can so easily be done in many of our sermon illustrations, will preach "Christ crucified" (1 Cor 1.23; 2.2). "We do not preach ourselves," Paul said, "but Christ Jesus as Lord, and ourselves as your bond-servants for Jesus' sake" (2 Cor 4.5–6). To do this it is imperative that the preacher spend time in the words of the inspired Evangelists: Matthew, Mark, Luke, and John. He must know these accounts that he may know Jesus intimately and proclaim Him thoroughly! This is the way to be the unashamed workman who accurately handles the word of truth (2 Tim 2.15).

Preaching that is worthy of the gospel is preaching done by a man who has full confidence in the *sufficiency* of the inspired Scriptures for a man's salvation (2 Tim 3.15) and his subsequent growth unto every good work (3.16). He's just got to believe that the Word will get the job done! If eloquence (Acts 18.24), or nice PowerPoint pre-

---

[46] From *kolakeías logo,* "flattering talk, blarney that gratifies one's vanity," J. Swanson, *Dictionary of Biblical Languages with Semantic Domains: Greek (New Testament)* (Oak Harbor: Logos Research Systems, Inc., 1997). "Excessive or insincere praise," Brannan, Rick, ed. *Lexham Research Lexicon of the Greek New Testament.* Lexham Research Lexicons. (Bellingham, WA: Lexham Press, 2020).

sentations, or engaging illustrations and anecdotes can be employed to support the message, let them prayerfully be placed in God's hands for that purpose. However, we can never allow these to trump a proclamation of the inspired text itself!

Preaching that is worthy of the gospel is not a venture which remains in the office where sermon preparation takes place. At some point it must "get its hands dirty" and *go to the people* who are needing the application of its message. "We proclaim Him," Paul says, but by means of the dirty work of "admonishing every man and teaching every man with all wisdom, so that we may present every man complete in Christ" (Col 1.28). It's not just preaching to big audiences but working with "every man." One cannot read our text here in 1 Thessalonians 2 without being impressed by the intimate, personal nature of Paul's work among these early Christians. He surely addressed groups from the "pulpit" at times, but he was also "imploring each one" (2.11). Judging from Paul's work in Ephesus, his typical practice involved teaching "publicly and from house to house" (Acts 20.20). It was a continual admonishing "each one with tears" (20.31).

So, there was this *individual* element that naturally produced an *emotional* one. A preacher cannot be this close to individual members and prospects without forming emotional ties. Thus, Paul's poignant statements about "having so fond an affection for" the Thessalonians, and they are becoming "very dear to us" (2 Thes 2.8). Of course, this also sets up the preacher for potential disappointment, frustration, and discouragement. It's the nature of getting close to people and loving them. Thus, in dealing with the carnally schismatic Corinthians we observe the gamut of Paul's emotions ranging from "affliction and anguish of heart" (2 Cor 2.4) to comfort (7.6–7), joy, and confidence (7.16). In "topping off" an extensive list of physical difficulties encountered in his preaching, Paul would add, "there is the daily pressure on me *of* concern for all the churches" (11.28). That's the risk of getting close to people in gospel preaching. One is investing of self in these people—one is imparting his own life and soul (1 Thes 2.8).

However, if working closely with immature brethren could frustrate Paul, it could also lift him to the highest levels of joy when they would follow God's word and do right. "For who is our hope or joy or crown of exultation? Is it not even you, in the presence of our Lord Jesus at His coming? For you are our glory and joy" (1 Thes 2.19–20; cf. 3.9; 2 Cor 1.14). Because Paul did not hide himself in an office, but worked with people, his life—whether unto fulfillment or failure—was largely intertwined with the lives of those same Christians (1 Thes 3.5; Gal 4.11; Phil 2.16).

This element of *human relationship* is, in fact, observed in the entire gospel process. So, of all the ways God might have chosen to save a man, he determines to do it through a preaching of the gospel (1 Cor 1.21) which had been placed in "earthen vessels" (2 Cor 4.7), that is, gospel preachers. Thus, the good news is from above but announced by humans to other humans. Paul himself first heard the gospel this way when God sent the preacher Ananias to him at the time of his conversion (Acts 9.10–17). When angels were employed in evangelism, it was to put the *preacher* in contact with the sinner. Consider the angel sending Philip to the Ethiopian Eunuch (8.26ff.) or putting Cornelius in touch with Peter (10.3ff.). This personal contact then continues beyond the initial conversion as evidenced by Paul's example of working among new Christians, even *individually*, to "present every man complete in Christ" (Col 1.28). He was so close to them that they were also aware of his secular work outside of preaching (1 Thes 2.9). This in turn was another kind of sermon for them by way of *example* (2 Thes 3.7–12). Along these same lines, when Paul was imprisoned in Rome, he not only reached unbelieving guards with the gospel *message* (Phil 1.13), but believers also with *his example* (1.14ff.). They were emboldened to preach outside the prison having observed Paul's preaching on the inside.

With the advent of Zoom, Skype, and other similar Internet platforms comes the opportunity to preach to people on the other side of the globe. At the same time, our Thessalonian text reminds us there is no real substitute for *in-person* preaching and teaching. It's not just a matter of imparting information (the gospel). The prospect or new convert is also learning by the *real-life example of the teacher!* So, let's continue to beseech the Lord of the harvest to send out workers (Matt 9.38) to follow up on contacts made virtually. Let's go into the homes and the coffee shops, even if in the less attractive neighborhoods or more difficult parts of the city—but let's be there with the gospel where it can be *heard* in word and *seen* embodied. After all, the gospel is about a God who not only *told* us of His love for us but *demonstrated* it (Rom 5.8). He didn't just impart the information, He *showed* us. He came to us from heaven, took on flesh and blood (John 1.14), entered our difficult human experience (Heb 2.10–18), and set us the example of obedience unto death so as to find life (1 Pet 2.21–24). Preaching that is worthy of this good news will follow suit.

Those of us *who preach* urgently need to follow the example of Paul here. We must begin with a message of truth, speaking not what pleases men but God. We must also imitate the character of Paul—the boldness in persecution, the giving up of "rights" as necessary, knowing how to be both gentle and forceful because we will be *spending time with people.* Above all, we need to carry a consciousness of having to one day give an account to the God who entrusted us with this message. And we need more men to do this! Note throughout our text the "we," "our," and "us." It was not just about Paul. It included others like the young evangelist in training, Timothy, as well as the lesser known but capable companion, Silas (1 Thes 1.1). These shared in Paul's sterling character, and these kinds of men can still be present today. Maybe you, young man, are reading this and feeling the urge to become the next Silas, Timothy, or Paul.

Is it demanding work? It absolutely is! It is a "labor"[47] and "striving"[48] that leaves one exhausted by day's end, but ready to go again the next day "according to [Christ's] power, which mightily works within" (Col 1.29) the preacher. I know preaching would be a lot more convenient if it only involved a "9 to 5" set of office hours. Nonetheless, that which is worthy of the gospel is carried out "night and day" (Acts 20.31; 1 Thes 2.9; 2 Thes 3.8), in the same way that the Object of the gospel began His day before dawn (Mar 1.35) and continued laboring long after sunset (1.32).

Be advised there is great reward if we will follow this pattern: the gospel we preach will not come in vain to those who hear it (1 Thes 2.1), we will have something for which to give thanks (1.2ff.; 2.13ff.), we will become dear to a people (2.8), and it will bring great joy (2.19–20)!

At the same time, those of us *who listen* to preaching need to consider the character of the preachers we listen to in considering his message as truth or error. Beware of those who use deceit. Remember, they will look like sheep (Matt 7.15), like servants of righteousness (2 Cor 11.14–15), so by its very nature outward appearance is not an adequate test—there must be more. Beware of those who are more interested in material benefits, who are not willing to give up anything in preaching the gospel, who run from persecution, conflict, or trouble in the church. Beware of those who speak only what the church wants to hear—who never "step on toes" but only "tickle ears" (1 Tim 4.3–4). May the preaching of Paul here in 1 Thessalonians 2 be at the forefront of our minds when thinking about the next preacher to hire for the local work or deciding what men will hold our gospel meetings.

---

[47] From *kopíao*, "to exert oneself physically, mentally, or spiritually, *work hard, toil, strive, struggle*" (BDAG 558). Same word used of the work of overseers in the local church in 1 Thessalonians 5.12.

[48] From *agonízomai*, "'to contend' in the public games, 1 Cor 9.25"; here, "to put forth every effort, involving toil" (Vine 2.235); "*to fight, struggle*" figuratively (BDAG 17).

If in fact we have been blessed by preachers who have displayed the character of Paul here, we have all the more reason to stand fast in what was taught by them. This brings us back to a question raised in our introduction and an application for us all. What was Paul's purpose in writing this? To the Thessalonians he says, "as you received from us ... that you excel still more" (4.1ff.). That meant things like abstaining from fornication (4.3ff.), increasing in love of the brethren (4.9ff.), being ready for the Lord's return (5.1ff.), submitting to elders, living in peace with the brethren, and working with the unruly, fainthearted, and weak (5.12ff.). All of us need to stand confidently in every doctrine of the Macedonian letters, indeed every doctrine of this apostle. We need to practice it, because it was the gospel "of God" (1 Thes 2.2, 8, 9), and it was preached in a manner worthy of the gospel!

Pray without Ceasing

Prayer That Is Worthy of the Gospel

Trevor A. Brailey

Near the beginning of Philippians, Paul spoke of a life worthy of the gospel:

> Only let your conduct be worthy of the gospel of Christ, so that whether I come and see you or am absent, I may hear of your affairs, that you stand fast in one spirit, with one mind striving together for the faith of the gospel, and not in any way terrified by your adversaries, which is to them a proof of perdition, but to you of salvation, and that from God. (Phil 1.27–28)[1]

Paul described a life worthy of the gospel as one that stands for the truth and is willing to speak forthrightly in its defense. A congregation acting in a way worthy of the gospel will be unified, working together for the gospel's sake, and fearless in the face of opposition. Every Christian, not just a few leaders, must be willing to suffer for the truth of the gospel (Matt 5.10–12; 1 Pet 4.12–14).

A life worthy of the gospel must be characterized by prayer worthy of the gospel. How can Christians meet that high standard in prayer? The Philippian and Thessalonian letters contain direct instructions about prayer and examples of prayer. We seek to follow those instructions, honor those examples, and improve our prayers

---

[1] Unless noted otherwise, all quotations of scripture are from the NKJV.

as individuals and in congregational worship. We want to consider first what "worthiness" requires.

What Does It Mean to Be Worthy?

To have worthy prayers, we must be truly serving God in all ways. We cannot live the wrong way, pray like nothing is amiss, and then expect to be blessed in our inconsistency. We cannot harbor resentment toward other Christians and expect to be strengthened (Eph 4.1–3; Col 1.9–12). When we have sinned, sincere prayers for forgiveness and help are worthy prayers that lead us back to worthy lives.

I have been struck by how the topic I was assigned has affected me. For years I was pained by the feeling that my prayers were never quite right, never meant quite sincerely enough, and I spent many additional hours trying to say things the right way, trying to mean the words more fully as I said them, or trying to pray for everything that I felt that I ought to have mentioned at that moment. These doubts were at times debilitating as I acted in an obsessive way. C. S. Lewis described having similar feelings about prayer as a youth, being concerned that he had not been thinking fully about everything he had said in prayer, which led to the attempt to pray better, and usually to the same concern of inadequacy regarding the second prayer, and so on, until prayer became a great burden.[2] From speaking with others with similar concerns in prayer I expect that having some degree of doubt about the worthiness of one's own prayers is not uncommon among Christians. As time passed, I grew better able to pray with confidence and to avoid being hamstrung by those obsessive thoughts. I believe a greater understanding of the love and mercy of God allowed me to improve.

Perhaps, having some perfectionist tendencies, I was trying to be worthy in the absolute sense, which no man except Jesus Christ has achieved. Understanding the sense of worth involved is key. Are our prayers or any of our other acts of devotion worthy in the sense of be-

---

[2] C. S. Lewis, *Surprised by Joy* (San Diego: Harvest/HBJ, 1956) 60–3.

ing equal to God's great love for us and great sacrifice on our behalf? Certainly not! However, when we simply act in the ways that He has commanded with true love and devotion, He gladly accepts us as we stand before Him. Forgiven and faithful, we are worthy in His eyes.

A lesser example can be found in human relationships. How do I show appreciation for my wife? I buy her flowers from time to time. I buy gifts. I compliment her frequently. Are those actions worthy of her? In the sense of being equal to all her good characteristics, no! She is worth much more than the flowers, gifts, and praise. However, is what I do worthy in the sense of being appropriate and acceptable? Yes!

> You are witnesses, and God also, how devoutly and justly and blamelessly we behaved ourselves among you who believe; as you know how we exhorted, and comforted, and charged every one of you, as a father does his own children, that you would walk worthy of God who calls you into His own kingdom and glory. (1 Thes 2.10–12)

The worthy (holy, righteous, and blameless) character of the teachers needed to be seen also in the behavior of the Christians they were instructing. Paul's worthiness was not absolute, as he emphasized in Ephesians 3.8. Our worthiness is not absolute, yet when we are living as we should (Col 1.10), our walk is deemed worthy of God despite our frailty.

We should notice how we can pray for the good works and even the faith of others; to pray for them does not violate their responsibility to choose to believe in God or their autonomy in choosing to obey God:

> Therefore we also pray always for you that our God would count you worthy of this calling, and fulfill all the good pleasure of His goodness and the work of faith with power, that the name of our Lord Jesus Christ may be glorified in you, and you in Him, according to the grace of our God and the Lord Jesus Christ. (2 Thes 1.11–12)

The Christians in Thessalonica, who were probably still recent converts,[3] were suffering without having done anything wrong to deserve it (2 Thes 1.4–5). They were not suffering because of diseases, natural disasters, or economic problems, which could affect anyone without regard to guilt or righteousness (2 Thes 1.6–10). They were suffering for the Lord's cause, and their continuing love and faithfulness through persecution affirmed that they were standing for truth and were worthy of the kingdom. When we endure hardship and remain faithful, we also are acting in a worthy way and bringing glory to Christ.

Instruction about Prayer

1 Thessalonians 5.17–18 contains the commands to "pray without ceasing, in everything give thanks; for this is the will of God in Christ Jesus for you." Many readers have wondered what Paul meant by praying without ceasing and have proposed widely varying answers.

Some people claim that everything they do is prayer. While prayers can be pictured as other acts of worship before God (Ps 141.2; Rev 5.8; 8.3–4), no instance of calling another act of worship a prayer is apparent in the New Testament.

Many people claim that being silent is a form of prayer. While there are groanings too deep for words (Rom 8.26), the expectation that we can wait and have God tell us something while we listen in silent "prayer" is dangerous.

Some people have tried to pray without stopping in a literal sense. One prominent example is in the 19th century Russian book, *The Way of a Pilgrim*.[4] The writer, or at least the narrator in the work, was a peasant with some education and a great deal of devotion. He had heard good sermons on what prayer was, the need for it, and its fruits,

---

[3] Relevant internal evidence includes Paul's having been away for a short time (1 Thes 2.17) and that Timothy was sent during that time to establish their faith (1 Thes 3.1–2).

[4] Anonymous, *The Way of a Pilgrim*. Trans. O. Savin (Boston: Shambhala, 1996).

but nothing on how to succeed in prayer. He was concerned that he was not practicing the kind of unceasing prayer that he thought 1 Thessalonians 5.17, Ephesians 6.18, and 1 Timothy 2.8 commanded.[5] He was advised to use the "Jesus Prayer," specifically "Lord Jesus Christ, have mercy on me!"[6] He began reciting the Jesus Prayer 3000, then 6000, then 12,000 times per day. Eventually he had no cares, concerns, or interests other than the unceasing prayer.[7] That kind of continual prayer differs greatly from the practical concerns about which we are told to pray in Philippians and Thessalonians. Eventually, the narrator identified prayer without ceasing with always remembering and praising God in all times, places, and circumstances.[8] The semi-mystical advice in the earlier part of the book seemed to have changed to include more relevant, helpful instruction.

What does praying "without ceasing" entail? Paul used a closely related word in 2 Timothy 1.3 to describe praying for Timothy as a regular part of his prayers night and day. Paul prayed about this as a regular practice, not something he did literally without stopping. The context also demonstrates this. Paul said to give thanks in everything in 1 Thessalonians 5.18. He did not mean that thanksgiving to God would be literally unending; some translations have "in every circumstance" or a similar phrase (RSV, NIV, NRSV, ESV) instead of "in everything." Prayer, including thanksgiving, is to be habitual but not continuous.

It is not enough to avoid the abuses of praying without ceasing; we must also positively practice what the verse teaches. Every Christian must spend time in prayer regularly. Kreeft correctly calls "taking time to pray" "the first thing, the hardest thing, and the most essential thing of all."[9] Nelson writes, "The ability to pray is the acid

---

[5] Ibid. 1 (First Narrative).

[6] Ibid. 10 (First Narrative).

[7] Ibid. 14–18 (First Narrative).

[8] Ibid. 97 (Fourth Narrative).

[9] P. Kreeft, *Prayer: The Great Conversation* (Ann Arbor, MI: Servant Books, 1985) 12.

test of faith" (Matthew 7.7–11; Luke 18.1–8), referring to repeated prayer without an apparent immediate response.[10]

Philippians contains a related instruction about prayer. Paul wrote, "Be anxious for nothing, but in everything by prayer and supplication, with thanksgiving, let your requests be made known to God; and the peace of God, which surpasses all understanding, will guard your hearts and minds through Christ Jesus" (Phil 4.6–7). God wants to hear our thanks and our requests regularly. He wants to hear about all our concerns. Prayer brings peace and is a productive means of dealing with stress, but its benefits are not merely psychological. Prayer resolves our needs through the power of God. Prayer is for everything, not just emergencies or the matters we feel we cannot handle ourselves. We can pray intensely without becoming anxious in a sinful way; Colossians 4.12 describes Epaphras as "laboring fervently" or "struggling" (ESV) in prayer for the Christians in Colossae.

Groeschel gives his readers a thought experiment about prayer: Suppose everything for which you had prayed on a given day were to be granted immediately. What would happen? Your relative and a church member you know would be healed of their illnesses suddenly. Your job would be pleasant. Your children would get along. You would have enough to eat and your house would be secure. Would that be all? There were probably things not listed that you had intended to include in your prayer but did not.[11] With God's great promises to grant our prayers (in His time), why let a lack of effort keep us from bringing those other important things before Him?

Paul addressed praying for other Christians when he wrote, "But we are bound to give thanks to God always for you, brethren beloved by the Lord, because God from the beginning chose you for salvation through sanctification by the Spirit and belief in the truth" (2 Thes

---

[10] R. Nelson, *First and Second Kings*. Interpretation. (Louisville, KY: John Knox Press, 1987) 59.

[11] C. Groeschel, *Altar Ego* (Grand Rapids, MI: Zondervan, 2013) 204.

2.13). Do we thank God for our fellow Christians? We see that Paul did so repeatedly and regularly. In the past, I was unsure about praying for the faith of others because individuals must make the choice to believe, and no one can do that for them. I learned that God had chosen these people in Thessalonica to believe, be sanctified, and be saved, but that did not take away their personal responsibility to choose to believe and obey. Paul prayed for them, but nothing that God would do in response to Paul's prayers would violate the Thessalonian Christians' free will.

In the closing of the first letter to the Thessalonians, Paul asked them to pray for him (1 Thes 5.25). Toward the end of the second letter he repeated the request with more explanation, writing, "Finally, brethren, pray for us, that the word of the Lord may run swiftly and be glorified, just as it is with you, and that we may be delivered from unreasonable and wicked men; for not all have faith" (2 Thes 3.1–2). Paul desired intercessory prayer. As he was praying for them, so they were to return the request for divine favor. Paul wanted his preaching to succeed in spreading the word and bringing others to faith. God's help never removes the obligation for the hearers to believe and obey, but He can and does help in many ways to make our preaching more effective if we are actually praying for it.

Examples of Prayer

Paul provided many examples of prayer in the letters to Philippi and Thessalonica.

> For God is my witness, how greatly I long for you all with the affection of Jesus Christ. And this I pray, that your love may abound still more and more in knowledge and all discernment, that you may approve the things that are excellent, that you may be sincere and without offense till the day of Christ, being filled with the fruits of righteousness which are by Jesus Christ, to the glory and praise of God. (Phil 1.8–11)

Paul prayed for others with the most love possible: the affection of Christ. Do we pray that others will grow in knowledge and wisdom? Do we pray that a struggling Christian will grow in love to the point that he will overcome temptation and be strong again? Praying for others does not relieve them of the need to study or obey, but the Lord will help them if they are open to Him. Paul interceded for the Philippians even though they were already spiritually strong. Growth in knowledge and wisdom will result in choosing the right things and living a righteous life (Rom 12.2).

> For what thanks can we render to God for you, for all the joy with which we rejoice for your sake before our God, night and day praying exceedingly that we may see your face and perfect what is lacking in your faith? Now may our God and Father Himself, and our Lord Jesus Christ, direct our way to you. And may the Lord make you increase and abound in love to one another and to all, just as we do to you, so that He may establish your hearts blameless in holiness before our God and Father at the coming of our Lord Jesus Christ with all His saints. (1 Thes 3.9–13)

Paul wanted to encourage these Christians and help them grow. While we may not know as many other Christians as Paul did, we all have many people for whom we can pray. In this short passage, Paul mentioned praying with thanksgiving, petition, and intercession, providing a model of rich and multifaceted prayer.

Paul was also grateful for the prayers of others on his behalf. He wrote,

> For I know that this will turn out for my deliverance through your prayer and the supply of the Spirit of Jesus Christ, according to my earnest expectation and hope that in nothing I shall be ashamed, but with all boldness, as always, so now also Christ will be magnified in my body, whether by life or by death (Phil 1.19–20).

Do we pray for others in extreme need, as he did while imprisoned? The Philippians were interceding for Paul, which, along with the work of the Spirit, was key to his success. Paul would continue to preach and glorify Christ. The Christians in Ephesus were also to pray for him in that way (Eph 6.19–20).

We can properly pray for the health and safety of ourselves and others, but Paul was content with life or death as long as it glorified Christ, just as he had been content with freedom or prison as long as it helped the cause of Christ. Do we have the kind of faith that puts Christ above personal comfort (Acts 20.24; 1 Pet 4.16)?

> We give thanks to God always for you all, making mention of you in our prayers, remembering without ceasing your work of faith, labor of love, and patience of hope in our Lord Jesus Christ in the sight of our God and Father. (1 Thes 1.2–3)

> We are bound to thank God always for you, brethren, as it is fitting, because your faith grows exceedingly, and the love of every one of you all abounds toward each other. (2 Thes 1.3)

Paul was thankful for these Christians, who were suffering but faithful. Are we praying for Christians who are suffering today? Do we give thanks for our brothers and sisters, both for their growth and for their love? Worthy action on the part of others ought to lead to worthy prayers of thanksgiving to God.

> I thank my God upon every remembrance of you, always in every prayer of mine making request for you all with joy, for your fellowship in the gospel from the first day until now, being confident of this very thing, that He who has begun a good work in you will complete it until the day of Jesus Christ; just as it is right for me to think this of you all, because I have you in my heart, inasmuch as both in my chains and in the defense and confirmation of the gospel, you all are partakers with me of grace. (Phil 1.3–7)

How much do we pray for others? Paul prayed with thanksgiving every time he remembered the Philippians, interceding for them in prayer (as he did for other Christians in Eph 1.15–16; Col 1.3–4). He had joy because they had been in fellowship with him, and he was confident that God would continue to help them fulfill their service. He remembered that they had shared in God's grace as they aided him in preaching the truth despite official opposition and persecution (Acts 16.12–40). Paul wanted them to be equipped by God with everything good (Heb 13.20–21). Are we praying for those who help us? Are we praying for those we help? Do we pray frequently for them?

> Now may our Lord Jesus Christ Himself, and our God and Father, who has loved us and given us everlasting consolation and good hope by grace, comfort your hearts and establish you in every good word and work. (2 Thes 2.16–17)

> Now may the Lord direct your hearts into the love of God and into the patience of Christ. (2 Thes 3.5)

> Now may the Lord of peace Himself give you peace always in every way. The Lord be with you all. (2 Thes 3.16)

Whether you call these passages benedictions, blessings, or prayers, Paul was interceding for these Christians. We are not going to change Christ's and the Father's choice to comfort and strengthen those who respond to the divine teaching, just as we will not change the choice of others to love and obey, but we still can pray for God to console them and expect that He will respond positively. It is not wrong to pray for what God has already promised to do.

Praying within the Will of God

We often speak of the will of God in two different ways. One is what God wants us to do, i.e., to obey the commands and principles given by divine revelation. Another way is what He allows to happen—for example, whether a natural disaster strikes or a serious illness occurs. Our prayers must be in accordance with God's will in the first sense, because we should not ask for what He has forbidden. We cannot know God's will in the second sense; our requests might not fit His plans in a particular situation, but that does not mean that our prayer has been sinful.

Our prayers to the Father must have the attitude of Christ: Your will be done (Matt 6.10; 26.42). That is true for both meanings of God's will. While we must work to please Him and show Him respect by following His rules, we also have to trust what He has determined about the future. When our main concern shifts from getting what we want to trusting God to work through us, we will pray in ways worthy of the gospel.

Paul also told the Thessalonians that they needed to follow "how you ought to walk and to please God" (1 Thes 4.1). If we want our prayers to be effective, we need to live in ways that are consistent with God's commands. Paul went on to show that worthy behavior would include avoiding sexual immorality, displaying brotherly love, working honestly, and living quietly (1 Thes 4.2–12).

The key to praying in a worthy way is being willing to change to better follow God. Unconfessed sin or a broken relationship that has not been handled according to Bible teaching (Matt 5.23–24) will interfere with praying properly.[12]

Sittser, after having read many great prayers of the Old and New Testament, noted that the speakers did not generally ask for a long life, perfect health, or worldly success. They asked for more knowledge of God's love, more purity, and more strength.[13] Solomon's request of the Lord at the beginning of His reign was like that (1 Kng 3.5–14). Sittser also said that asking for the world to change without

---

[12] D. DeWelt, *Sweet Hour of Prayer*. Adapted by S. Tippett (Joplin, MO: College Press Publishing Company, 1999) 10.

[13] J. Sittser, *When God Doesn't Answer Your Prayer* (Grand Rapids, MI: Zondervan, 2003) 129.

being willing for the self to change is worthless.[14] He writes, "Either we can view the world as a place that needs changing for our sake, or we can ask God to use the world to change us for his sake."[15] Fosdick noted that the Prodigal Son's words to his father had changed from "Give me" in Luke 15.12 to "Make me" in 15.19, reflecting a rejection of greed and a willingness to be changed into a humble servant.[16]

Prayers need to be honest and backed up by a willingness to change even in painful ways. As an example of a "dangerous" but beneficial prayer, Groeschel uses Psalm 139.23–24:[17] "Search me, O God, and know my heart; Try me, and know my anxieties; And see if there is any wicked way in me, And lead me in the way everlasting."

Simple Suggestions for Worthy Prayer

Anyone who loves and desires to obey God can pray in a way worthy of the gospel, and everyone should want to improve in prayer. In this section, paragraphs with applications of Bible teaching will be followed by suggestions about how to implement the teaching in prayer. Most of these suggestions can be applied to individual, family, and congregational prayers.

Paul wrote a list of qualities our thoughts should have. He wrote, "Finally, brethren, whatever things are true, whatever things are noble, whatever things are just, whatever things are pure, whatever things are lovely, whatever things are of good report, if there is any virtue and if there is anything praiseworthy--meditate on these things" (Phil 4.8). This list of praiseworthy things outlines many characteristics of worthy living and subjects of worthy prayer. What is in our thoughts will affect what is in our prayers.

Suggestion 1: Set aside some time each day for serious thought in prayer. You might find it helpful to organize your prayers in a vari-

---

[14] Ibid. 163–4.

[15] Ibid. 174.

[16] H. Fosdick, *The Meaning of Prayer* (New York: Association Press, 1915) 24.

[17] C. Groeschel, *Dangerous Prayers: Because Following Jesus Was Never Meant to Be Safe* (Grand Rapids, MI: Zondervan, 2020) 31–2.

ety of different ways. You might think about needs in areas of your life, in your family's lives, and in the congregation's work. You might think about the friends that you would like to see reached and then about various places that you would like to see the gospel preached. You might think about some specific efforts the church is making to preach to non-Christians, to teach Christians, and to help Christians in need. A prayer given time and careful consideration will be more effective than a prayer without those things.

Worthy prayer will also encompass different kinds of prayers found in the Bible. 1 Timothy 2.1 lists four types of prayer, though they can overlap: supplications, prayers, petitions, and intercessions. Prayers may also contain thanksgiving, praise, confession, or lament. My own rough tally of the content of New Testament prayers puts petition as the most frequent topic, followed closely by thanksgiving and intercession.

Suggestion 2: Look for balance in the content of your prayers. If you have been mostly asking God for things in prayer, spend some time thanking Him for what He has already given you. If your prayers have mostly concerned your own needs (or those of your closest family and friends), dedicate time to praying about the needs of others. If you have not praised God in prayer recently, set aside a few minutes to keep your focus upon that. Balancing "please" and "thank you," or balancing requests for yourself with requests for others, can improve your spiritual focus inside and outside of prayer.

The Psalms were often directly addressed to God (as is prayer), they are sometimes classified in many of the same ways that prayers are (petition, thanksgiving, intercession, and praise), and, most importantly, several of the Psalms call themselves prayers (Ps 17.1; 72.20; 86.1, 6; 90.1; 102.1; 142.1). Brueggemann wrote of the Psalms and prayer, "We find in the psalms both models and permits. We stand under their discipline, and we are authorized by their freedom."[18] He noted that the Psalms also show us that God is not "easily offended" by strong emotion or expressions of confusion and frustration; fearing to speak to God in those ways can leave our prayers bereft of seriousness and effectiveness.[19] He also writes, "It is evident that Israel's prayer [in the Psalms]—even though stylized and therefore in some ways predictable—is rarely safe, seldom conventional, and never routine."[20] Lewis states that the Psalms express the delight in God that made David want to dance.[21]

Suggestion 3: Choose a psalm. Think about how God is addressed. Think about how some of the Psalmist's thanksgivings, petitions, intercessions, praises, or lamentations might apply to your life. Pray accordingly. For congregational worship, consider the praises expressed in prayer in many passages (Matt 6.9; Luke 11.2; Acts 4.24; 2 Cor 9.15; Heb 13.15) and work similar words of praise into public prayer.

Paul instructed Christians in Corinth who exercised spiritual gifts to ensure that others could understand what they were saying. Praying while using a gift also needed to be done "with the understanding" so that all the members could understand what was being said and be edified (1 Cor 14.14–19). Even though Christians no longer have supernatural spiritual gifts (1 Cor 13.8–10), each man leading prayer should still work to help all listeners understand the prayer and be edified. I believe that one of the most simple and effective ways to improve public worship in most congregations would be to emphasize putting more thought and effort into public prayer.

Suggestion 4: Men who lead prayers could avoid archaic phrases that some people might not really understand. They could also encourage deeper thought by rephrasing parts of their prayers to avoid

---

[18] W. Brueggemann, *The Psalms and the Life of Faith* (Minneapolis: Augsburg Fortress, 1995) 34.

[19] Ibid. 58.

[20] Ibid. 50.

[21] C.S. Lewis, *Reflections on the Psalms* (San Diego: Harvest/Harcourt, 1958) 45.

cliches. Additionally, men leading prayer could incorporate lessons from sermons, classes, and songs in their prayers, thus reinforcing the teaching. Opportunities to edify the congregation could include praying for the evangelists that the congregation supports and expressing praise and love to God directly in prayer.

Many of these suggestions need only a small amount of preparation. When people who are praying individually or publicly take some time to plan what they will say and then speak in simple and thoughtful ways, they promote spiritual growth and health.

Conclusion

As Christians, we are commanded to pray regularly, expressing our requests and our thanks to God. We also need to intercede in prayer for others. We can pray for the spiritual health and growth of other Christians, even though we cannot override others' free will or remove their personal responsibility.

Worthy prayer presupposes a willingness to accept the will of God and change whatever is necessary to conform to it. Thinking about different areas of our lives and different types of prayer can make our prayers more effective. Public prayer is an opportunity to help many people grow together spiritually and unite their desires before the Lord.

While our prayers are not worthy of the gospel in an absolute sense, the New Testament counts our prayers as worthy when we faithfully serve God and repent after we have sinned.

How do we fulfill the command to "pray without ceasing?" Reciting "Lord Jesus Christ, have mercy on me!" thousands of times per day will not help (Matt 6.7). Instead, regularly speaking what is heartfelt and true, even something as short and plain as "God, be merciful to me, a sinner!" (Luke 18.13–14) when needed, will be fully acceptable to the Lord.

To Walk in a Way Worthy of the Gospel

Benjamin Lee

The church in Thessalonica is one of the best examples of a local congregation. This church, which had its beginnings rooted in suffering, provides churches and Christians today an example of what is possible when we trust in God.

The church in Thessalonica was established during Paul's second missionary journey.

> Now when they had traveled through Amphipolis and Apollonia, they came to Thessalonica, where there was a synagogue of the Jews. And according to Paul's custom, he went to them, and for three Sabbaths reasoned with them from the Scriptures, explaining and giving evidence that the Christ had to suffer and rise again from the dead, and saying, 'This Jesus whom I am proclaiming to you is the Christ.' And some of them were persuaded and joined Paul and Silas, along with a large number of the God-fearing Greeks and a number of the leading women (Acts 17.1–4; NASU).

The young congregation remained faithful to God despite Paul's quick departure due to persecution. According to some, Paul may have been in Thessalonica for only three weeks. Consider the following from Weaver:

> Paul's statement in his first letter that the Thessalonian converts had 'turned to God from idols, to serve the living and true God'

(1 Thess. 1.9) raises some question about whether Luke reports the full story about his evangelistic work in the city. The book of Acts tells only of the success in the synagogue, whereas the information provided in the Thessalonian letter implies that the great majority of converts during his time there came from those who had not believed in God. This would mean that there was a 'turn to the Gentiles' mission not mentioned in the Acts account that would likely have taken more time than the three week period reported by Luke. Paul makes specific reference to the Jewish opposition to their work among the Gentiles (1 Thess. 2.16). Some have concluded that this would have required a visit of at least several weeks, and perhaps even a few months.[1]

Arnold states,

The total length of Paul's stay in Thessalonica may actually have been longer than three weeks; this is merely how long his welcome lasts in the synagogue. We know that he stays long enough to receive a monetary gift from the Philippians (Phil. 4.16) and that he spends time working in the city to earn his support (1 Thess. 2.9). His stay in the city, however, lasts no more than a couple of months.[2]

However long or short, Paul's visit was highly effective.

The saints in Thessalonica became imitators of Paul and Jesus in how they suffered.

But the Jews, becoming jealous and taking along some wicked men from the market place, formed a mob and set the city in an uproar; and attacking the house of Jason, they were seeking to bring them out to the people. When they did not find them, they began dragging Jason and some brethren before the city authorities, shouting, 'These men who have upset the world have come here also; and Jason has welcome them, and they all act contrary to the decrees of

---

[1] W, Weaver, *The Books of 1 and 2 Thessalonians:* (Guardian of Truth Foundation), 13.

[2] *Zondervan Illustrated Bible Backgrounds Commentary*, Volume 2, 381.

Caesar, saying that there is another king, Jesus.' They stirred up the crowd and the city authorities who heard these things. And when they had received a pledge from Jason and the others, they released them. The brethren immediately sent Paul and Silas away by night to Berea and when they arrived, they went into the synagogue of the Jews. (Acts 17.5–9).

Paul would speak about their suffering as well throughout his first letter to them: "You also became imitators of us and of the Lord, having received the word in much tribulation with the joy of the Holy Spirit" (1 Thess 1.6); "For you, brethren, became imitators of the churches of God in Christ Jesus that are in Judea, for you also endured the same sufferings at the hands of your own countrymen, even as they did from the Jews" (1 Thess 2.14). Despite suffering, they still had joy! Their joy was rooted in Christ and not in their circumstances. Can we say the same when we endure suffering for Christ?

Paul's letters to the Thessalonians read differently from some of his other epistles. There are few rebukes, compared to other epistles like first and second Corinthians. The epistles to the Thessalonians are filled with Paul's commending the brethren of their love, faith, and hope in Jesus. The report Paul received from Timothy (while in Corinth) was a great source of encouragement to him. Paul said to the Thessalonians, "But now that Timothy has come to us from you, and has brought us good news of your faith and love, and that you always think kindly of us ..." (1 Thess. 3.6).

Weaver states,

Hendriksen captures the real motive that gave rise to the writing of the first letter, as well as its intent, when he says that Timothy's report '... was so encouraging that the heart of the great missionary was filled with joy and thanksgiving. 'Now I (really) live,' said Paul, as Timothy brought him the wonderful news of the undiminished faith and love of the infant church (cf. 1 Thess. 3.8). Not only did the arrival of Silas and Timothy and the information which they conveyed add zest to his preaching (Acts 18.5), but he also decided to express his feeling of gratitude in a letter to the Thessalonians. This was to be a letter of encouragement, the tenor of which would be 'You're doing fine, continue to do so more and more (cf. 1 Thess. 4.1). Do not let persecutions get you down. These are necessary; also, they are to be expected, just as I told you when I was still with you.' (cf. 1 Thess. 3.2–4)[3]

While Paul encouraged the saints, there were also matters he addressed to strengthen and to safeguard them from potential wicked influences. As Weaver states,

> He wanted to address certain moral issues, which suggests that there was a tendency for them to slip back into certain heathen ways of moral misbehavior. There is no indication that any actually had turned back, but Timothy's report must have called attention to the danger, so Paul stresses the holiness that is required of the Christian (1 Thess. 4.1–8; 5.22–24). Guthrie describes Paul's instruction on this subject by saying that 'he points out the superiority of Christian morality over pagan,' and that this was 'probably to safeguard them from pagan attempts to make new converts to Christianity revert to their old standards.'[4]

Paul also addressed other issues, like the second coming of Jesus and idleness.

Despite these matters, what we find overall is a group of Christians who had been transformed by the gospel of Jesus Christ! The word of the Lord they had received was working in them. "For this reason we also constantly thank God that when you received the word of God which you heard from us, you accepted it not as the word of men, but for what it really is, the word of God which also performs its work in you who believe" (1 Thess. 2.13). Let's consid-

---

[3] Weaver, 11–12.
[4] Ibid., 566.

er a few passages from 1 Thessalonians that demonstrate how their lives had been transformed.

> We give thanks to God always for all of you, making mention of you in our prayers; constantly bearing in mind your work of faith and labor of love and steadfastness of hope in our Lord Jesus Christ in the presence of our God and Father ... (1 Thess 1.2–3).

> You also became imitators of us and of the Lord, having received the word in much tribulation with the joy of the Holy Spirit, so that you became an example to all the believers in Macedonia and in Achaia (1 Thess 1.7).

> But now that Timothy has come to us from you, and has brought us good news of your faith and love, and that you always think kindly of us, longing to see us just as we also long to see you, for this reason, brethren, in all our distress and affliction we were comforted about you through your faith; for now we really live, if you stand firm in the Lord (1 Thess 3.6–8).

The Thessalonians walked in a way that was well pleasing to God. Paul, like a father would encourage his son, encouraged these Christians to walk in a way worthy of the gospel. In Thess. 2.10–11 Paul said, "You are witnesses, and so is God, how devoutly and uprightly and blamelessly we behaved toward you believers; just as you know how we were exhorting and encouraging and imploring each one of you as a father would his own children, so that you would walk in a manner worthy of the God who calls you into His own kingdom and glory."

Then, in 1 Thess. 4.1 Paul said, "Finally then, brethren, we request and exhort you in the Lord Jesus, that as you received from us instruction as to how you ought to walk and please God (just as you actually do walk), that you excel still more."

This church, born in suffering, did not swerve into apostasy. Rather, they served God faithfully. Paul reminded the Corinthians that their ambition was to be pleasing to God: "... we have as our ambition, whether at home or absent, to be pleasing to Him" (2 Cor. 5.9). This was the ambition of the Thessalonians. This should be our ambition as well.

What did "pleasing to God" look like for the Thessalonians? How were they able to make it their ambition to be pleasing to God? What about the Philippians, who were also conducting themselves in a way that was well pleasing to God? How were they able to make it their ambition to be pleasing to God? We can find the answers when we consider the Macedonian letters. While this idea of "being pleasing to God" is not as big as other themes in the Macedonian letters, it is a theme that should be at the heart of all we do. Let's investigate the scriptures to see what we can learn so we can walk in a way that is worthy of the gospel, that is, a way that is pleasing to God.

Words in the Word

First, let's consider the words in the word of God that were used by Paul and others as they spoke about being pleasing to God. Paul told the Thessalonians in 1 Thess. 4.1, "... how you ought to walk and please God (just as you actually do walk), that you excel still more." To please God means, "To be pleasing, to be acceptable to."[5]

"The Greek word in this passage is 'aresko' which means 'to please.' The general sense of 'pleasing' someone conveys the idea of making a favorable impression on others. This usage is evident in Acts 6.5; Rom.15.2; 1 Cor. 7.33ff.; 10.33; Gal. 1.10; and 2 Tim. 2.4. Romans 15.3 states that Christ chose not to please himself during his life on earth. This same idea is indicated with respect to human beings pleasing God in 1 Cor 7.32 and in 1 Thess 4.1. The impossibility of unbelievers pleasing God is indicated in Rom. 8.8 and in 1 Thess 2.15. Romans 15.1 records the exhortation not to please oneself (cf. also 1 Thess 2.4). In Matt. 14.6 and Mark 6.22, a unique

---

[5] *Vine's Expository Dictionary of Old and New Testament Words.*

use of "aresko" suggests that Herodias' dancing before her stepfather king Herod may have pleased him in an erotic way." [6]

"Areskeia is a noun derived from the verb aresko (see above) that occurs only in Col 1.10, where the believers are exhorted to live a life wholly 'pleasing' to God." [7]

"Euaresteo is a synonym for aresko (see above) and occurs only three times, meaning 'to please.' Heb.11.5 refers to the patriarch Enoch, who was said to have pleased God. Heb. 13.16 affirms that a selfless concern for other people constitutes a sacrifice that is pleasing to God. Heb. 11.6 claims that is impossible to please God without the possession of saving faith." [8]

"Euarestos is an adjective derived from euaresteo (see above) and is consistently translated 'acceptable' or '(well) pleasing' in each of the nine contexts in which it occurs. The majority usage of euarestos centers on those things that are 'pleasing' to God, such as whole-hearted service to God (Rom. 12.12; Phil 4.18; Heb. 13.21), and also service to Christ (Rom. 14.18). 2 Cor 5.9 and Eph. 5.10 contain exhortations to live lives pleasing to God. The obedient submission of children to parents, and slaves to masters, evokes a pleasing response from God in Col. 3.20 and Titus 2.9, respectively." [9]

"Eudoeo is a verb meaning "to be (well) pleased," "please," or "take pleasure in" in most of its twenty-one occurrences. When predicated of God, eudoeko refers to God's being pleased with his son Jesus, expressed through explicit divine testimony at the outset of, and during, the public ministry of Christ (cf. Matt 3.17, 12.18, 17.5; Mark 1.11; Luke 3.22; 2 Pet 1.17). In contrast, God was not pleased with most of the Israelite people during their sojourn in the wilderness en route to the land of Canaan (cf. 1 Cor 10.5). See also Heb. 10.38. As far as human beings are concerned, the godless are said to

---

[6] *Expository Dictionary of Bible Words,* 740.

[7] Ibid.

[8] Ibid.

[9] Ibid, 741.

take pleasure in unrighteousness in 2 Thess 2.12. Paul refers to those who 'were pleased' to make a significant contribution to the plight of the poor in Rom. 15.26ff." [10]

These words in the word of God should have a tremendous impact on us. It is possible for us to be pleasing to God, and it is possible to be displeasing to God. Our goal in all we do is to please Him. We can know what He desires. We find a few examples in the letters to the Thessalonians and the Philippians about what it looks like to be well-pleasing to God. This is not exhaustive in nature, but it will help us to see how we can walk in a manner worthy of the gospel.

The Church in Thessalonica
"This is the will of God…"

Paul was clear to the Thessalonians what the will of God was for them (1 Thess. 4.1–3). They had already been instructed earlier by Paul while he was in Thessalonica. Yet, this young congregation needed to be reminded again. Like the Thessalonians, we need to be reminded as well. Peter did the same thing as Paul, as he reminded brethren who were already walking in a worthy manner.

> Therefore, I will always be ready to remind you of these things, even though you already know them, and have been established in the truth which is present with you. I consider it right, as long as I am in this earthly dwelling, to stir you up by way of reminder, knowing that the laying aside of my earthly dwelling is imminent, as also our Lord Jesus Christ has made clear to me. And I will also be diligent that at any time after my departure you will be able to call these things to mind. (2 Pet. 1.12–15)

This is an important reminder for us.

As Paul reminded them about God's will, there was a sense of urgency in his tone. "Finally then, brethren, we request and exhort you in the Lord Jesus …" (1 Thess. 4.1). In his request, there was

---

[10] Ibid.

an urgent plea. What Paul had to say to them was intended to catch their attention. It was to be taken seriously. It should be the same for us as we seek to please God.

Paul's requests and exhortation to them was "in the Lord Jesus..." (1 Thess. 4.1). Weaver writes, "This prepositional phrase has been interpreted in one of three ways."[11] One view is that Paul is appealing to the authority of Jesus. The second is that it "indicates close fellowship with the Lord."[12] The third view is that,

> This phrase indicates connection with the Lord. Lenski prefers to word it this way. He says the phrase means, 'in connection with the Lord,' and that it shows that 'both the writers and the readers acknowledge this Lord who has saved and made them his own and has set out his apostles (1.5). His authority as well as his grace are back of this fraternal request and admonition. No statement that is made in the following comes only from men.[13]

As we consider the commandments Paul gave to the Thessalonians, let us remember they are from the Lord Jesus. They are authoritative in nature and are not to be disregarded.

As we consider doing the will of God, like the Thessalonians, we do not have to guess what God expects from us. Paul told the Thessalonians, "... that as you received from us instruction as to how you ought to walk and please God (just as you actually do walk), that you excel still more. For you know what commandments we gave you by the authority of the Lord Jesus" (1 Thess. 4.1–2). They knew what God desired and expected from them as new creatures in Christ. These commandments Paul delivered to the saints were not optional. Willis states,

> The word **ought** (dei) actually means 'it is necessary' (AG171). It is often used of obligations that are imposed by God, such as showing

---

[11] W, Weaver, 231.

[12] Ibid.

[13] Ibid, 303

compassion to a fellow servant (Matt. 18.33), being about the Father's business (Luke 2.49), being merry at the return of the young son (Luke 15.32), always being engaged in prayer (Luke 18.1), or obeying God rather than men (Acts 5.29). Not one of these things is (was) optional. Christians not merely 'ought' **to walk and to please God,** but they must do so.[14]

One big area Paul discussed was the matter of sexual immorality.

"Abstain from sexual immorality..."

Abstaining from sexual immorality was the will of God for them. Paul says, "For this is the will of God, your sanctification, that is, that you abstain from sexual immorality" (1 Thess. 4.3). This is how they could be well pleasing to God. What made Christianity so distinct throughout the centuries was the disciples of Jesus abstaining from sexual immorality. Sexual immorality has always been one of the great dangers for the people of God. Paul's letter to the Corinthians reminds us of the devastating effects of sexual immorality. "It is actually reported that there is immorality among you and immorality of such a kind as does not exist even among the Gentiles, that someone has his father's wife" (1 Cor. 5.1). Therefore, it was important to remind the Thessalonians that they needed to abstain from this kind of behavior. Many of these Christians had turned from idols to the living God (1 Thess. 1.9–10). Much of idol worship involved sexual immorality. Consider the following thoughts regarding the gods and goddesses worshiped at Thessalonica:

> Just like any other city in the Mediterranean world, Thessalonica had an array of cults. The Greek deities Zeus, Asclepius, Aphrodite, and Demeter were popular among the people. By far the most popular cult of the city was the cult of the Cabirus. Not well known, this cult had a wild, bloody, and sexually perverse set of features. The central myth of this cult involved two brothers killing a third, decapitating

---

14 Ibid., 234.

the body, and burying the head at Mount Olympus. One of the key symbols of the cult was the male genitals. In a similar way, the cult of Dionysus gave prominence to phallic symbolism in addition to the drunken revelry that went along with the celebrations of the god. These two cults certainly had a powerfully negative impact on the social ethics of the city. Converts from these cults had a long way to go in appropriating a distinctively Christian lifestyle. In addition to these traditional deities, the Thessalonians also revered the Roman rulers as divine. During the reign of Caesar Augustus, a temple was built for the ruler cult to honor Augustus and his successors.[15]

No doubt, overcoming this background for some of the saints may have been difficult, but it was possible with God's strength. They had turned to the true and living God. Therefore, they were to be holy.

This is what Paul emphasizes as well. Sanctification is first mentioned in verse three of this chapter. It means "to be made holy or treated as holy. The kindred term 'holiness' was used in (3.13), but there it referred to a state of holiness (as in verse 7), whereas here the word for **sanctification** describes a process. The Christian is to live a life of **sanctification**, a life set apart for or dedicated to God. This involves growth in holiness; becoming sanctified or concentrated to God by living a life of separation from all that is unclean, or from all that is sinful."[16] According to 1 Thess. 4.4, they were to honor their bodies. In 1 Thess. 4.5, Paul instructed them not to act like the Gentiles, where they would be controlled by their lustful passion. Rather, they were to be holy and to live with self-control. None of them were to sin and defraud one another in this matter (1 Thess. 4.6). What is the "matter" Paul is referring to? None of them were to have someone else's spouse or engage in any other sexual immorality. The New Living Translation says, "Never harm or cheat a Christian brother in this matter by violating his wife...." Could this really

---

[15] *Zondervan Illustrated Bible Backgrounds Commentary*, page 378.

[16] Weaver, 239.

happen among brethren? The answer is: Yes! It had already happened in Corinth. Willis states,

> Green has given a good description of why such a warning would be appropriate for Christians in the close knit relationship that existed among them in the first century: 'In the intimate meetings held in the tight confines of the home or homes of fellow believers, Christians of both sexes were thrown together in a close, interpersonal setting that could easily have given rise to relationships that were outside the lines of morality. Such offenders went beyond the bounds and so sinned against both the Lord and the spouse of the person with whom they had an affair. Sexual sin was not simply about a sinful liaison between two people. Their relationship with God and the community was prejudiced (197).'[17]

How serious was this matter to God? In the second half of verse six, Paul said, "... because the Lord is the avenger in all these things, just as we also told you before and solemnly warned you." This manner of immoral living was not who the Thessalonians were to be. Thankfully, they were walking in a manner well pleasing to God! Yet Paul is strong with his language in 1 Thess. 4.8 in that those who rejected his words were really rejecting the will of God. This is a great reminder for us when it comes to how we hear the words of the apostles. They are not mere words for us to casually glance at and quickly dismiss. Rather, they are the very words of God (cf 1 Thess. 2.13).

One way we can be pleasing to God is by abstaining from sexual immorality. While this is not the only example Paul provides for us in this chapter in how we are to walk, this conduct takes up a good portion of the chapter and for good reason. Not much has changed since the days of the Thessalonians. Sexual immorality is still rampant in our world and sadly at times in the body of Christ. This kind of behavior is not pleasing to God. It is sinful in nature. Nothing good will ever come from it. The devil wants us to think that sexual

---

[17] Ibid, 254.

immorality is where we will find pleasure and satisfaction, but it will only bring about regret, pain, terrible consequences, and separation from our God. Therefore, let us "Flee immorality" (1 Cor. 6.18).

We have only considered one way in which the Thessalonians were pleasing to God. The rest of chapter four shows how they could be pleasing to God in other areas of their lives (love for one another, how they conducted their daily affairs, how they worked and handled their money, and their view of death and the resurrection). What about the Philippians? In what way were they pleasing to God? Let's consider one example.

The Church in Philippi
"You sent a gift more than once for my needs."

As Paul finished his letter to the church in Philippi, he spoke about the blessing they had been to him. Like the Thessalonians, the Philippians had been pleasing to God. How? One way was by their financial assistance to Paul in his ministry.

> You yourselves also know, Philippians, that at the first preaching of the gospel, after I left Macedonia, no church shared with me in the matter of giving and receiving but you alone; for even in Thessalonica you sent a gift more than once for my needs. Not that I seek the gift itself, but I seek for the profit which increases to your account. But I have received everything in full and have an abundance; I am amply supplied, having received from Epaphroditus what you have sent, a fragrant aroma, an acceptable sacrifice, well-pleasing to God. And my God will supply all your needs according to His riches in glory in Christ Jesus. (Phil. 4.15–19)

The saints in Philippi were living the words of Jesus: "It is more blessed to give than to receive" (Acts 20.35). They were generous in nature. They shared in Paul's work. "As he did in 1.5, Paul acknowledged the Philippians' financial partnership in the gospel."[18]

---

[18] *Philippians;* Aaron Erhardt Publications, 96.

The word of the Lord was working in them as well! Their financial assistance Paul described as a "fragrant aroma, an acceptable sacrifice, well-pleasing to God" (Phil. 4.18). Let's consider this idea of fragrant aroma. Fragrant aroma "… is an image that moves us from the accountant to the priest, and relates their gift to God. The same language is used of Christ's death in Ephesians 5.2. What they did to help Paul and his mission was also pleasing service to God (cf. Gen 8.2; Exod. 29.18; Lev. 1.9, 13; Ezek. 20.41)." [19]

While more could be said about what it looked like for the Thessalonians and Philippians to be pleasing to God in their daily lives, another question must be answered. How did these two congregations get to the point where their goal was to be pleasing to God? We know what the result looks like, but how was it their number one priority? This question is important for us as well. We know we should be pleasing to God. Yet, it can often be the case that we seek to be more pleasing to ourselves or to others. Let's consider a few thoughts that will help us to make pleasing God our number one priority.

How to Make It Our Ambition to be Pleasing to God
Have an "I am third" mentality

The saints in Macedonia had an "I am third" mentality. That is to say, "God was first in their lives, their brethren and neighbors were second, and they were third." They had a great love for God! They had the attitude of Christ. In Phil. 2.3–8, Paul said,

> Do nothing from selfishness or empty conceit, but with humility of mind regard one another as more important than yourselves; do not merely look out for your own personal interests, but also for the interests of others. Have this attitude in yourselves which was also in Christ Jesus, who, although He existed in the form of God, did not regard equality with God a thing to be grasped, but

---

[19] A, Ash, *The College Press NIV Commentary: Philippians, Colossians, and Philemon,* 130.

emptied Himself, taking the form of a bond-servant, and being made in the likeness of men. Being found in appearance as a man, He humbled Himself by becoming obedient to the point of death, even death on a cross.

Jesus put the Father first. He always sought to do the will of God! Jesus put mankind second. He sacrificed Himself so that we could be saved. Jesus had an "I am third" mindset.

Like the Macedonian Christians, we need to have the same attitude. Those in Thessalonica fully turned and followed the true and living God. The Father and His will were first. They excelled in loving one another! Remember, Paul said, "Now as to the love of the brethren, you have no need for anyone to write to you, for you yourselves are taught by God to love one another; for indeed you do practice it toward all the brethren who are in all Macedonia. But we urge you, brethren, to excel still more ..." (1 Thess. 4.9–10). They excelled in their love for one another because of their love for God. They had put the interests of their brethren above their own. They were third!

The same could be said about the Philippians! How were they able to give so freely to Paul, as described in Phil. 4.15–18? It was possible because God and His will were first. They too had a great love for God. They had been walking in the will of God: "So, then, my beloved, just as you have always obeyed, not as in my presence only, but now much more in my absence, work out your salvation with fear and trembling; for it is God who is at work in you, both to will and to work for His good pleasure" (Phil. 2.12–13). The brethren and saving souls were second. Their personal interests were third. This is the attitude we must have if our ambition is to be pleasing to God. Sadly, in America this arrangement is often reversed. People often put themselves and their interests first, while others are second, and God is third. If we are not careful, God can be left out of the equation as we seek to please ourselves and others. God must be first in all we do.

"...Some of them were persuaded..."

How did these disciples have this great love for God? How could the saints in Macedonia put God first? It's because they were fully persuaded of who He is and His Son Jesus Christ. In Acts 17.4, Luke said, "And some of them were persuaded and joined Paul and Silas, along with a large number of the God-fearing Greeks and a number of the leading women." The fact that they were "persuaded" by the evidence Paul gave to them as he explained how Jesus is the Christ and risen from the dead means that they were fully convinced. Their faith was rooted in evidence. Jackson states,

> Some of Paul's auditors 'were persuaded.' The Greek word is peitho, meaning to become convinced, to believe (Arndt, 1967, 645), even to obey (cf. Jn. 3.36b ASV). W.E. Vine (1991, 560) says that peitho is that obedience which results from being persuaded; it issues from "trust" (pisteuo)—a kindred term. At the conclusion of Paul's preaching, some obeyed the gospel. These new converts then "consorted" (literally to cast a lot toward) with Paul and Silas; as we might say it—they threw in with them.[20]

These Christians were all in! This point is important as we consider how they made it their ambition to be pleasing to God. They were fully convinced of God's love, mercy, and grace for them and the price that was paid for their sins. They were fully persuaded that Jesus was raised from the dead and that hope comes because of the empty tomb.

This persuasion led them to repentance and obedience to the gospel. They were fully devoted to God. They fully turned to God. "For they themselves report about us what kind of a reception we had with you, and how you turned to God from idols to serve a living and true God and to wait for His Son from heaven, whom He raised from the dead, that is Jesus, who rescues us from the wrath to come" (1 Thess. 1.9–10). There is great application for us as we think

---

[20] W, Jackson, *The Acts of the Apostles from Jerusalem to Rome,* 202.

about making it our goal to be pleasing to God. When one is fully persuaded about something, there is no turning back. There is only moving forward. Like the saints in Ephesus who burned their magic books (Acts 19.19), the saints in Thessalonica left their former lives and sinful practices behind. Their hearts were pricked by the gospel message, the love of Christ, and an understanding of their Creator. This is why they were able to endure suffering. They experienced and endured suffering because they fully believed in the suffering servant, Jesus. There was no turning away like the rich young ruler when a great price was to be paid. They had been fully persuaded.

When we are fully persuaded of who Jesus is, then we too will make it our ambition to be pleasing to Him. The question is, are we fully persuaded? Have we been fully persuaded Jesus is the Christ? Have we turned from our idols (self, wealth, power, etc.) to the true and living God? Have we burned our books (sinful practices and allegiances) and become fully devoted to Jesus? This is how we can walk in a way that is well pleasing to God. God wants us to be fully convinced of who He is and who His Son is. As we consider our lives, God does not want us to have balance between Him and our other responsibilities. He wants all of us. As someone once said, "There is no balance when it comes to God." He desires to always be first. The Thessalonians were fully persuaded. Are we?

"…You accepted it not as the word of men, but for what it really is, the word of God…"

Their belief in Jesus as the Christ is seen in their action and response to the word that was preached to them. They loved and believed the words of Paul as being the very words of God. "For this reason, we also constantly thank God that when you received the word of God which you heard from us, you accepted it not as the word of men, but for what it really is, the word of God, which also performs its work in you who believe" (1 Thess. 2.13). The Thessalonian hearts were filled with God's word! The word of God changed their hearts and kept them focused on the true and living God. How were they able to make it their ambition to be pleasing to God? By the way they had received God's word when Paul initially preached to them and how they continually received his word as God's word. There are several thoughts from this passage that will help us to make being pleasing to God our ambition and goal.

Paul was constantly thankful for the hearts the Thessalonians had in the way they received the gospel message. They realized it was not the word of men, but rather the very word of God. Weaver states,

> The gospel message accepted by the Thessalonians is 'not the word of men.' It is **of God** and is not a humanly devised message. What was being preached by the charlatans and quacks in Thessalonica was indeed the word of men, but the message preached by Paul and others who were with him, the word of the Thessalonians heard and accepted, **is in truth the word of God.** Paul stresses this fact by introducing this phrase with the word **but** in truth the word of God. To say that the message the Thessalonians had received is **in truth** the word of God is Paul's way of emphasizing what it *actually* is— **the word of God.**[21]

Paul said the "…word of God which also performs its work in you who believe." The word they had received had been working in them! Their faith and love grew. "We give thanks to God always for all of you, making mention of you in our prayers; constantly bearing in mind your work of faith and labor of love and steadfastness of hope in our Lord Jesus Christ in the presence of our God and Father…" (1 Thess. 1.3). In his second epistle, Paul spoke even more about their love and faith being enlarged. "We ought always to give thanks to God for you, brethren, as is only fitting, because your faith is greatly enlarged, and the love of each one of you toward one another grows ever greater; therefore, we ourselves speak proudly of you among the churches of God for your perseverance and faith

---

[21] Weaver, 160.

in the midst of all your persecutions and afflictions which you endure" (2 Thess. 1.3–4). Why did their love and faith grow even in difficult situations? Because their desire was to be pleasing to God. This is even more impressive when we consider how they persevered through times of affliction.

We know that the word of God had transformed their hearts because they had become "imitators of the churches of God in Christ Jesus that are in Judea, for you also endured the same sufferings at the hands of your own countrymen, even as they did from the Jews" (1 Thess. 2.14). Wright states, "But now we hear that the Thessalonians, too, have already suffered for their new-found **faith**. Indeed, Paul gives this as the reason, at least in part, why he can tell that the **gospel** of Jesus had had its effect in them, not as a mere human message but as the word of God himself. If it had been a merely human message, one might expect that when the hearers began to be persecuted for accepting it they would turn back and give it up. But they have not." [22]

There was a constant hiding of God's word in their hearts. There was a constant reminder of His great promises and His great love. How can being pleasing to God be our number one priority? We need to continue to receive God's word in our hearts. The challenge for many Christians is that there is often so much stuff that gets in the way of receiving God's word. There's a constant competition for our attention. One person has said, "Attention equals influence." That is true. Where we put our attention is what will influence us. It's not that many Christians don't know God's word to be true. But rather, we have allowed so many other influences to get in the way of God's word working in us. Therefore, we must be intentional when it comes to receiving God's word. We must make room in our schedule, where we can hear from God. Like Jesus, who arose early in the morning to pray (Mark 1.35), we must be intentional to have time alone with God. We need

---

[22] N.T., Wright, *Paul for everyone: Galatians and Thessalonians,* 101.

to decrease the daily demands we put in our lives, the entertainment we consume, and the time we waste on social media, so that there will be room in our day for God's word to increase in our hearts. We must carefully examine our daily habits and make the necessary changes. But there is more that we must do as we receive God's word.

We will have to be both doers and hearers. It's not enough to merely hear God's message. This is what those in the days of Ezekiel did.

> But as for you, son of man, your fellow citizens who talk about you by the walls and in the doorways of the houses, speak to one another, each to his brother, saying, 'Come now and hear what the message is which comes forth from the LORD.' They come to you as people come, and sit before you as My people and hear your words, but they do not do them, for they do the lustful desires expressed by their mouth, and their heart goes after their gain. Behold, you are to them like a sensual song by one who has a beautiful voice and plays well on an instrument; for they hear your words but they do not practice them. (Ezek. 33.30–33)

What's important is how we hear God's message. Those in the days of Ezekiel heard God's message, but seeking to be pleasing to God was not their desire. Rather, they were only concerned about pleasing themselves. This recipe will never work! God's word must be not only heard but also applied. Like the Thessalonians, we need to be reminded of the commands of God (1 Thess. 4.1–3).

Conclusion

Is it possible to be pleasing to God? Yes! Enoch walked with God and was pleasing to God (Heb. 11.5). The saints in Macedonia walked in a manner that was well pleasing to God. We can do the same. What it will require is a daily choice. It will require that we are intentional when it comes to being pleasing to God. We can learn what His will is and how to be pleasing (Eph. 5.7–10). We can live in a way in which He will be pleased! To God be the glory.

Consider Others as More Important
Humility that is Worthy of the Gospel

Jonathan Brown

One of the most important themes of the New Testament is that we are to follow Jesus as our example. In fact, the very name, "Christian," implies "Christ-likeness." To be a disciple of Jesus is to want, more than anything else, to be just like the Master. What is interesting, though, is that every single time the scriptures specifically mention an attribute of Jesus to follow as an example, the lesson is one of service, humility, submission, and dying to self. For example, when Paul discusses the advantages of being single in 1 Corinthians 7, he did not use Jesus as an example when he certainly could have. When Paul taught us to pray without ceasing in 1 Thessalonians 5.17, it would have been the perfect time to use Jesus as an illustration, but he did not. Jesus is never held up by the apostles as an example of being a great evangelist when He could have been. Instead, in the New Testament, Jesus is cited as an example of becoming a servant, a slave, an example of humility, one who offers forgiveness, and an example of selflessly dying for others (cf. Eph 5.1–2; 1 Pet 2.20–23; 1 John 3.15–16). The reason for that is because humility is at the very core of Christianity, and it must, therefore, be at the very core of how we see our role within the church, the home, work, school, and every aspect of our daily living.

Perhaps the premier passage in all of Scripture that expresses the example of humility and service displayed in our Master is in Philippians 2.1–11. In this passage, Paul calls upon the Philippians to put aside their selfish ambitions and empty conceit and follow the example of Christ Jesus who showed us what true humility is.

The Context (Philippians 1.27–2.2)

In Philippians 1.27 Paul urged the brethren in Philippi to, "conduct yourselves in a manner worthy of the gospel of Christ." In doing so, he said that in his absence, he would want to hear that they were, "standing firm in one spirit, with one mind striving together for the faith of the gospel." This was an exhortation to stand as one unit against a common foe. Paul went on to describe the kind of mindset that would be needed to stand up against their opponents who would cause them to suffer. He did this by striking courage in them so that they would "in no way" be "alarmed" by their opponents. In short, the end of chapter 1 explains that there would be an external opponent, and it provides the correct attitude needed to face that difficulty.

But beginning in chapter 2, Paul lets the Philippians know that there would also be internal struggles that form, and it was just as important to have the right attitude in those conflicts as well.[1] Paul turns to consider the kind of disposition they must maintain if they are to be united among themselves as Christians. He begins this section with an appeal to the Philippian church's experience (verse 1). Paul uses the words, "if there is" (*ei tis*) four times in this verse to point out four things that the Philippian brethren had experienced.[2] At some point in their Christian lives they had all been: 1) encouraged by their brethren to realize that they belonged to Christ ("encouragement in Christ"), 2) been aware of their brethren's comforting love ("consolation of love"), 3) delighted in the sense of be-

---

[1] That is the connection made with the word, "therefore" (*oun*), in 2.1.

[2] This is a first class condition in Greek. "If" does not express doubt about these things in Paul's mind. He assumed each one of these things to be true for the sake of his argument.

longing to the fellowship of God's people with the Holy Spirit ("fellowship of the Spirit"), and 4) received wonderful compassion from their brethren in times of suffering ("affection and compassion"). The argument the apostle makes is this: "If these blessings are what have been your experience (verse 1)[3], then here is how you must behave (verse 2). What this means for you as a Christian is that you owe the same blessings to others."

Paul then tells them that they must be unified, expressed by four phrases in verse 2. The first and last of the four are almost identical in the original language,[4] however, translators often translate them differently. The NASB reads, "being of the same mind," and, "intent on one purpose." The ESV says, "the same mind," and, "of one mind." The bookends of these phrases emphasize the oneness of their thinking. Paul wanted the brethren to be in agreement with each other. The two middle phrases reinforce the main thought of having one mind. "Maintaining the same love," and, "united in spirit," describe what it means to have, "one mind." Their love was to be directed toward the same things and they were to be joined in soul. Essentially, all four points mean the same thing, but in them, Paul brings in the mind (same mind), the heart (same love), and the soul (united in spirit). In other words, they needed to be wholly united in every aspect of their beings. If the Philippians would recognize this point and live by it, it would make Paul's "joy complete." This was given as a motivation to be unified, but it is also possible Paul was trying to show the Philippian brethren, "that the key to joy consists in shifting our attention away from ourselves and onto the needs of others."[5]

---

[3] "If then your experiences in Christ appeal to you with any force" [Lightfoot, J.B. *St. Paul's Epistle to the Philippians*. (Grand Rapids: Zondervan Publishing House, 1963) 106].

[4] "*To auto phronēte*," and "*to en phronountes*."

[5] Silva, Moises, *Philippians*. 2nd Ed. BECNT. (Grand Rapids: Baker Academic, 2003) 86.

Paul's Solution for Unity: Humility
(Philippians 2.3–4)

Verse 3 elaborates on how to be of the same mind with one another. Stated negatively at first, Paul says, "nothing from selfishness or empty conceit" should be done or contemplated. Unity cannot exist among brethren when a selfish person wishes to be over others because he thinks "more highly of himself than he ought to think" (Romans 12.3). Division occurs when a person thinks that his ways are always right and are the best ways of accomplishing a task.

Instead, Paul said, "with humility of mind regard one another as more important than yourselves." This is a humility before God that leads to a humility in our relations with other people (see 1 Peter 5.5–6; Romans 12.10). To have this attitude towards God and one's fellow man is to be aware of one's own failings and unworthiness. We have sinned making us unworthy before God (Romans 3.23). The fact that we have "all sinned" should cause us to realize that we each individually are no better than anyone else.

Interestingly, the word translated, "humility of mind" (*tapeivophrosunē*) is never found in secular writings before the New Testament was written. This is probably due to the fact that the pagans did not view humility as a virtue, but as a shortcoming, much as it is viewed today. When the adjective form of this word was used outside the Bible, it was of slaves who were viewed as the lowest of society.[6] Its lack of usage in secular writings might also be explained by the fact that while humility before God does not require that one is poor and downcast, it is more likely found in people who are.

Christians must, "regard (count, consider) one another as more important than" themselves. The true obstacle to unity is not differences of opinions, but self-centeredness. Shifting our attention away from ourselves becomes the challenge (1 Cor 10.24). To clarify, it is not that we *are* less important than others, but we need to treat oth-

---

[6] Hawthorne, Gerald F. *Philippians*. Word Biblical Commentary 43. (Waco: Word Books, 1983) 69–70.

ers better than ourselves and put their needs before our own. They are not better, but their needs surpass my own.

Verse 4 continues the pattern in verse 3 of "not this, but this." Again, first stated negatively, true humility requires that one, "not look out for your own personal interests." The word translated, "look out" (*skopountes*) is the word from which we get our English word, "scope." It means, "fixing the attention upon, with desire for or interest in... Hence often to aim at."[7] Instead of "scoping in" on ourselves, more positively stated, we are to "scope in" on, "the interest of others." Paul did not mean that we should not consider our own feelings and needs, but this should not be our priority. This is suggested by the word, "also" (*kai*), in the second half of the verse.[8] Paul assumes you will look out for your own interest, too. Translators have supplied the word "merely" to help out this idea. The interests (things, feelings, needs, and concerns) of others are to be put above our own. However, selfishness and empty conceit (v. 3) are what keep us from doing that. Humility of mind is what allows us to put others first.

The Great Example of Humility: Christ Jesus (Philippians 2.5)

What follows in verses 5 through 11 may be the most important verses in the epistle. "By anyone's reckoning, 2.6–11 constitutes the single most significant block of material in Philippians."[9] It is probably the most difficult passage in the book to interpret because of the nature of its content: the incarnation. It may also be the single most important Christological passage in the whole Bible. However, despite the vast amounts of time and debating that has been spent on dissecting the pre-existence, the deity, and the humanity of Christ from this passage, that is actually not the point of this section of

---

[7] M. Vincent, *Word Studies in the New Testament, Vol. 3, The Epistles of Paul.* (Grand Rapids: Wm. B. Eerdmans Publishing Co., 1957) 430.

[8] However, *kai* is missing in many mss.

[9] G. Fee, *Paul's Letter to the Philippians.* NICNT. (Grand Rapids: Wm. B. Eerdmans Publishing Co., 1995) 39.

scripture. While those elements are assumed and implied here, the incarnation is used by Paul as the ultimate example of the humility he demanded in verses 3 and 4. What better way to reinforce the importance of humility than by reminding the Macedonians of the attitude and conduct of their Lord, Christ Jesus?[10]

This point is made clear in verse 5 when Paul writes, "Have this attitude in yourselves which was also in Christ Jesus." The Greek sentence begins with the word "this" (*touto*), which consistently in Philippians points backward rather than forward.[11] As a result, Paul is saying that the attitude of humility and putting others' interests first is the attitude you *must* have (*phroneite* as an imperative) "in yourselves." It was the attitude that "was also in Christ Jesus." Although many commentators[12] believe that the phrase, "in Christ Jesus" (*en Xristō Iēsou*), should be taken in the typical Pauline sense of, "of those united in Christ" (i.e. the attitude of the Christian community at large), the context seems to focus on the humble attitude of Christ Jesus Himself. The attitude that Christ Jesus had towards others is what His followers should have. That is reflected in the example of Christ Jesus in the following verses. As Bockmuehl has written, "The key to a citizenship 'worthy of the gospel of Christ' is in fact none other than to adopt the mind of Christ."[13]

Many believe that what follows in verses 6–11 may have been an early Christian hymn that Paul quoted to make the case for the humility of Jesus that we are to emulate. This view was seen as early as 1897 by J. Weiss, but gained a larger following after Lohmeyer's dissertation and commentary in 1928. Much scholarly work has been done to provide analyses of the passage's poetic pattern. While many

---

[10] Paul did the same thing in 2 Cor 8.9 to admonish the Corinthians to contribute generously for the sake of the poor in Jerusalem.

[11] cf. 1.7, 22, 25; 3.7, 15; 4.8, 9—with the exception being in 1.19.

[12] *E.g.* R. Martin, *Philippians.* TNTC 11. (Downers Grove: Intervarsity Press, 1987) 103. and Silva, *Philippians* 97.

[13] M. Bockmuehl, *The Epistle to the Philippians.* BNTC. (New York: Hendrickson Publishers, Inc., 1998) 121.

agree that there is an undeniable rhythm, repetition and a Hebraic-sounding parallelism, "there is no way of identifying such a hymn in our case with any degree of confidence."[14] We can be for certain that whether Paul used a hymn that was already known in the first century or he created his own poetic lines, the Holy Spirit guided him to record these thoughts in order to illustrate his main point about humility.

As God, Christ "Emptied Himself" (Philippians 2.6–7)

The Holy Spirit wonderfully claims that before coming to this world Jesus, "existed in the form of God" (v. 6a). This does not mean that He *appeared* to be like God. The word translated, "form," (*morphē*), is a difficult word to define because the only other place outside of this passage that it is found in the Scriptures is Mark 16.12 and it has limited use in early Christian and Hebrew writings. "It covers a broad range of meanings and therefore we are heavily dependent on the immediate context to discover its specific nuance."[15] The immediate context of the next verse (v. 7) gives us some clarity. There it says when Jesus came to earth He took on "the form of a bond-servant." Jesus did not merely *appear* like a bond-servant, He *was* one. He lived and functioned as a bond-servant, because He was one. Likewise, verse 6 teaches us that Christ enjoyed real equality with God because He was God. This is a statement of who He was before coming to this earth (cf. John 1.1ff). Jesus functioned as God before becoming a man. Furthermore, Jesus is said here to have "equality with God." The word translated "equality" (*isos*) carries the idea of two things that are equal (*e.g.* am isosceles triangle is a triangle with two equal sides). The Father and the Son are equally God.

Yet, amazingly, Jesus, "did not regard equality with God a thing to be grasped" (v. 6b). In other words, equality with God was not

---

[14] Ibid. 117.

[15] Silva, *Philippians* 101.

"something to be exploited."[16] Jesus did not use His equality with God as something to be used for His own advantage. Jesus did not use His God-ness to become a man and be served as an egotistical worldly king. Instead, as is seen in verse 7, He made Himself nothing and became a servant. He did not use His God-ness for His own advantage, but for the interest of others. "Jesus refused to act selfishly with regard to his pre-incarnate state in relation to God."[17] This is consistent with Romans 15.3, where Paul wrote, "Christ did not please Himself." It is also in contrast with most of mankind whose goal it is to only please themselves. A prime example of this is the first man, Adam, who did not have equality with God, yet considered it something to be seized (Genesis 3.5–6). He tried to become like God by grasping. However, Christ, who is God, became a man by releasing.[18]

Instead of exploiting His deity for His own personal self-service, Christ Jesus "emptied Himself" (v. 7a). The word, "but" (*alla*) at the beginning of the verse draws a contrast of how we might expect someone in a position of deity as described in verse 6 to act. The gods of Roman and Greek mythology would use their powers for their own selfish purposes. The Philippians may have used their positions of power in the congregation to get their own way. Jesus could have used His deity and insisted on His rights and personally profited from His equality to God. "But" instead, He chose to empty Himself.

This does not mean that Christ emptied Himself *of* something. For example, He did not empty Himself of deity when He came to earth. The words, "form of God," in verse 6 are separated from the word, "emptied," at the end of verse 7 by the word, "but," at the beginning of verse 7. Therefore, it is grammatically impossible that the "form of God," is the object of the verb, "emptied." Christ Jesus

---

[16] D.A. Carson, *Basics for Believers* (Grand Rapids: Baker Books, 1996) 54.

[17] Bockmuehl, *The Epistle to the Philippians* 130.

[18] Although this Adam-Christ theme appears in Paul's letters (1 Cor 15.21–22, 45–49; Rom 5.12–21), "there is not a single linguistic parallel to the Genesis narrative here in this passage" (Fee, *Paul's Letter to the Philippians* 209). But the point is an interesting contrast, nonetheless.

continued to be God. In fact, that is what makes His incarnation remarkable and this passage even more powerful. Furthermore, Jesus did not empty Himself of the attributes of deity.[19] If he would have, He would not be God. We have an old saying, "If it walks like a duck, quacks like a duck, it is a duck." If it has all the attributes of a duck (bill, webbed feet, feathers, swims, and flies) it is a duck. If you take away any of those attributes of a duck, whatever you have left will not be a duck. Likewise, if you take away the attributes of deity from the Son, He ceases to be deity.

Instead, the expression seems to mean that "he gave up all His rights," or something similar. The NKJV and KJV say that He "made Himself of no reputation" to express the idea. The NIV interprets this, "He made himself nothing" (not literally, of course, or He would cease to exist). Jesus abandoned His rights and became a nobody. In truth, Christ Jesus emptied Himself *of Himself.* "Christ did not empty himself *of* anything; he simply 'emptied *himself,*' poured himself out."[20] We should not be so concerned so much with of *what* He emptied Himself, as much as what He did and how He acted to show His humble mindset. He poured Himself out, putting Himself at the disposal of others (cf. Isa 53.12). This is what He calls on us to do as well. This is the essence of humility.

The next two participles in verse 7 describe how Jesus "emptied Himself." First of all, He took on "the form of a bond-servant." Being a "nobody" in society is the defining characteristic of a slave. People afford them no rights and very little value. And yet, Jesus entered into our history, not as "Master," but as "a slave" (*doulos*). "The form of a bond-servant," as noted already, is in contrast to *"the form of God"* (v. 6) in which He had all the rights of deity. He was one with God. Because of that, He did not perceive His equality with God something to be exploited, but became "a nobody." But in

---

[19] Also known as the "kenosis" theory from the Greek word found here: *ekenōsen.*

[20] Fee, *Paul's Letter to the Philippians* 210.

doing this, Jesus did not exchange one "form" for the other. He did not give up being God to become a bond-servant. When He became a bond-servant, He took on another role (similar to when a husband becomes a father). He possessed both "forms" at the same time.

Secondly, to do this, Jesus was, "made in the likeness of men" (v. 7c). This paritciple phrase is a further explanation and elaboration of the first one. It describes how and when Jesus took on "the form of bond-servant." The idea is not that Jesus just *looked like* a man, but was not actually human (like some Gnostics in the first century believed). It means He became a being fashioned this way, and only humans are fashioned like humans. Remember, "If it quacks like a duck, then it must be one." Christ Jesus had always been God, but at His birth, He also became something He had not been: human. "He was God living out a truly human life."[21] Many New Testament passages declare this (*e.g.* Rom 8.3; 1 Tim 2.5; Heb. 2.7, 14–18; 4.14–16; 1 John 4.2–3; 2 John 7).

Admittedly, it is difficult for our finite minds to understand how Jesus was both human and God in the womb of a woman and as a baby in a manger. However, there are many mysteries about God that we do not understand. As Doy Moyer has written, "We are working with finite minds, and we will find ourselves getting into trouble when we try to limit Deity with our own finite limitations."[22] Just because we do not understand the "how," does not negate the reality.

As Man, Jesus Humbled Himself (Philippians 2.8)

The first participle phrase in verse 8 ("being found in appearance as a man") summarizes the two previous participle phrases in verse 7. Christ presented Himself as a man when on this earth. As much as verse 6 emphasized Christ's deity, verse 8 emphasizes His once-held humanity. His "appearance as a man" is what others "found" (or discovered or recognized) when they saw Jesus walking on earth. They

---

[21] Ibid. 213.

[22] T.D. Moyer. "Did Jesus Give Up His Deity?" *Gospel Anchor* July 1990.

"found" Him as man, because He looked like one. Although He was much more, He did not look like more. His appearance was the same as other men. No doubt, that is why many who merely focused on His appearance mistook Him to be *just* a man. There were no clues from outward appearances that He was sinless or divine.

As a man, "He humbled Himself." This is an act, not a disposition (i.e. not, "He was humble"). This describes an act that occurred after He "emptied Himself" (v. 7), not the emptying itself. The emptying occurred when He became man. The humbling of Himself occurred after He became man. So, how did He humble Himself? "By becoming obedient to the point of death." While Christ's death is a reality, it is not the emphasis in this phrase. Instead, the emphasis is on His humble obedience. Christ's humble and complete obedience led to His death. He went as far as death in His obedience to the Father and in His service to others. "Obedience to the point of death" does not always involve death, but in Jesus' case, it did. There cannot be a greater example of humility.

Jesus' decision to come to become man occurred in heaven. This was emptying Himself as God. But as a man, He humbled Himself to do the Father's will. Weaver tells us that the word "becoming obedient" (*genomenos*) "indicates that his obedience was rendered from the time he was first on earth." [23] We see it as early as when Jesus was twelve years old and He said He "had to be in His Father's (things)" (Luke 2.49). Certainly it would have been seen before that. We see it in the Garden of Gethsemane (Mark 14.36), and we see that obedience all the way to His death (Matt 26.39).

Understand, however, that it was no ordinary death in which Jesus was called to participate in humble obedience. It was the most humiliating death that existed at the time: "even death on a cross." This shows us the depth of His humility. If this section of Philippians was indeed an ancient hymn or poem that Paul quotes, this line

---

[23] W. Weaver, *Philippians*. Truth Commentaries. (Bowling Green: Guardian of Truth Foundation, 1996) 96.

sticks out from the flow and rhythm of the rest. This has led some scholars to conclude that Paul added this part as emphasis to the lowly death that Jesus died. The idea of God dying on a Roman cross may have even been something that was a difficulty for Paul to accept before he became a Christian.[24] Even if not, we know it was something that the first-century Jews stumbled over (1 Cor 1.17–18). It is difficult for us, 2,000 years removed, to fully appreciate the shocking overtones Paul used of the cross here. For us, the cross has become such a domesticated symbol, but for the original recipients of this letter, it was the Roman tool of execution. The cross was designed to humiliate. Only the worst criminals among the slaves and foreigners underwent crucifixion.[25] "Scholars have gone through every instance of the word 'cross' and related expressions that have come down to us from about the time of Jesus and shown how 'crucifixion' and 'cross' invariably evoke horror."[26] It was so humiliating that a Roman citizen was not allowed to be crucified without approval from the emperor. In fact, our word, "excruciating," is rooted in the same Latin word as "crucifixion." Thus, the word "crucifixion" "was considered too cruel—so shameful that the word itself was avoided in polite conversation."[27] This sheds light on what the Jewish leaders were trying to do to Jesus—not just get rid of Him, but completely humiliate Him as they did so. Yet, here is Paul suggesting that our Lord was so humble that He subjected Himself to the revolting death of a cross, reserved for the dregs of the criminal justice system. The language is meant to shock, and it does!

Jesus left the glories of heaven with His Father and emptied Himself of everything to become like us. He made Himself a nobody. He

---

[24] F.F. Bruce. *Paul: Apostle of the Heart Set Free* (Grand Rapids: Eerdmans, 1977) 70–1.

[25] D.H. Wheaton. "Crucifixion" in J.D. Douglas, ed., *The New Bible Dictionary* (Grand Rapids: Wm. B. Eerdmans Publishing Co., 1962) 281–2.

[26] Carson, *Basics for Believers,* 56.

[27] Ibid.

became a slave. Once He was a man, He humbled Himself to the Father's will and the service of man even to the point of death; and not just any death- the humble death of the cross. That is the Lord whom we serve! The language is designed to shock us into thinking, "If He could humble Himself, then certainly I should, too." ("Have this attitude…"; v. 5).

Now, God Has Exalted Him as Lord of All (Philippians 2.9–11)

Verses 5–8 focused on what Jesus did in putting others' interests first. Verses 9–11 focus on what God (the Father) did for Jesus in response to His humble service, resulting in God's glory.[28]

In verse 9, the phrase, "for this reason," indicates that Jesus' deep humility led to high exaltation. "Highly exalted" translates the word *huperērsosen* (hyper-exalted or super exalted). God "exalted him to the highest possible decree."[29] Although not specifically stated here, this exaltation of Christ must have occurred at His ascension and coronation at God's right hand. This exaltation was not comparative, but superlative. In other words, this exaltation was not a promotion above His pre-earthly state (comparative), but a lifting up from His earthly state back to His pre-earthly state (superlative). Jesus went from His low state on earth where He was despised and degraded as a slave and ended in death on a cross, to a height of which there is no higher.

In doing so, God, "bestowed on Him the name which is above every name" (v. 9b). The word translated, "bestowed" (*echarisatō*) means to "give freely or graciously as a favor."[30] Jesus' humiliation resulted in God giving Jesus the gift of this "name." There is a defi-

---

[28] Fee points a chiastic structure in verses 9–11 that emphasizes this fact (Fee, *Paul's Letter to the Philippians* 219).

[29] Ibid. 221.

[30] W. Arndt, F.W. Gingrich, F. Danker, and W. Bauer, *A Greek-English Lexicon of the New Testament and Other Early Christian Literature* (Chicago: University of Chicago Press, 1979) 876.

nite article before "name" (*to onoma*) indicating a specific name in mind (as opposed to the KJV's "a name"). In the Hebrew way of thinking, the concept of "name" stood for the whole character and personality of an individual. The term represented or stood for who a person was. It included everything involving the person referred to by the word.[31] That is why God put so much emphasis on not taking His name in vain (Exodus 20.7). It is much more than just the pronunciation of nomenclature. Therefore, Paul was saying considerably more than that the Father simply "renamed" Jesus once He got to heaven. What is meant here is that God assigned Jesus a name that reflects what He has achieved and that acknowledges who He is.[32] It appears from verse 11 that the specific name that Paul had in mind was, "Lord." It echoes from Isaiah 42.8a where God declares, "I am YHWH; that is My name!" When translated into Greek, YHWH was rendered "Lord" (*kurios*), which is the same word used in verse 11. This is fascinating, because the very next phrase in Isaiah 42.8 says, "I will not give My glory to another." Thus, for the Father to "bestow" on Jesus the title of, "Lord" is tantamount to confessing Jesus' deity. It is not that Jesus did not have that equality with God before His death, burial, resurrection, and ascension (that is shown in verse 6). It is now that His position is universally recognized in a way that it was not before His incarnation. This is similar to Paul's assertion in Romans 1.4 that Jesus, "was declared the Son of God with power by the resurrection from the dead." It was not that He became the Son of God at the resurrection, but that it was proven at that point.

Jesus' exaltation should result ("that"—*hina*—"in order that") in universal praise to Him (v. 10). Because of who Jesus is exalted to be (deity, at the right hand of God), "every knee should bow." This is an honor only fit for God (Matt 4.10; Acts 10.25–26; Rev 19.10; 22.8–9). The verbs "bow" and "confess" in verses 10 and 11

---

[31] Weaver, *Philippians* 100.

[32] Carson, *Basics for Believers,* 57.

are aorist subjunctives but translate like future indicatives.[33] Therefore, "should," must not be understood as a possibility, but rather as
a matter of fact. Every being *will* bow their knee at some point in the
future. Most likely Paul was referencing Isaiah 45.22–25 (especially
v. 23). If so, Paul is absolutely connecting Jesus with YHWH (deity).

There should be a universal recognition of who Jesus is after His
exaltation "of those who are in heaven and on earth and under the
earth." The phrase, "those who are" has been added by translators,
but it expresses the idea of rational beings rather than all creation
(unintelligent beings and inanimate objects do not have knees and
tongues). There are three classes of beings: 1) Those "in heaven" (an-
gelic beings and souls that have already died), 2) Those "on earth"
(people still living), and 3) Those "under the earth" (departed spirits;
probably evil). The point of this statement is that every being should
acknowledge the authority of who Jesus is.

Not only should every knee bow in worship to Jesus, but also
"every tongue should confess that Jesus Christ is Lord" (v. 11). In
keeping with the reference from Isaiah 45.21, "every tongue" may refer to every nation (Isaiah 45.20, 22 refers to the Gentiles). The same
recognition of Jesus' lordship that should cause them to bow their
knees also causes them to "confess" His lordship with their tongues.
The word translated, "confess," (*ezomologēsetai*) indicates a profession
of faith (cf. 1 Tim 3.16). This is not a confession with the tongue that
results in salvation (cf. Rom 10.9–10), but a universal acknowledgment of Jesus' lordship. "This universal worship is inevitable: many
will 'bow the knee' to Him in joyful adoration, though some who
were His enemies may find themselves doing so in shame."[34] In Romans 14.10–12, Paul quotes Isaiah 45.23 to refer to judgment. Even
Isaiah 45.24 seems to indicate that some of those who "confess" will
do so grudgingly ("all who were angry at Him will be put to shame").

---

[33] W. Hendriksen, *Exposition of Philippians*. HK. (Grand Rapids: Baker Book
House, 1962) 116.

[34] Bockmuehl, *The Epistle to the Philippians* 146.

This universal confession will result in "the glory of God the Father." All of the emptying of Jesus (His becoming a man), His dying on a cruel cross, and the exaltation that followed resulting in universal praise brings the Father glory. That was the ultimate motivation for all Jesus did. Jesus did not humble Himself to be exalted to heaven. He already had that. He humbled Himself, "to the glory of God the Father." The point is: we must, too!

Humility That Is Worthy of the Gospel

The reason Paul wrote about Christ Jesus coming down to this earth and humbling Himself to the point of crucifixion is not because he wanted to be poetic, but because he wanted to be practical. If effect, he was saying, "Listen here, church, you serve a God who became 'lesser than' for you. That means you need to be willing to become 'lesser than' for each other." Clearly, this is what Paul was speaking of when he said, "Have this attitude in yourselves which was also in Christ Jesus" (v. 5). From this beautiful passage and the passages that follow in Philippians we learn several things about the essence of humility that our Lord modeled for us.

First of all, humility is essential for unity. This was the springboard for Paul's whole discourse on the incarnation in verses 1–4. Little time should be spent on this subject in this lecture due to the fact that the next lecture is dedicated to this topic from this passage. However, it is sufficient to say that pride is at the root of every division that exists, whether it be in the church, in the home, or any other relationship. We learn in chapter 4 that the Philippian church had two women of its members, Euodia and Syntyche, who were not getting along (Phil 4.2–3). There is no way of telling what their issue was, but it was big enough that Paul did not mind naming names and telling the whole church these two ladies needed some help. Most likely, this was not a doctrinal problem or Paul would have addressed it, as he is always quick to do in this letter and in his other epistles. The bigger problem that they had was that neither sister was considering the other better than herself. When one is looking out for their own "personal interests" before the "interests of others," it will always result in division. If unity is lacking in any of our relationships, we would do well to examine ourselves and ask, "In what way is humility lacking in my life?"

Jesus was not the only example Paul used in chapter 2 of someone who put the interest of others first. He wrote of his own sacrificing for the Philippians in verses 16–18. He described Timothy, "who will genuinely be concerned for your welfare," in contrast with those who "all seek after their own interests" (vv. 20–21). He also commended the Philippian church to Epaphroditus, who, "came close to death for the work of Christ, risking his life to complete what was deficient in your service to" Paul (v. 30). These are all examples of ones who were willing to give up their own pleasures and comforts for the sake of others. Humility leads us to do the same. This may mean giving up our rights. It may mean a sacrifice of time, money, or energy that many would want to spend on themselves. Humility like this put into practice would radically change our homes, our churches, and our communities.

Secondly, Christ-like humility refrains from *"empty conceit"* (*kenodozian*) (v. 3). The only other time this word is used in the New Testament is in the adjective form in Galatians 5.26 where it is translated as "boastful." Literally, it is a compound word that means "empty glory." "This word occurs throughout the Greco-Roman world to describe those who think too highly of themselves,… those whose 'glory' is altogether baseless."[35] Empty conceit is a subcategory of pride, yet goes one step forward. Pride deludes us into thinking we are great, but empty conceit desires for *others* to think we are great. It is the craving for honor, glory, recognition, and approval of others. Those with empty conceit are not so concerned about being the best as much as they are about other people thinking that way about

---

[35] Fee, *Paul's Letter to the Philippians* 187.

them. They will seek to do whatever will bring them the most public applause, whether it is deserving or not. Empty conceit causes us to be more concerned with our reputation than who we actually are. Image is everything. It is what causes us to go along with the crowd just so that we fit in. It causes us to exaggerate our accomplishments. It tempts us to gossip about others so that we are seen as better than others, or as the one with all the knowledge of the situation. When a person is full of empty conceit, he hides his true self so that no one sees the ugliness that would bring us down in others' eyes. This sin tempts us to do good deeds in order to be seen by men (cf. Matt 6.1–18) and to boast about what we have done in the kingdom of our Lord. However, this is the opposite disposition of Christ who emptied Himself and became a servant by seeking, "the glory of God the Father" (v. 11). Our focus as followers of Christ ought to be to bring glory to God and not ourselves (cf. Matt 5.16).

Thirdly, in connection with the previous point, the humility of Christ in us results in service to others. This passage impresses upon us not just that Jesus came our way, but the way in which He came. When Jesus came down to this earth, He really did come *down*. He made himself nothing, taking the form of a servant. Again, if He had assumed the status of a powerful man, that would have been amazing. But He did not take the status of a man that was greater than everybody. He took the status of a man that was less than anybody. This is exemplified by Jesus the night before He died when His disciples were all gathered around a table for the Passover meal. There, He took a basin of water and washed His disciples' feet, even though He was their Master and God. He then told them that His disciples are to follow His example (John 13.1–17). Jesus came to this world not, "to be served, but to serve, and to give His life a ransom for many" (Matt 20.28). We, then, must also "have this attitude" of humble service towards others. Many Christians do not mind doing acts of service for other people. What we often have a problem with is when we do those acts of service and then we are treated like a servant. A true test of one's humility is when one can humbly serve, even when we are taken for granted, overlooked, and/or unnoticed. Such was the humility of our Lord.

Fourthly, Jesus demonstrated His humility, "by becoming obedient to the point of death" (v. 8). We must have the same attitude. In fact, that seems to be the direct application Paul makes following this passage: "*So then*, my beloved, just as you have always obeyed, not as in my presence only, but now much more in my absence, work out your salvation with fear and trembling" (Phil 2.12, emp. JB). We should have a serious and humble attitude about our duty, with a proper fear of our Master should we fail in any way. Instead of trying to impose our own will on God, a lowly servant submits to God's will, humbly recognizing that His agenda is better than what we would have chosen on our own. Disobedience to God is always traced back to pride (cf. Gen 3.6; Rom 1.21–23).

Fifthly, humility is also expressed in contentment. Continuing in Philippians 2, Paul says, "Do all things without grumbling or disputing" (v. 14). This refers to petty disputes and questionings that grow out of discontentment with one's circumstances. Such discontentment is the result of one thinking that he deserves better than what God has given him. Did Jesus not deserve better than how He was treated on earth? Yet, not once did He ever complain about His circumstances (cf. 1 Pet 2.21–23). Moreover, when a person has the humble attitude of Jesus, he will be content with his lot in life. This contentment is something Paul said later in the letter that he "learned" to be, "in whatever circumstance" he was. Those circumstances included getting along "with humble means," "going hungry," and "suffering need" (Philippians 4.11–12). By following the example of Christ's incarnation we learn to do the same.

Lastly, humility results in exaltation. Christ's deep humility resulted in God highly exalting Him (v. 9). The implication in this passage is that those who humble themselves and put others first as Christ did in the incarnation and crucifixion, will also be glorified someday as He was. This is always the divine order of things. Jesus stated, "Whoever exalts himself shall be humbled; and whoever humbles himself shall be exalted" (Matt 23.12). The irony of the Scriptures is that the humble person does not practice his humility in order to be exalted. He does it as a lowly servant out of recognition of the reality of his own standing before God. He humbly does what he does only "to the glory of God the Father" (v. 11). Yet, in the end, the promise of God is this: "Humble yourselves in the presence of the Lord, and He will exalt you" (James 4.10). The humble Christian looks forward to these words from his Master: "Well done, good and faithful slave… enter into the joy of your master" (Matt 25.21, 23).

Conclusion

It is truly amazing to think about what Jesus did. He went from the height of heights to the depth of depths. How remarkable it is to think about the staggering implications of what it meant for the holy, glorious, eternal Son of God to take on human flesh. In doing so, He did not take on the flesh of a king, but of a servant. Stooping even lower, He willingly and obediently went to the cross, not for Himself, but for our best interest. It was the sins of all mankind that put Him there. As Isaac Watts put it, "Love so amazing, so divine, demands my soul, my life, my all."[36] May we all have the attitude that was also in Christ Jesus.

---

[36] Watts, Isaac. "When I Survey the Wondrous Cross." *Psalms, Hymns, and Spiritual Songs,* Sumphonia Productions, LLC, 2012, p. 230.

Standing Firm in One Spirit with One Mind

Unity that is Worthy of the Gospel

Phillip W. Martin

In the beginning, the story of humanity opens with the wonder and amazement of creation. Imagine it as an inspired painting brought to life in the words of Genesis. Situated within the temple of creation, God and mankind are united. In what seems like an instant, the slippery tongue of the serpent slithers in and shatters any sense of harmony. This story is a cyclic tragedy that is the plague of mankind. We build broken cities[1] of our own design in an effort to numb our once tender consciousness.

God eventually washes the slate of creation clean. He scrubs the rubble of mankind and scatters the people that emerge. Yet, the hearts of men are then on full display as the Tower of Babel rises in Genesis 11.1–9. Oh, what wonders they may accomplish with their grand schemes. The Babelites[2] banded together and unified themselves with a common language. They had a single mind to build a

---

[1] The longstanding conflict of Gardens and Cities is well recognized in the Bible's narratives. See Phil Roberts, "The City of God," in *The Gospel in the Old Testament*, ed. Daniel W. Petty, Florida College Annual Lectures (Temple Terrace, FL: Florida College Bookstore, 2003), 234.

[2] Thematically, when we read of Babel is it wise for us to see it as emblematic of Babylon, Egypt, and Rome, it is the representation of the enemy of God's people in any age.

tower. We might retort from the gilded throne of our "modern sensibilities," "what good is that low tower? We build them to the heavens now." However, the scriptures explain further: "And the Lord said, "Behold, they are one people, and they have all one language, and this is only the beginning of what they will do. And nothing that they propose to do will now be impossible for them" (Genesis 11.6).[3] In other terms, a unified people with a unified language of disobedience to God is a rebellion in need of reckoning. It should be easy to acknowledge that this story had already played out on the earth at least once. Its end had every man doing what was right in their own eyes. So, for the Babelites, not even the sky would be the limit. God scatters them for his own reasons. The most obvious reason is their unwillingness to spread out and fill the earth. Instead, they clung together and built a single city.[4]

The consequences of this event still burden all of humanity. Languages divide us more than the lines we draw on a map. As the nations separate themselves, God's people often do the same. Just as Israel would let the malfeasance of their neighbors seep into their hearts, the Kingdom of Christ is all too willing to do the same. The deep need for disciples to unify themselves is a demanding and daunting journey. Jesus has called his disciples to be known for their care of each other: "By this all people will know that you are my disciples, if you have love for one another." (John 13.35)

God Unites Us in Christ

In a wonderful return, God has upended the division of mankind and has made us one in Christ (1 Cor 12.13–27, Gal 3.26–29, Eph 2.16). This change in relationship dynamics is core to the unity of the citizens in the grand Kingdom of the Son (Matt 28.18–20, Rom 12.5, 1 Cor 12.13–13). The very substance of that

---

[3] Unless otherwise noted, all quotations of scripture are from the ESV.

[4] K. A. Mathews *Genesis 1–11.26*, vol. 1A, The New American Commentary (Nashville: Broadman & Holman Publishers, 1996), 467.

renewed connection, rebuilt by the transformation of each new soul, should engender unity, togetherness, and fellowship, as the body of Christ supplies back to every joint and member (1 Pet 3.8, Eph 2.21, 1 Pet 2.5).

A unity worthy of the gospel stands on two pillars. First, we must complete our growth to maturity by submitting to the authority of Jesus Christ. We need to squash every tug on our hearts that calls for us to adopt the language of self from the corners of our hearts. Secondly, we must adopt the attitudes that are commended by King Jesus in our hearts, directed towards our fellow citizens. These changes will require a kind of effort that needs contestant tending.

This need for consistency is why, within the unified pleas and prayers of Christ, Paul and James roundly call for disciples in Christ to make every conceivable effort to be united in mind and spirit. As the anointed of God made his prophesied move to the cross, his ardent prayer was that his followers would share in the form of unity foreshadowed by the divine unity of God. (John 17.17–23) Paul evokes the name and the authority of Christ when he appeals to the disciples in Corinth. He centers his plea on Jesus. "Is Christ divided? Was Paul crucified for you? Or were you baptized in the name of Paul?" (1 Cor 1.13) James slices to the heart of the issues that fuel the disorder in these crucial areas. This disharmony is the direct result of personal rebellion. It is the absence of wisdom. "But the wisdom from above is first pure, then peaceable, gentle, open to reason, full of mercy and good fruits, impartial and sincere." (Jam 3.17)

Consider well the alarming wisdom from the Proverbs: the capstone of hatred is "one who sows discord among brothers." (Pro 6.19). The God of creation demands that we pay attention to how we interact with others within the kingdom. This decree is so clear that God judges the one who sows discord among his brothers as the worst of the worst!

Unity Worthy of the Gospel is Stable
(Philippians 1.27a)

Only let your manner of life be worthy of the gospel of Christ, so
that whether I come and see you or am absent, I may hear of you
that you are standing firm in one spirit… (Philippians 1.27a)

The language of unity is stable amidst a backdrop of discord. Paul
breathes out a radical message of humility that hints at a reality that
may shake your senses. As G. B. Caird quipped, "Salvation in the
New Testament is always an intensely personal, but never an individual, matter."[5] Paul expected Kingdom citizens to live in a manner
of such stability that he, being absent from those at Philippi, would
hear of their resolute faith. "Worthy"[6] defines the nature of our citizenship and the obligations that come with it. The gospel is at the
center of this. Earlier in the epistle, Paul knit himself with them
through this joint cause. (Philippians 1.5, 7, 12, 15). What he had
anticipated before, he now will fully explain. God calls us to live
faithfully as genuine citizens in a world. Gordon Fee says the verb
thus means (literally) to "live as citizens:"[7] not as Romans, but as
Christians. "Paul's concept of dual citizenship can be conveyed by
an expanded paraphrase: As good citizens of Philippi and as good
citizens of heaven, live in a manner worthy of the gospel of Christ"[8]

As Paul desired to live long enough to be of personal encouragement to their spiritual progress, we should also expect this and more

---

[5] As quoted in Gordon D. Fee, *Paul's Letter to the Philippians.* The New International Commentary on the New Testament. (Grand Rapids, MI: Wm.B. Eerdmans
Publishing Co., 1995), 235n23.

[6] The wider context of Phil 1.27–2.18 demands that we consider that our conduct is seen within the communal relationships that are shared in the community of
disciples. For a larger discussion see P. Hartog, 2008. "'Work Out Your Salvation':
Conduct 'Worthy of the Gospel' in a Communal Context." *Themelios* 33 (2): 19–33.

[7] Fee, *Paul's Letter to the Philippians*, 163.

[8] G. Hansen, *The Letter to the Philippians*, The Pillar New Testament Commentary (Grand Rapids, MI; Nottingham, England: William B. Eerdmans Publishing
Company, 2009), 95.

of ourselves in a way that helps others to grow into a fuller way of life. Paul expected to be with them in the future, but until that day, he sought for them to live a worthy life in the gospel. The idea here is for their "manner of life" (politeuomai) to be fitting across the full range of their lives. They were to be worthy, as they were not of this world but still in it. Paul's full request is that those at Philippi behave in such a manner that their speech and actions are well suited to the gospel of King Jesus. The practicality is that God indeed holds our lives to a kingdom standard. In all this, He expects us to have a firmness that echoes a house built upon the rock called Christ.

Unity Worthy of the Gospel is Shared (Philippians 1.27b)

...with one mind striving side by side for the faith of the gospel (Philippians 1.27b)

The language of unity is shared in the life of a Christian. It should be one that is in tune with their fellow disciples. There are three areas of note that need to sound together to make this chord complete. They must stand, contend, and not be intimidated as one.[9] The key to that goal is that they accomplish this task "in one Spirit." By contrast, the people of "Babel" were united in rebellion against God's expectation that they go forth and populate the earth. God's solution to scramble their communication was sufficient to force the people to the needed behavior. For disciples, the converse is true. If we choose the language of unity, we are compelled to behave as we should. I would suggest that this is accomplished in part during our initial transformation into Christ and continues over the course of our lives.

---

[9] Fee, *Paul's Letter to the Philippians*, 163. He spells out specifically three coinciding matters he hopes to hear about "their affairs": (1) that by standing firm in the one Spirit (2) they are contending together as one person for the faith of the gospel; and (3) that in so doing they are not themselves intimidated in any way by the opposition that is responsible for their present suffering.

The spiritual language of Christians is truth: "God is spirit, and those who worship him must worship in spirit and truth." (John 4.24) Disciples united by this language will consequently become knitted as: "one soul." It will be the sign of their lives together. The fastest way to build that rapport is through adversity. As disciples suffer together, they will learn the value of their shared spiritual experience.

Unity Worthy of the Gospel is Sure (Philippians 1.28–30)

and not frightened in anything by your opponents. This is a clear sign to them of their destruction, but of your salvation, and that from God. For it has been granted to you that for the sake of Christ you should not only believe in him but also suffer for his sake, engaged in the same conflict that you saw I had and now hear that I still have. (Philippians 1.28–30)

The language of unity requires security. People who have knit themselves to become one spirit and one soul have found a power that exceeds any individual. As such, Paul admonishes that we should not be fearful of our adversaries. When the saints of God are of one spirit and soul, they make for a powerful people. Who would stand against us? In context, it would be those who are at first not unified with them and those who do not share a common interest.

This resolute trust in God displays the flimsy assaults of the unconverted. It is also evidence of our own salvation. We see the power of this security in the contrasting ends of those who suffer for the sake of Christ and those who oppose the Kingdom. Christians have been given what the outsider could see as a strange gift, but to "suffer on his behalf" is roundly seen as a blessing. Paul told the Thessalonians that suffering was what God had appointed them to do (1 Thes 5.9). It is possible, then, that we can read this section as a reflection of what we see in the text of Job. As much as God permitted the suffering of Job, God is also an agent of our suffering. The words *and that from God* indicate that it is God who is the indirect agent of this persecution.[10]

This connection of suffering should be the expectation of all those who choose to follow Christ. Peter explains that our suffering then is the result of our sympathetic relationship with Jesus. We suffer as he suffered because we seek to walk as he walked!

> For what credit is it if, when you sin and are beaten for it, you endure? But if when you do good and suffer for it you endure, this is a gracious thing in the sight of God. For to this you have been called, because Christ also suffered for you, leaving you an example, so that you might follow in his steps. (1 Pet 2.20–21)

Thanks be to God, though, that we who suffer are never truly alone. We not only have those who have gone before us, but we are united to a family who shares in that suffering. Jesus empowered John to write for us: "Do not fear what you are about to suffer. Behold, the devil is about to throw some of you into prison, that you may be tested, and for ten days you will have tribulation. Be faithful unto death, and I will give you the crown of life." (Revelation 2.10)

Much like the Law is a tutor that leads us to Christ (Gal 3.24), shared suffering should lead us to unity.

Unity Worthy of the Gospel is About Service (Philippians 2.1–4)

> So if there is any encouragement in Christ, any comfort from love, any participation in the Spirit, any affection and sympathy, complete my joy by being of the same mind, having the same love, being in full accord and of one mind. Do nothing from selfish ambition or conceit, but in humility count others more significant than yourselves. Let each of you look not only to his own interests, but also to the interests of others. (Philippians 2.1–4)

---

[10] R.P. Martin, *Philippians: An Introduction and Commentary*, vol. 11, Tyndale New Testament Commentaries (Downers Grove, IL: InterVarsity Press, 1987), 95.

The language of unity requires us to learn to serve others. This requirement is the core of genuine unity in Christ. Consider the first disciples in Jerusalem as they banded together after the resurrection. They had all things in common; they gave freely to serve the needs of the community of disciples that surrounded them. This service is a stark contrast to the often partisan view of unity we see practiced. The message of the world says, "align with my polemics, and we will be united." However, any unity that does not find itself in the service of others is, at best, shallow and, at worse, vain.

We may understand this passage better if we take the time to lay out the four verses in three sections:

I.

A   Therefore, if there is any encouragement in Christ,

    B   if there is any consolation of love,

        C   if there is any fellowship of the Spirit,

            D   if there is any affection and compassion,

II.

A   fulfill my joy by being of the same mind,

    B   maintaining the same love,

    B'   united in spirit,

A'   intent on one purpose.

III.

A   Do nothing from selfishness or empty conceit,

    B   but with humility regard one another as more important than yourselves.

A'   Do not look out for your own interests

    B'   but also for the interests of others.[11]

---

[11] D. Black, "Paul and Christian Unity: A Formal Analysis of Philippians 2.1–4," *JETS* 28.3 (1985). David Black offers this excellent arrangement for the translation of the message. This layout brings to light the core ideas of the message as intended by Paul.

This arrangement of the passage simplifies the message for clarity: (1) the **criteria** for Christian unity, (2) the **outcome** of Christian unity, and (3) the **manifestation** of Christian unity. These three steps are where we, as disciples, need to grow.

The **criteria** for Christian unity begins with a soft shift in tone. Chapter one closed with the sorrow of suffering shared, and now Paul expresses a tender call to encouragement. The four concepts summarize the blessings found within genuine communities of Christians. These four truths represent what those in Christ need to demonstrate toward each other.

First, we need to become encouragers. The world around us is drab and gray with criticism and failure. However, in Christ, we have a hope that does not disappoint. God calls us to be a light to the world around us. (Matt 5.16)

Second, we need to become adept at the kind of love that exemplifies Jesus. We live in a world that misunderstands love in ways that swirl hearts into a cynical abyss. True love comforts the hearts of the broken and mends their wounds. (1 Cor 13.1–13)

Third, we need to become truly invested in the spiritual bonds that unite us. We need to drop the false facade of unity that is superficial and be willing to unite through our shared faith. For too long, we have allowed the petty tyrant of personal wants to supersede our need to be as one. (Col 3.12–15)

Finally, we must grow to like each other. It is one thing to accept the command to love your brother, but genuinely loving our brethren might be the toughest test of forgiveness. The expectation is that we care for each other and that, in all situations, we seek to help each other overcome the world, and not let it overcome us.

The **outcome** of Christian unity that Paul seeks can be found in us today. The focus on learning about the Kingdom should allow us to quickly dispel the illusions offered as unity. A united people will not look the same. They will not dress the same. They may not even speak the same language! A united people will, instead, share the same mind of Christ. They would rather serve one another than demand to be served. They would rather suffer as their Lord did than renounce their faith in the idols of this generation. They would rather unify with the purpose of heaven than the calls of politicians and rulers of this age.

The **manifestation** of Christian unity can be seen in the sacrifice of preferences and perceived rights in the service of the King. The trappings of the Roman Empire surrounded the disciples in Philippi. Any citizen of Rome (like Paul) had the right to vote, hold office, purchase, possess, sell, and bequeath property, enter a legal contract, have a fair trial, and appeal to Caesar.[12] These rights were tied to their responsibilities to return service to the empire. In the spirit, Paul called them to be willing to set aside their "rights" for the betterment of their brethren. Consider again: "each one looking not to their own interests, but rather each to the interests of others" (Phil 2.4)[13] For the final real test of our heart's willingness to unify is simply this: what will you give up in service to your brother?

Coda: Unity Worthy of the Gospel is Lived (Philippians 4.2–3)

> I entreat Euodia and I entreat Syntyche to agree in the Lord. Yes, I ask you also, true companion, help these women, who have labored side by side with me in the gospel together with Clement and the rest of my fellow workers, whose names are in the book of life. (Philippians 4.2–3, ESV)

The language of unity requires us to reconcile. The two who were once able to work side by side with Paul and others in gospel work

---

[12] Hoehner, Comfort, and Davids, Cornerstone Biblical Commentary: Ephesians, Philippians, Colossians, 1&2 Thessalonians, Philemon., vol. 16 (Carol Stream, IL: Tyndale House Publishers, 2008), 166.

[13] Seth M. Ehorn and Mark Lee. "The Syntactical Function of Alla Kai in Philippians 2.4." *Journal of Greco-Roman Christianity and Judaism* 12 (2016) 9–16. Ehorn and Lee argue that this is the best translation of the manuscripts.

are now an example of a lamentable echo. It pulses from the garden tragedy through the tower and, in a sad discord, bears diseased fruit in us. When we find ourselves at odds with those who hold a share in the kingdom, we are called upon and encouraged to be of the "same mind in the Lord."

Like Paul and James, I feel compelled to beg all who would seek Christ to think deeply about what they can do to rebuild unity among the family of God. Pause for a moment and remember, if you raise your voice to demand that others serve your "right," you have already lost. There is a time for the bold defense of the faith, but I beg you to consider, is your love bolder than your voice? If so, you will finally see unity that is worthy of the gospel.

Bibliography

Allred, Tyler. "Philippians 4.2–3 : An Alternative View of the Euodia-Syntyche Debate." *Priscilla Papers* 33 (4) 2019 4–7.

Black, David A. "Paul and Christian Unity: A Formal Analysis of Philippians 2.1–4," *JETS* 28.3 (1985).

Brown, Derek R. *Philippians*. Edited by Douglas Mangum. Lexham Research Commentaries. (Bellingham, WA: Lexham Press, 2013)

deSilva, David Arthur. *An Introduction to the New Testament: Contexts, Methods and Ministry Formation*. Downers Grove, IL: InterVarsity Press, 2004.

Ehorn, Seth M., and Mark. Lee. "The Syntactical Function of *Alla Kai* in Philippians 2.4." *Journal of Greco-Roman Christianity and Judaism* 12 (2016) 9–16.

Fee, Gordon D. *Paul's Letter to the Philippians*. The New International Commentary on the New Testament. (Grand Rapids, MI: Wm.B. Eerdmans Publishing Co., 1995)

Hansen, G. Walter. *The Letter to the Philippians*. The Pillar New Testament Commentary. (Grand Rapids, MI; Nottingham, England: William B. Eerdmans Publishing Company, 2009)

Hartog, Paul. 2008. " 'Work Out Your Salvation': Conduct 'Worthy of the Gospel' in a Communal Context." *Themelios* 33 (2): 19–33.

Hoehner, Harold W., Philip W. Comfort, and Peter H. Davids. *Cornerstone Biblical Commentary: Ephesians, Philippians, Colossians, 1&2 Thessalonians, Philemon.* Vol. 16. (Carol Stream, IL: Tyndale House Publishers, 2008)

Keener, Craig S. *The IVP Bible Background Commentary: New Testament.* (Downers Grove, IL: InterVarsity Press, 1993)

Kurek-Chomycz, Dominika."Fellow Athletes or Fellow Soldiers? *Synathleō* in Philippians 1.27 and 4.3." *Journal for the Study of the New Testament* 39 (3): (2017) 279–303

Mathews, K. A. *Genesis 1–11.26*, vol. 1A, The New American Commentary (Nashville: Broadman & Holman Publishers, 1996), 467

Martin, Ralph P. *Philippians: An Introduction and Commentary.* Vol. 11. Tyndale New Testament Commentaries. (Downers Grove, IL: InterVarsity Press, 1987)

Melick, Richard R. *Philippians, Colossians, Philemon.* Vol. 32. The New American Commentary. Nashville: (Broadman & Holman Publishers, 1991)

Moo, Douglas J. *A Theology of Paul and His Letters: The Gift of the New Realm in Christ.* Edited by Andreas J. Köstenberger. Biblical Theology of the New Testament. (Grand Rapids, MI: Zondervan Academic, 2021)

Motyer, J. A. *The Message of Philippians.* The Bible Speaks Today. (Downers Grove, IL: InterVarsity Press, 1984)

Silva, Moisés. *Philippians.* 2nd ed. Baker Exegetical Commentary on the New Testament. (Grand Rapids, MI: Baker Academic, 2005)

Taught by God to Love One Another
Relationships That are Worthy of the Gospel

Adam Shanks

Love is an ill-defined concept, often made confusing by a culture that grossly misunderstands and misappropriates the word. The Church, as God designed it, is to be the beacon that lights the path to real love, as God defines it, for a world that desperately needs to be loved, as God declared it. The famous John 3.16 declares God's love for His created world, but because the world poorly understands the word, they have no idea what this passage truly means. The world misinterprets the word as tolerance and acceptance. Therefore, if God loves them by that definition, God tolerates their sins and accepts them. The world bends the word to give approval for all to do whatever they want, however they want, whenever they want, to whomever they want. In this case, God must allow them freedom of expression. The world misinterprets the word as merely a feeling, meaning God must feel "lovingly" toward them, and therefore He would never punish those whom He loves. The misunderstanding of this basic word leads to many false conclusions, leading to false theologies that lead people away from God instead of towards Him.

It is unsurprising that the world struggles to understand God's love, but it is sometimes embarrassing how badly Christians choose to ignore the abundant teaching from the Bible. There are at least one hundred "one another" (*allélón*) commandments found in the

New Testament, revealing to us how to relate to one another, including "be at peace," "do not grumble against," "accept," "tolerate," "forgive," "be kind to," "confess to," and "give honor to." Unsurprisingly, "love one another" is the most cited *allélón* commandment. While we might be well aware of the commandment, we often miss the application of what it means for us. Or maybe we ignore it. Perhaps we don't understand it. Worse case, we intentionally disobey it. No matter the reason, the teaching is there, in plain sight for the student of the Bible. It's written on the pages like a blinking, florescent message, proclaiming the Bible's intention as a book that promotes relationships between God's people.

Admittedly, the word "love" is difficult to define. Definitions, by their nature, seek to help us understand words through synonymous terms to provide further context for understanding. Love is not an object that is easily identified because it is an ideal. Is love a feeling? Is love an action? Is it a determination or matter of the will? Is it something that one can grasp intellectually or only experience emotionally? Love is no easier to define to someone who doesn't understand it than it is to describe a color to a blind man. Living in a world of "love-blind" people, we are trying to explain the nature of something often beyond their grasp.

Seeing how debased the understanding of love is in our modern society doesn't require much effort. Social media has made this abundantly clear as "friends," fans, and fiends have 24-hour access to our lives, which they fill with criticism, complaints, and comparisons. These critical relationships rob them of any desire for deeper connections. Modern counselors teach against "interdependency," redefining love based on selfish terms, even using Scripture to defend such a point of view by arguing that the Royal Law teaches self-love before the love of others.[1] Modern marriages are struggling because they cannot live

---

[1] Some will argue that "Love your neighbor as you love yourself" requires a "love of self" that proceeds loving others. Ironically, these same people will not argue that a man should love himself before considering his love of his wife, as their logic if

up to the expectations of an erroneous view of love. The following explanation of marriage describes these conflicting expectations:

> Marriage was an economic institution in which you were given a partnership for life in terms of children and social status and succession and companionship. But now we want our partner to still give us all these things, but in addition I want you to be my best friend and my trusted confidant and my passionate lover to boot, and we live twice as long. So we come to one person, and we basically are asking them to give us what once an entire village used to provide: Give me belonging, give me identity, give me continuity, but give me transcendence and mystery and awe all in one. Give me comfort, give me edge. Give me novelty, give me familiarity. Give me predictability, give me surprise. And we think it's a given, and toys and lingerie are going to save us with that.[2]

Modern marriages are often made of husbands who seek intimacy on their terms and wives who despise the biblical teaching of submission, neither finding fulfillment, comfort, or support in the marriage. The Beatles' declaration of "All you need is love" has been replaced by the Stones' cry of "I can't get no satisfaction." No satisfaction comes when there is no understanding of love.

Even when it comes to friendships, modern society struggles with their explanation of love, often equating affection with lust, and relational intimacy is confused with erotic fantasy. Men shun any depth of relationships with another man because they do not want to be misidentified as homosexual. Women hear that feelings of closeness with another woman must mean they are lesbians. What would in years gone by have been perceived as the innocent affection of friendship is now redefined as illicit and intimate sexual desire.

---

consistently applied, would teach in Eph 5.28. Even the "Golden Rule" in Matt 7.12 is warped to say that we should consider what we want first, then treat others that way, essentially putting our own desires before the good of others.

[2] E. Perel. "Are We Asking Too Much Of Our Spouses?" By Guy Raz, *TED Radio Hour* (April 25, 2014): *https://www.npr.org/transcripts/301825600.*

Ancient friendships, like that shared between Gilgamesh and En-kidu, or Achilles and Patroclus, have been reinterpreted by modern academics as homosexual when their expressions of love were long understood to be platonic and moral. Gone are the days when David could cry about the death of his friend "whose love was better than any woman's" (2 Sam 1.25–26).³ No longer can one man declare his love for another without immoral conclusions being supposed.

Christians live in this same world and can struggle with the same blindness. Attempting to better understand, Bible students have often resorted to poorly performed word studies, understanding love by de-fining "The Four Loves."⁴ The difficulty with this is that language does not work as cleanly as this view demands, arguing that Greek has four words for various types of love. In reality, Greek has many more than four words that translate as love (of which the New Testament only uses three), many of those words overlap in their meaning, and the Bible does not use these various Greek words consistently enough for us to make conclusive statements about various types of love.

In 2 Samuel 13 (LXX), both ἀγαπάω (*agapaô*, to love) and the cog-nate ἀγάπη (*agapê*, love) can refer to Amnon's incestuous rape of his half sister Tamar (2 Sam 13.15, LXX). When we read Demas forsook Paul because he loved this present, evil world, there is no linguistic reason to be surprised that the verb is ἀγαπάω (*agapaô*, 2 Tim 4.10). John 3.35 records that the Father loves the Son and uses

---

³ Gilgamesh dreamed of his friendship before it happened, with the words "There will come to you a strong one, a companion who rescues a friend.... You will fall in love with him and caress him like a woman" (*Epic of Gilgamesh*, p. 106, lines 261–266). Achilles shared his special armor with his friend and expressed the deep-est sorrow upon his death, "A mist of black grief enveloped Achilles. He scooped up fistfuls of sunburn dust and poured it on his head fouling his beautiful face. Black ash grimed his fine-spun cloak…, and lay there, tearing out his hair with his hands" (Illiad, p. 284, lines 7–10). These expressions are surprisingly similar to David's words and experiences with Jonathan.

⁴ C.S. Lewis's *The Four Loves* is one example of this. Many have taken Lewis's conclusions to the extreme, drawing wrong conclusions that Lewis himself did not make.

the verb ἀγαπάω (*agapaô*); John 5.20 repeats the thought, but uses φιλέω (*phileô*)—without any discernible shift in meaning. The false assumptions surrounding this pair of words are ubiquitous.[5]

How God-like was the love the Pharisees had for the best seats (Luke 11.43)? How unconditional was the love the backsliders had for gain from wrongdoing (2 Pet 2.15)? There are many other examples of *agapaô* being used in ways that do not match our modern understanding.[6] We cannot demand that love fit into neat categories, nor should we want to use language to reinforce an idea that strays far away from biblical teaching. "*Agape* love" is not the oft presented unfeeling, emotionless, matter of the will. It is not the justification for "I-love-them-but-I-don't-have-to-like-them."

This leaves us with no definition, but we are not hopeless. Christians have an advantage. We know God—and "God is love" (1 John 4.16). Therefore, if we know God, we can better understand what the world cannot, because we know the story of Scripture: "This is how we have come to know love: He laid down His life for us" (1 John 3.16). We can know love by knowing Christ, who displayed incredible love for us. Admittedly, love is hard to define in words because it is something that is better experienced or witnessed, but this is how God defines love. Not by particular Greek words but by displaying it so "that you also should do just as I have done for you" (John 13.15). Paul admits that this love can be both understood while also being beyond understanding (cf. Eph 3.17–19). It is his (and my) prayer that we comprehend what we can but recognize no matter how much we think we understand, we still cannot fully grasp how far love can go.

Even Paul's "love chapter" in 1 Corinthians 13 does not define love as much as it describes what love looks like between breth-

---

[5] D.A. Carson, *Exegetical Fallacies* (Grand Rapids: Baker Academics, 1996) 31–32.

[6] cf. John 3.19, 12.43; 2 Tim 4.10; 1 John 2.15; and Rev 12.11.

ren. Its patience, kindness, and selflessness are every day, practical ways to love others within the community of God's people. "For the whole law is fulfilled in one word: 'You shall love your neighbor as yourself'" (Gal 5.14). This one word is not "neighbor," nor is it "yourself." Love is the principal concept and foundation for everything we do, the defining characteristic of our relationship with God and one another.[7] This command demands community, something increasingly ignored over the centuries. "In the beginning the Church was a fellowship of men and women centering on the living Christ. Then the Church moved to Greece, where it became a philosophy. Then it moved to Rome, where it became an institution. Next it moved to Europe where it became a culture, and finally, it moved to America where it became an enterprise."[8] When we have redefined our relationships in God's Church to fit in a consumer mindset, we fail to recognize the value of fellow believers and for what they exist. They are not there for my good nor to serve me. They are there for me to serve, love and encourage. They exist as a way for me to exercise God's love for others. The irony is that if the church functions as an enterprise filled with consumers trying to be served, no one ends up satisfied because everyone is waiting for someone to meet their needs while no one does the work. If it exists as a community of servants, everyone ends up being served and we end up receiving more than we give.

This community is on full display in the Macedonian letters. The expressions of love between brethren help us better understand what God was creating in the Church and the strength it provides to its community, knowing that if we emulate these examples, we will experience more extraordinary and satisfying love.

---

[7] Love is the shared imperative when Jesus discusses the two greatest commandments. (cf. Matt 22.36–40; Mark 12.28–34; Luke 10.25–28).

[8] Origin Unknown.

Love One Another Through Prayer

The first expression of love in each of the Macedonian epistles is found straight away in the introductions. Paul expresses his love through admitting they are in his prayers, complimenting them for the way they have partnered with him in the gospel (Phil 1.3), the good work God is doing through them (1.6; 1 Thes 1.3), and for the love they show to one another (1 Thes 1.3; 2 Thes 1.3). This constant remembrance in prayer in both letters is revealing. Paul is in continuous contact with the Church in Philippi, as they send him regular support for his ministry, as mentioned in Philippians and 2 Corinthians. He depends on their support (although he admits that God is the one who provides what is needed) and has a great appreciation for them because of their continued financial fellowship. In the letters to the Thessalonians, Paul's recent departure under duress gives him ample concern for the Christians to remain faithful despite the persecution they saw him endure, which is reflected in his prayers on their behalf.

These prayers are a common theme throughout Paul's letters.[9] To hear the prayers of Paul would be both remarkable and tiring, considering the number of people for whom he admits praying. His

---

[9] "I constantly remember you in my prayers at all times" (Rom 1.8–19); "My heart's desire and prayer to God for the Israelites" (Rom 10.1); Paul prays for their unity (Rom 15.5–6); Paul prays for their hope and joy (Rom 15.13); "I always thank God for you" (1 Cor 1.4–9); Paul prays for their comfort (2 Cor 1.3–7); Paul prays for their innocence (2 Cor 13.7–9); "I have not stopped giving thanks for you, remembering you in my prayers (Eph 1.15–23); Paul prays for their strength and that they would know Christ's love (Eph 3.14–21); "I thank God every time I remember you" (Phil 1.3–6); Paul prays for their abounding love (Phil 1.9–11); "The grace of the Lord Jesus be with your spirit" (Phil 4.23); "We always thank God the Father of our Lord Jesus Christ, when we pray for you" (Col 1.3–14); "We always thank God for all of you" (1 Thes 1.2–3); Paul prays thanks for their acceptance of truth (1 Thes 2.13–16);""How can we thank God enough for you? (1 Thes 3.9–13); Paul prays for blessings on them (1 Thes 5.23–24); "We ought always to thank God for you" (2 Thes 1.3–4; 2.13–14); Paul prays for their worthiness (2 Thes 1.11–12); Paul prays for their hearts and peace (2 Thes 3.1–5, 16); "I constantly remember you in my prayers (2 Tim 1.3–7); Paul prays for mercy on the house of Onesiphorus (2 Tim 1.16–18); "I always thank my God as I remember you in my prayers" (Phlm 4–7).

prayers overflow with not just praise for God but praise for God's people. He even mentions this as one of the "persecutions" he endures when he says, "There is daily pressure on me: my concern for all the churches" (2 Cor 11.28). This continual concern is a display of love. How much more should we be on our knees regarding our people, fellow citizens, and family? As Paul says, "It is right for me to think this way about all of you" (Phil 1.7). It is right for us to do the same. Notice the differing scenarios for prayers in these two churches. According to the context of his letter, Paul would be praying thanksgiving for his fellow believers in Philippi. The situation is optimistic and filled with gratitude and appreciation. Paul would be expressing his concern and petitioning for his brethren in Thessalonica, considering their aforementioned situation. Our prayers for our brethren should not merely be when the going gets tough but appreciation when the tough get going. We should preach "in season and out of season," and we should pray likewise. "Pray without ceasing," Paul states, "giving thanks in all circumstances" (1 Thes 5.17–18). When we love our brethren, we pray for them.

Love One Another Through Selflessness

Paul also displays love through the command, "Do nothing out of selfish ambition or conceit, but in humility consider others as more important than yourselves. Everyone should look not to his own interests, but rather to the interests of others" (Phil 2.3–4). This "others-focus" is essential in our expression of love.

> The believers, as children of God, become what sociologists call a fictive kinship group, that is, a collection of people who are not genealogically related but who nevertheless consider one another as family, attempting to relate at that higher level of intimacy, belonging and mutual commitment. As sisters and brothers, believers share honor within one household, working together toward the advancement of the honor of all members of the family rather than competing with one another for honor as if between unrelated individuals.... Paul

urges his friends in Philippi to lay aside all rivalries over recognition in the Church, choosing instead "in humility [to] regard others as better than yourselves" (Phil 2.3). Instead of clinging to claims of certain recognition, the Christians are simply to relinquish those claims (seedbeds of factionalism that they are) and offer recognition and honor to the other members of the body.[10]

Paul even visualizes this in terms of human relationships in 1 Thessalonians. He speaks of the gentleness of a nurse nurturing her children. He speaks of a father with his children, encouraging, comforting, and imploring them to walk worthy. He declares that he sought not to "burden" any of them, speaking of financial strains, working doubly hard so that he would not distract them from the gospel (1 Thes 2.9; 2 Thes 3.8).

All of this displayed clearly that Paul considered them more highly than himself. He was "them-focused" instead of self-focused. He was not in this work for gain or his own glory. Instead, he sought their glorification and exaltation as they served the Lord.

Paul continues with the statement that "all seek their own interest," excluding Timothy, who "is like-minded" and "who will genuinely care about your interests" (Phi 2.20–21). "Love begins when someone else's needs are more important than my own."[11] Paul here shows that displaying love is a rare and desired quality. Timothy loves properly. Epaphroditus also clearly understands love, worrying about the saints, putting Paul's needs above his own, and anticipating his return to his spiritual family in Philippi so they could "rejoice when they see him" (Phil 2.28).

Similarly, we should also focus on the good, the glory, and the godliness of others. This first requires self-resistance. Our culture teaches self-care, self-focus, self-image, self-esteem, self-love, self-defense,

---

[10] D. DeSilva. *Honor, Patronage, Kinship, & Purity* (Downers Grove, IL: Inter-Varsity Press: 2000) 76.

[11] G.D. Fee, *Paul's Letter to the Philippians, The New International Commentary on the New Testament* (Grand Rapids: Wm. B. Eerdmans Publishing Co.: 1995) 185.

self-image, and self-assurance; ultimately it teaches self-love. Instead, Christians focus on selflessness. We must feel about our brethren as John did when he spoke to his disciples when they came complaining about the growing popularity of Jesus, "He must increase. I must decrease" (John 3.30). This does not mean we must practice self-punishment or self-debasement. Instead, we must learn the attitude of C.S. Lewis, who states, "He will not be thinking about humility: he will not be thinking about himself at all."[12] The goal is to get our thoughts off self and onto others. God should be a consuming focus (cf. Heb 12.29), but along with Him, we should be mindful of (read that mind-filled with) God's people. We should be interested in the interests of others. We should seek to find ways to serve by engaging in the good works of working good. We practice this by benevolence[13] and

---

[12] C.S. Lewis, *Mere Christianity*, book 3, chapter 8, *The Great Sin*.

[13] Consider the benevolence and work of the early church. "All the believers were together and held all things in common. They sold their possessions and property and distributed the proceeds to all, as any had need. Every day they devoted themselves to meeting together in the temple, and broke bread from house to house. They ate their food with joyful and sincere hearts, praising God and enjoying the favor of all the people" (Acts 2.44b-47a). By the time you get to the end of chapter four, even though we do not know how much time has passed, it says, "The entire group of those who believed were of one heart and mind, and no one claimed that any of his possessions was his own, but instead held everything in common" (Acts 4.32). We often get sidetracked into a debate of whether this is necessary or not in today's world, so far removed from the culture and circumstances that existed in the early church. This is both beside the point of the text, yet also displays the point that we do not love as they loved. We are concerned with *what* is mine instead of *who* is God's. This self-focus that prompts us to protect what is our own is contrary to what we see in Philippians and Thessalonians, or in Jerusalem. Paul was clearly supported financially by the Macedonian brethren (cf. 2 Cor 8.1ff). It states that they gave "according to their ability and even beyond their ability, of their own accord" (8.3). This kind of generosity did not come from their excess funds, being that they suffered extreme poverty, but because they saw supporting their beloved brother Paul as a privilege and an honor to share the opportunity of the gospel with those who did not yet have the truth. Their generosity is called an "act of grace." They were gift-giving, not just to Paul but to those whom Paul would teach. This was an act of love, humility, and service. They were lifted up as an example to the much more affluent brethren of Corinth to emulate. They should be an example to us too.

hospitality.[14] Loving our brethren requires us to live open-handed instead of tight-fisted. We must look for opportunities to share and consider such moments with abundant joy. "God loves a cheerful giver" (2 Cor 9.7).

Other times, "putting others first" will consume our time, an even more precious resource. We are to feed the hungry, quench the thirst of the thirsty, take in the stranger, clothe the naked, care for the sick, and visit the incarcerated (Matt 25.35–45). We find the widows and orphans, care for these less fortunate, and love them through their distress (Jam 1.27). We have a responsibility to teach those who need truth (2 Tim 2.2). Those who serve the Lord will take time to teach patiently, rebuke gently, and work with those who struggle with the truth because God can use those efforts to turn people to the truth (2 Tim 2.24–26). Being a Christian is starting to sound like a full-time job–because it is. It is not merely something we do but something we are, and you cannot take time off from being who you are.

Love One Another with Emotional Attachment

Love is not expressed through apathetic duties, but promotes emotional attachment, made evident by Paul's expression in Philippians 1:

> Indeed, it is right for me to think this way about all of you, because I have you in my heart, and you are all partners with me in grace, both in my imprisonment and in the defense and confirmation of the Gospel. For God is my witness, how deeply I miss all of you with the affection of Christ Jesus. And I pray this: that your love will keep on growing in knowledge and every kind of discernment, so that you may approve the things that are superior and may be pure and blame-

---

[14] The early church was hospitable. Early Christians would even bring unwanted children in to their homes as a part of their hospitable works. "These impious Galileans (Christians) not only feed their own, but ours also; welcoming them with their agape, they attract them, as children are attracted with cakes... Whilst the pagan priests neglect the poor, the hated Galileans devote themselves to works of charity, and by a display of false compassion have established and given effect to their pernicious errors. Such practice is common among them, and causes contempt for our gods (Julian the Apostate, Epistle to Pagan High Priests)."

less in the day of Christ, filled with the fruit of righteousness that comes through Jesus Christ to the glory and praise of God (1.7–11).

Paul's heart is on full display in these words, which are tender and loving. He appreciates their support. He longs to see their faces. He wants the comfort of being with them. He is proud of their stand for truth and firm determination to follow the Lord. He longs for their success. He considers them partners in his work but also partners in life. Their fellowship is not based on being together, like fair-weather friends, but he feels that partnership even while separated from them: he is in prison while they are still free.

The letter to the Philippians continues Paul's emotional expressions of praise. He conditions the health of the family and the foundation of its unity on "love" and "affection" (Phi 2.1). He mentions their mutual gladness and rejoicing when they consider one another (2.18). He calls them his "dearly loved and longed for brothers and sisters" (4.1) These statements and appellations are abundantly emotional. Paul's heart is wide open in his affection.

Paul's opening statement to the Thessalonians carries similar sentiments of appreciation. He calls them loved by God, commends their evangelism efforts with pride, and identifies how the word had spread from them into Macedonia and Achaia. In Paul's second letter, he admits that he even brags about them to other churches. While we cannot see Paul's face, it is not hard to imagine his eyes lighting up when the brethren of Thessalonica are mentioned. The same smile would be inevitable when the brethren of Philippi are brought up in conversation.

Paul commands them to preach and labor in love (Phil 1.16; 1 Thes 1.2), to be united in love and display affection among God's people (Phil 2.2), to share Christ's love for one another (2.5), and to "overflow with love for one another and everyone" (1 Thes 3.12). Paul demands them to have an emotional attachment to one another. It brings to mind the lyrics from the Sister Hazel song, "This kind of love is what I dream about; yeah, it fills me up. Baby, it leaves no doubt."[15] This kind of love, affection, tenderness, and longing is clearly felt from the heart, displayed by actions, and would leave no doubt to the shared relationships among brethren.

When Christians share love, affection, and longing for one another, there is no doubt about the quality of their relationship. An interdependency exists, with brethren leaning on brethren, holding one another accountable. There is a brokenness that spreads when one sins. There is a rejoicing that applies when one repents. This kind of love demands Christians to give themselves to one another. The Thessalonians were doing this for their local congregation and all of the brethren in Macedonia (1 Thes 4.10).

What about our relationships today? Do we feel deeply for our brethren? Do we find ourselves breaking down with them in their sorrow and rejoicing over victories? Do we find ourselves longing for our brethren? Would we qualify our emotions for the brethren as "overflowing?"

The covid pandemic of 2020–2021 was an interesting case study of God's people. While no official surveys exist among local churches belonging to Christ, the general consensus is that the pandemic exposed a problem within the Church. Many churches went into panic mode, initiating quickly decided protocols of "distance worship," most online through onscreen bible classes or video presentations of worship. Many churches did what was necessary, legal, and prudent as we learned more about the virus. Whether this was right or wrong is a topic for another article.

The problems began appearing when it was time to start coming back together. Some wanted to, while others were fearful. Some thought it wise to meet, others thought it foolish to expose others to unnecessary risks. Churches began fighting. Leaderships began panicking. Problems began multiplying. In some ways, it would be easy

---

[15] Sister Hazel, "This Kind of Love." Track 10 on *Absolutely,* Adrenaline/Wandering Hazel Records. 2006, digital.

to blame it all on the virus, government interference, or leaderships for making the wrong decisions.

The truth is that the virus exposed something that has long been a problem among God's people. In decades of teaching that we just come together to worship and learn, focusing on God and no other, people decided they could do that at home. They could sing at home. They could break bread at home. They could bow their heads at home. They could hear a sermon at home. In the early "separation," the only major issue most churches faced was how to contribute. If all the Church does is provide opportunities to worship, what else did they need?

Soon, it was realized that fellowship is included in Acts 2.42 for a reason. God's people need one another. When doors started opening again, too many had become comfortable worshipping in their pajamas with coffee on the side table, arguing they were getting everything they needed from the Church at home. This problem was self-created by the "anti-fellowship" teachings taught for so long.

It is hard to imagine this being a problem in the churches of Macedonia. Despite what they would do during an emergency situation (to meet or not to meet, that is the question), there is no doubt that as soon as they were able, they would desire to be with their beloved brethren again. Paul longed to see them. They longed to see Paul. They loved being together. They were emotionally knit together like a quilt; each patch sewed to another until they made a masterpiece. They were a body where every member needed every other member for the strength and health of the whole. They were a building where every brick was required to provide stability. They were a flock, where every sheep mattered, and none would rest until all were safe within the fold.

The Church, as designed, is an interdependent organization of people. We need one another. We should long to be together because of what we can provide for one another. Strength. Kindness. Support. Affection. Faith. Wisdom. Fellowship. Consolation. Comfort.

Encouragement. Love. These require togetherness. These require emotions. These require one another.

Increasing Our Love for One Another

This work of love is never complete. Paul prays that the Philippians' "love will keep on growing," that the Thessalonians would "increase and overflow with love for one another and everyone," and that "the love each one of you has for one another is increasing" (Phil 1.9; 1 Thes 3.12; 2 Thes 1.3). Even though Paul admits that the Thessalonians did well at loving one another, he says, "Now as to the love of the brethren, you have no need for anyone to write to you, for you yourselves are taught by God to love one another; for indeed you do practice it toward all the brethren who are in all Macedonia. But we urge you, brethren, to excel still more."

There is always more work to do when it comes to love. This is easy to see when it comes to marriage. When have you loved your spouse enough? Is there a limit to how much they need? Can you put a ceiling on affection? Is there a checklist for completion? Love, understood as "action only," certainly can be finished. Dishes? Check. Vacuum? Check. Said "I love you?" Check. Yet, this kind of love leaves people feeling disconnected. Treating people like a chore is not love.

Likewise, there is no checklist for loving your brethren. Even the list found in 1 Corinthians 13 is not something that can be checked off. When have you finished patience, kindness, or having a lack of jealousy? Those qualities are not qualifications. They are not a to-do list to verify completion but a quality list that presents a continual challenge. Christians must grow in patience, kindness, and selflessness, just as Christians must increase in love.

When is my task of loving my brethren complete? Never. Not now. Not even in eternity. There is never a time when you've done enough for your brethren, served them enough, or accomplished enough good on their behalf. "Let us not lose heart in doing good, for in due time we will reap if we do not grow weary. So then, while we have opportunity, let us do good to all people, and especially to those who are of the household of the faith" (Gal 6.9–10). Or to keep this within the context of the Macedonian epistles, "it is right for me to think this way about all of you, because I have you in my heart" (Phil 1.7) or "love one another... we encourage you, brothers and sisters, to do this even more" (1 Thes 4.9–10).

Our task, every day, is to love our brethren more. We must take every burden, every struggle, every fight against the devil and bear it like it is our own. We must rejoice and celebrate with our brethren. All of this takes time. It takes effort. It takes knowing them intimately. It requires getting to know them deeply, learning more about them, and sharing more about ourselves. It necessitates us putting our schedules aside to fit them in. It requires humility to be all things to all people and to fight against our desire for selfishness. We must desire community more than confinement, friendship more than quarantine. On top of it all, we must practice love in increasing measure as a part of the community of God.

The Most Surprising Aspect of Love

This kind of love does not take long to develop. According to most estimates, the second missionary journey took less than two years, meaning Paul was only in the Macedonian region for a few months. Some of this time was spent in Philippi, some in Thessalonica, but how much time in each location is unknown. By the time the Philippian letter was written, Paul had grown his relationship with the Church through continued fellowship and a sharing of financial support, making his deep relationship with these brethren easy to understand. On the other hand, Paul's loving statements to the Thessalonians are astonishing. He had only been there mere weeks before he was forced to leave town. By the time he had gone through Berea, Athens, and then Corinth, where he writes this letter, it had been no more than a few months.

Imagine a preacher coming to a congregation, teaching for a few weeks before moving on. How much of a relationship have you built with this man? How deeply connected are you? I would imagine, in our modern culture that holds people at bay, not much. We tend to only spend our time on those we believe warrant such effort. A temporary stay by a traveling preacher would deserve some small talk, but probably not much more. Yet, the depth of relationship Paul builds with these brethren is astonishing.

Add to that the amount of turmoil they must have been facing. They had watched their establishing preacher, the one who taught them, who brought the gospel, get run out of town under threat of death. They had watched Jason, and some of the other brothers, brought before city leaders, accused, and fined (Acts 17.5–9). It seems if Paul is being literal with his figurative language, that some had already died by the time he writes the letter (1 Thes 4.13ff). Maybe those deaths were natural and unrelated, but they were those who had died with a hope of resurrection. Persecution may have escalated to the point of martyrdom.

This astonishing depth of relationship was built almost immediately. The simple explanation is that this love was supernatural, made by God, for God, and through God for God's people. As already stated, this love was also more acceptable culturally. Ancient people depended on one another more than we do today. We live self-sufficient lives, feed ourselves, commute by ourselves, and build fences around our properties to keep others out. We live disconnected, even though we are more "connected" than ever through technology. We've replaced authentic relationships with mere associations, detaching ourselves from needing anyone or anything. Through self-dependence, we've learned to be anti-dependent. This societal change has affected the relationships we build within the Church. The modern and thoroughly unbiblical sentiment is thus expressed well, "The strongest man in the world is he who stands alone."[16]

---

[16] Henrik Ibsen. *An Enemy of the People* (Compass Circle: 1882) foreword.

More in keeping with the biblical pattern is J.R.R. Tolkien, who says, "All have their worth and each contributes to the worth of others."[17] The God-designed Church is countercultural, creating interdependency among the brethren, filled with individual Christians who are reliable, and who provide strength for others instead of discouragement. This biblical concept of fellowship is the foundation of the instructions found in 1 Thessalonians 5.14–15. "And we exhort you, brothers and sisters: warn those who are idle, comfort the discouraged, help the weak, be patient with everyone. See to it that no one repays evil for evil to anyone, but always pursue what is good for one another and for all." These instructions require the foundation of a loving relationship. Warning the idle requires knowing the struggling brother well enough to identify the idleness, knowing how they will best receive correction, and having enough of a relationship that the idle would realize they are being warned out of love. The same is true for comforting the discouraged or helping the weak. The relationship helps identify the problem and is the basis for the conversation that leads to the solution.

A significant problem in many churches today is that the relationships between brethren and between shepherds and flock consist of such flimsy stuff that none can rebuke, correct, warn, comfort, and help others without people becoming offended and leaving. Shepherds disfellowship from brethren they have not seen or talked to in months (sometimes even years). A sister in sin cannot be corrected because no one "knows her" well enough. An angry brother cannot be quenched because he doesn't have enough respect for anyone in the congregation and everyone knows it. This is a betrayal of how God designed the Church. We are together for the good of one another. We are to build relationships that promote faithfulness and build strength. We are to watch for weaknesses in one another so we can be helpful and mend brokenness. This love is called the "armor

---

[17] J.R.R. Tolkien, *The Silmarillion* (London: Harper Collins, 2012) 35.

of faith and love" (1 Thes 5.8). Having these loving relationships between brethren is what protects us from the world, from the devil, from our selfishness, and from temptation.

The High Standard

Paul was preaching to the choir, so to speak. Philippians overflows with commendations. Paul compliments the Thessalonians: "About brotherly love: You don't need me to write you because you yourselves are taught by God to love one another. In fact, you are doing this toward all the brothers and sisters in the entire region of Macedonia. But we encourage you, brothers and sisters, to do this even more" (1 Thes 4.9–10).[18]

Paul says, "Do this even more." How far do we go with this? How do we know when we've done enough? While the obvious answer is that we can never do enough, this becomes such a vague answer that it does nothing to motivate us to do more. Jesus lays out a standard for us that the Thessalonian Church accomplished that is worth considering.

There are several textual connections between this passage and Paul's compliments in 1.8–9. In both cases, there's nothing Paul feels they lack in their understanding. In both texts, the brethren are excelling. Their work has increased their reputation in Macedonia (and Achaia) in both scenarios. Paul speaks of their faith, evangelistic efforts, and acceptance of the truth. Paul says their "labor is motivated by love" (1.3). He commends them for their love and admits they are so successful that there is no need for more teaching.

This is precisely the way Jesus says love would work in His Church. "I give you a new command: Love one another. Just as I have loved you, you are also to love one another. By this everyone will know that you are my disciples, if you love one another" (John 13.34–35). Jesus is clear that if we love one another correctly, as the Macedonian brethren were accomplishing, considering their grow-

---

[18] Also consider Paul's prayer that they "increase and overflow with love for one another and for everyone" (1 Thes 4.12).

ing reputation, we would be known for our love. This love itself would convince the world that we belong to Jesus.

What does the world say about God's people? That we are judgmental. We are disagreeable. We are intolerant. We despise the world. We fight, bicker, and squabble with each other. We are bigots. We think we are the only ones going to heaven. Whether you agree with these statements or not, these judgments reveal something about us. The world does not know God's people as loving to the world or one another. In the past, we have sought to be known as the guardians of truth and, through such, became known as the haters of men. We have taken to our keyboards and computer screens and publicly spit hatred at one another. We've done what Paul warned us against in 1 Corinthians when he warned the Christians not to sue one another because of the damage it would do to the reputation of the Church and Christ. We have waved our dirty, soiled, and disgusting laundry in the air so that all the world can catch a whiff of the stink and laugh at the stains.

Our love should be so apparent, so obvious, so "in-your-face," that the world sits up and takes notice. They should see our good deeds of service and love that they "give glory to [the] Father in heaven" (Matt 5.16). The love we share for our brethren is not merely our protection against the world but our message to the world. If we do not love our brethren enough, the world will never listen to the truth we have to share with them. The banner over us with which we march into battle is a banner of love. The king we have marching before us is a bloodied lamb, stained with the marks of His sacrificial love. The stains the world sees on us should look similar.

Practically, this means we need to do a better job. Spend more time with one another. Have deeper conversations. Support one another during hard times. Put aside our obligations so we might meet with others when they need us. Bear with one another's foolishness and know others are bearing with our own. Put the needs of others before our own and seek their good. Become emotionally attached so that when they hurt, we hurt. Rejoice with one another and share times of rejoicing. Prefer our time with God's people because they are our eternal community. Learn to confess our sins to one another instead of suffering alone in embarrassment. Remember those one hundred "one another" (*allélón*) commandments? Do them all. Then do them again. Then "excel still more" in each of them.

Conclusion

All of these commandments on love, and examples of how that is practiced, began with God's loving us first. He only asks us to do for one another what He has first been willing to do for us. He loves us, not because we deserve it, and not because we are worth it, but because He is love. He loves because He wants to love. He loves us because He chooses, and His choices cause Him to feel deeply about us.

We make the same choice to love our brethren. We have thousands of ways to show it daily, as long as we choose to do so. We must open our hearts to feel deeply about them the way He feels about us. If He can love His enemies, the essence of the entire gospel story, then we can certainly love our brethren whom the gospel has saved.

Admonish Him as a Brother

Correction that is Worthy of the Gospel

Joe Works

"Brethren" (2 Thes 3.6, 13) are the ones who Paul addresses in our text. Paul commands these brethren to treat the one in question as a "brother" (2 Thes 3.6, 15). Could it be that we have become so accustomed to using the words "brethren" and "brother" that we have lost sight of how significant they are in the application of challenging passages?

These two words are found twenty-eight times in the Thessalonian letters. The letters use them in all three texts related to the topic of idleness and disorderliness (I Thes 4.10; 5.14; II Thes 3.6, 13). In light of their usage throughout the epistles, we should seek to intensify our appreciation of our sibling relationship. This appreciation is especially necessary when it comes to brothers and sisters who are *not* following the will of our Father, nor the example of our older brother, Jesus (Heb 2.12; Psa 22.22).

If we fail to see ourselves correctly in God's family, we will certainly not treat our spiritual siblings who are struggling in sin as we should. A classic example of this is the story of The Prodigal Son(s) (Luke 15.11–32). Even after the younger brother returns to the Father, the Pharisaic brother refuses to welcome him back into the family. This hostile reception is not due to a lack of love for the brother, but a failure to follow the example of the Father in the parable. The older son may not have been prodigal in a classical sense, but he was certainly wasteful of the resources offered by the Father. He saw himself as perfect and under-rewarded (Luke 15.29). Before we can effectively admonish a brother, we must first love him as a brother. Before we can love him as a brother, we must see ourselves as undeserving sons and daughters of the Father.

Warning Worthy of the Gospel

This failure to properly see a fellow child of God as our sibling can find us failing in at least two differing ways. We may not have enough love for the erring one's soul to correct them at all, or we may correct them with a harshness often not seen even in the world.

We might say or think, "I love that person too much to jeopardize my relationship with him. I cannot tell him that he is wrong and walking in darkness." Of course, this kind of "love" is selfish love. It values our need to avoid rejection too highly, while dismissing the need for the other person to be right with the Father. It may also betray a "what's in it for me?" mentality. Consider Eli's refusal to properly rebuke his sons and the motive God revealed for Eli's weak reprimand. "Why do you kick at My sacrifice and My offering which I have commanded in My habitation, and honor your sons more than Me, to make yourselves fat with the best of all the offerings of Israel My people?" (2 Sam 2.29). Does our failure to address a wayward brother betray some selfish motive on our part?

On the other extreme, some brethren appear to relish an opportunity to put another Christian in his place. What causes someone to enjoy kicking a sinning Christian to the curb? Pride, low self-esteem, jealousy, and other self-centered attitudes can cause us to approach the situation in an opposite spirit to the one that God would have us uphold. "God, I thank You that I am not like other men ..." (Luke 18.11) is not only a condemnable prayer, but also a self-exalting attitude that will prevent us from truly seeking to save the sinning brother.

Our Lord knew how to admonish! In Jesus' most passionate condemnation of the religious hypocrisy of His day, He spoke with a clear and strong voice: "Woe to you, scribes and Pharisees, hypocrites!" (Matt 23.1–36). In almost the same breath, He manifested His absolute desire to protect and care for them: "How often I wanted to gather your children together, as a hen gathers her chicks under her wings, but you were not willing" (Matt 23.37–39).

Like Jesus, Paul rebuked others powerfully, but notice the constant attitude Paul displayed for those whom he admonished. Paul wept for those who had made themselves enemies of the cross (Phil 3.18). For his fellow Jews who had rejected the Savior, Paul had "great sorrow and continual grief" in his heart (Rom 9.2). As Paul reflected on his harsh words concerning the immoral man and the church's attitude toward him (1 Cor 5), he remembered his "affliction and anguish of heart" (2 Cor 2.4) as he penned that letter. Can you not see the tears on parchment that must have stained 1 Corinthians?

Admonition Is of the Lord

Paul commends their present obedience to the Lord's commands (2 Thes 3.4) and expresses confidence concerning their obedience in the future. Perhaps we should see 2 Thessalonians 3.3–5 as an introduction to 3.6–15. Is it possible Paul is expressing his confidence in their willingness to follow the Lord's commands so that they will pay closer attention to the difficult command they are about to hear? The brethren would certainly need a strong dose of "the love of God" and "patience (steadfastness) of Christ" (2 Thes 3.5) in order to fulfill the command to withdraw from a disorderly brother.

The word "command" is then used by Paul three more times in our text at hand, thus emphasizing the seriousness of Paul's instructions. In each usage, Paul deals with the same general topic but with an emphasis on different aspects of disorderliness or laziness and how we must address it.

In the first instance, Paul commands the congregation to withdraw from the unruly brother. "But we *command* you, brethren, in the name of our Lord Jesus Christ, that you withdraw from every brother who walks disorderly and not according to the tradition which he received from us" (2 Thes 3.6). In the second usage Paul reminds them of his teaching while he was among them (Acts 17.1–9). "For even when we were with you, we *commanded* you this: If anyone will not work, neither shall he eat" (2 Thes 3.10). Evidently some had failed to respect the instructions Paul gave while among them. In the third usage of the word "command," he informs that they needed to get their bodies busy working and cease being busybodies. "Now those who are such we *command* and exhort through our Lord Jesus Christ that they work in quietness and eat their own bread" (2 Thes 3.12).

Paul addressed the issues of laziness and disorderly conduct twice in his previous letter to these saints (1 Thes 4.9–12; 5.14). In both texts, he emphasized the importance of obedience, using words like command and exhort. "But concerning brotherly love you have no need that I should write to you, for you yourselves are taught by God to love one another; and indeed you do so toward all the brethren who are in all Macedonia. But we urge you, brethren, that you increase more and more; that you also aspire to lead a quiet life, to mind your own business, and to work with your own hands, as we *commanded* you, that you may walk properly toward those who are outside, and that you may lack nothing" (1 Thes 4.9–12). Paul instructs them to grow in their brotherly love by working to aid others. We achieve a quiet life by being occupied with worthwhile endeavors, thereby having no time to meddle in the affairs of others. "Now we *exhort* you, brethren, warn those who are unruly, comfort the fainthearted, uphold the weak, be patient with all" (1 Thes 5.14).

Work Ethics

May it not escape our attention that Paul took the subject of laziness and disorderliness so seriously that he taught it to the Thessalonians in person (2 Thes 3.10), twice in his first letter (1 Thes 4.9–12; 5.14), and then closes his second letter to them with a longer explanation of God's expectation (2 Thes 3.6–15). Do we take the sin of laziness in our own idleness or that of our brethren as seriously as Paul did?

Laziness can take the extreme form that Epimenides described, as quoted by Paul, "Cretans are always liars, evil brutes, lazy gluttons" (Tit 1.12). It may also be subtly deceptive, leading one to justify his lack of work, as in the case of the "wicked, lazy servant" described in Matthew 25.24–29. Perhaps the unwillingness to work, found in some Christians in Thessalonica, came from their misunderstanding about the return of our Lord. How foolish to think that mooching off hard-working saints was wise in anticipation of our Savior's appearing. Whether the Lord is coming soon or not, let us become more active, not less! Letting our lights shine through honest work is commended by the Lord (Eph 6.5–8; Col 3.22–25; 1 Tim 6.1; Tit 2.9–10; 1 Pet 2.18–25).

The Danger of Scripture Soup

It is tempting to take all the passages regarding church discipline, throw them in a sermon pot, stir them radically, and then make them say the same thing. Not all admonitions are equal. We understand that sentiment in parenting and the corporate realm. We ought not to treat the employee who shows up late for work once or twice a year the same as the individual who is embezzling from the company. Different circumstances would suggest different reactions. Similar circumstances, likewise, would warrant similar reactions. It would be extremely rare for two situations to be exactly the same and require the same reaction. When it comes to nearly any Bible subject, it is crucial to consider the circumstances as they are revealed and search for scriptures that are applicable, but it would be a mistake to make all those passages say the exact same thing. Without careful thought, we might wrongly warn or admonish the fainthearted and weak as much as the unruly (1 Thes 5.14).

Some situations are private and ought to remain as such. Matthew 18.15 describes the ideal private situation where the admonition of a "brother" (there is that word again) is required. No one else needs to know what has taken place when both parties behave as they should. Perhaps someone(s) else needs to become involved. While not stated in the text, we see the wisdom in finding a mature individual to become a witness to the conversation and help initiate the needed repentance (Matt 18.16). The church should become involved only as a last resort (Matt 18.17). At this point, options have been exhausted. The guilty, unrepentant brother is to be treated differently: as a heathen and a tax collector. The heathens and tax collectors are two unflattering groups to be compared with; the Jews would have no fellowship with them, yet Jesus constantly sought to bring about their repentance. We should not cast aside a person who refuses to repent forever, or never contact them again. His actions have caused him to leave our Father's side and should thereby sever our fellowship. However, we must remember how Jesus was ready to call and welcome the tax collectors who had a change of heart: Levi (Luke 5.27–32) and Zaccheus (Luke 19.1–10). A word of caution, though, must be given lest someone seek license to go beyond the meaning of Matthew 18.15–17. Jesus accepted the tax collectors who came "near Him to listen to Him" (Luke 15.1). Tax collectors and Gentiles who continued to reject His teaching found themselves outside of Jesus' fellowship and God's grace (Rom 1.18–32).

Sometimes we must decide whether we can fellowship with another person when considering his teachings. In Romans 16.17–20, Paul urges us to note and avoid those who cause division. We must exercise judgment in distinguishing between someone who has not yet come to a proper understanding of a biblical subject versus one who uses flattering speech to deceive and divide. Simply put, not everyone who teaches something false ought to be labeled a false teacher. This evaluation can be illustrated easily by answering the question, "Do you agree with everything your preacher or elders teach on every subject?" Hardly anyone would affirm they do. Would that make those preachers or elders false teachers, then? If so, would that make you a follower of false teaching, or at least accepting of it? Let us be cautious in using the label "false teacher" without careful consideration.

On the other hand, there are those seeking a following, fame, and fortune by perverting the gospel. Those individuals ought to be exposed and shunned (Rom 16.17). "Bad company corrupts good morals" (1 Cor 15.33) may be commonly applied to young people needing to avoid the bad influences of the world, but Paul's application concerns the teaching that is taking place within the church. A false doctrine regarding the resurrection can indeed cause some to loosen their morals and act in ungodly ways (1 Cor 15.32–35). We can compare some teachers today with those Jude described: "ungodly men, who turn the grace of our God into licentiousness and deny the only Lord God and our Lord Jesus Christ" (Jude 4). Wisdom would demand we carefully apply the teachings of Romans 16 and 1 Corinthians 15 to the present AD 70 doctrine, which is popular in too many pulpits today. You may want to listen for a tone of arrogance in some of those leading this movement. They proclaim an insight that allows them to turn Jesus' plain teaching on things like marriage and divorce into meaningless words.

When Families Collide

One of the most challenging and polemical scenarios is when a disorderly brother is also a member of the physical family. What do we do in those situations? The brief answer is simple: trust God's commands and follow through with His instructions. While this brief article cannot address every situation, let us make some clear points that should guide us if we find ourselves in this nightmarish situation. First, the passages that deal with "church discipline" do not provide any exception clause for physical or blood relatives. Second, if an exception is to be understood, it must come from another principle or command found elsewhere in the Bible. The command is given to the congregation. If the blood relative is a part of the body of Christ, then his family members must obey the commands of our Lord.

Some situations can be extremely challenging. Could there be a situation when an older widow acts like a busybody and allows her tongue to gossip (1 Tim 5.1–16)? Would the child or grandchild of that older widow still be expected to fulfill his obligation to care for the elderly lady (1 Tim 5.4)? Can that be done while still applying the command to "withdraw" (2 Thes 3.6–15)? Some judgment may come into play in how they achieve that goal. The child ought to decide how to proceed based on all that his Father in Heaven has said on the subject. Often, questions arise regarding an unrepentant child who has left the house and is living on their own. Godly parents are facing the unenviable task of withdrawing from their own child. All compassion and support ought to be given to those parents as they make, what is likely, the most painful steps imaginable in removing themselves from the familiar and familial relationship. Trust God. Trust His ways. Resist the temptation to be "mindful of the things of man." Reject the tendency to love your physical relationship with a loved one more than your spiritual relationship with the One who loves you perfectly. Recognize that the separation God expects is to bring the loved one back: first to the Head, then to the body. If the situation creates enmity, it is not because you caused it. Your loved one decided to walk a different path than the Way you are following. Believe in God's wisdom. If the relative is to return, let him return because he saw your determination to follow Jesus' example. When our Lord's family thought He had lost His mind and wanted to bring Him home (Mark 3.21), Jesus made it clear that His family was comprised of those who submitted to His Father (Mark 3.31–35). Who are your mothers, brothers, and sisters?

Preventative Maintenance

The best of teaching programs cannot guarantee that all will reain faithful. The world influences also. Our adversary, indeed, "walks about like a roaring lion, seeking whom he may devour" (1 Pet 5.8). Free will exists, and some will walk away from the Father's message, refusing to return (John 6.60–66). Jesus had those in His closest circle who tried to rebuke Him (Mark 8.31–33), forsook Him in the garden (Mark 14.50–52), denied Him publicly (Mark 14.66–72), doubted His resurrection (Mark 16.11), and even completely and totally betrayed Him (Mark 14.10–11). Some will fall away!

These facts should give us such great cause for alarm. We must be determined to equip our brothers and sisters with as much armor as possible.

We must emphasize strong Bible teaching for the youngest of ages. As Bob Waldron once said, "throw the fluff out of the classrooms!" Find resources that do not entertain, but rather teach. Good sources are available, but also remember that teachers need to teach, not babysit or moderate. Reevaluate your curriculum, making sure there are 66 subjects covered: "the whole counsel of God" (Acts 20.27), if you will.

Intensify your search for songs that acknowledge, honor, and praise God as our Creator, Sustainer, Savior, and Judge! Learn new songs without forgetting the old ones. God has blessed us with modern-day Mattaniahs (Neh 12.8) who have written songs that truly draw our hearts to a deeper relationship with God.

Does anyone pray enough? "Pray without ceasing" (1 Thes 5.17). "Brethren, pray for us" (1 Thes 5.25). "Be anxious for nothing, but in everything by prayer and supplication with thanksgiving let your requests be made known to God" (Phil 4.6).

Have family reunions often. Once a week for an hour or two on Sunday is not enough. In the first century, the saints sought out one another daily (Acts 2.46). With the modern technology available to us, determine that you will make greater efforts to know your brothers and sisters and be there for them.

Above all else, let us "be patient with all" (1 Thes 5.14).

Rejoice in the Lord Always
Joy that is Worthy of the Gospel

Daniel Broadwell

I am searching for the blue flower,
I am searching and never find it,
I have a dream that my good fortune
Will flourish in that flower.

I am hiking with my harp
Through countries, cities and wetlands,
To behold the blue flower
Anywhere in the earthcycle.

I am hiking for a long time,
For a long time I hoped, I trusted,
But alas, I have not yet
Beheld the blue flower anywhere.[1]

Thinkers and philosophers across the world and throughout history have concluded that the goal of life is something like joy. Different people have expressed it in different ways (happiness, inner peace), but the idea is the same: to live the good life is to achieve a state of

---

[1] Joseph Freiherr von Eichendorff, "Die blaue Blume"; translated from German at https://lyricstranslate.com/en/die-blaue-blume-blue-flower.html. The motif of "the blue flower" (common in Romanticism) is mentioned by C.S. Lewis in *Surprised by Joy,* and discussed in more detail by Dr. Jerry Root in his video lecture, "A Book Observed: C.S. Lewis's *Surprised by Joy*" available on the C.S.L.I. YouTube channel (https://youtu.be/_PVTR4j-SlE).

fulfillment which transcends ordinary pleasure and is not affected by other people or external circumstances. The suggested paths to that goal, however, are as many and varied as the people espousing them, revealing the elusive quality of this fulfillment. Joy, we might say, is the blue flower. Our friends and neighbors may not be so philosophical, but we can observe in them the same dilemma, namely that everyone wants to be happy, but not many people are.

As Christians, we look at the world's searching for happiness and shake our heads, saying (correctly) that true joy is found only in Christ. If that's true (which it is), are we in fact a joyful people? Am I a joyful person (and how would I know)? Is joy a clear, distinguishing mark of Christians and their churches? We may not be as confident answering these questions, because it is likely that they reveal that we as the people of God are floundering in our pursuit of joy as well. Maybe joy is our blue flower too.

If it's true that we have difficulty *obtaining* joy, it is likely because we have difficulty in *defining* joy. What exactly is joy? How would we explain it to someone? Is it different from happiness, inner peace, or personal fulfillment? If so, how? These questions are themselves hard to answer, and if we struggle to do so, we are not in a good position for successfully pursuing joy. We set out, therefore, to first explore the nature of joy and its place in the biblical story. From there, we will highlight the particular aspects of joy in Paul's letters to the churches of Macedonia. Finally, we will reflect on what it means to rejoice and how it is that we obtain the joy for which everyone is searching.

What is Joy?

Understanding (and explaining) joy is not straightforward because there are a number of conflicting elements, even within the use of the term in Scripture. For example, is joy a feeling? Or is it something more objective and observable, like a decision or a conviction? To say that joy is a feeling is perhaps the most intuitive way to describe it, and popular definitions resort to using that word. For example, John Piper says that "Christian joy is a good feeling in the soul, produced by the Holy Spirit, as he causes us to see the beauty of Christ in the word and in the world."[2] By "good feeling," Piper does, in fact, mean a "pleasant emotion." When Paul tells the Christians in Philippi that he thanks God in "all my remembrance of you, always offering prayer with joy in my every prayer for you all" (Phil 1.3–4)[3], it is surely true that the memory of his dear brethren evokes a "good feeling" or "pleasant emotion" within the apostle.

We may, however, be uncomfortable describing biblical joy as a feeling or emotion. Perhaps in a reaction against the abuses and distortions of emotionalism in Christianity, we tend to be 'anti-emotion,' preferring instead the security of rationalism or the tangible proof of action. We might describe joy as a decision, citing the instruction of James to "consider it all joy, my brethren, when you encounter various trials" (Jam 1.2). We might also describe joy as action, citing Paul's command (four times in the Macedonian Epistles) to "Rejoice" (Phil 3.1; 4.4; 1 Thes 5.16). Is God requiring that we summon "feelings," which so often arise and dissipate outside of our control?

The question of control sparks a similar group of questions. Who is in control of joy—who 'makes it happen'? Is joy something we do, or something done to us? Is it something external which we pursue and attain, something we summon from within ourselves, or simply a by-product that results naturally when we live as we should?

---

[2] John Piper, "How Do You Define Joy?" www.desiringgod.org/articles/how-do-you-define-joy; July 25, 2015. Piper's explanation of joy is simply one example, but one that is worth reflecting on critically. He is explicit about the fact that his Calvinism shapes his view of the subject (i.e. man's depravity makes joy impossible, so God is commanding emotions and making them happen within a person). He also distinguishes joy "in the soul" from joy "in the body," making more distinction between soul and body than I believe is appropriate or helpful.

[3] All scriptural quotations are taken from the New American Standard Bible (1995) unless otherwise noted.

Again, there are biblical passages which imply that joy has all of these apparently conflicting characteristics. The Holy Spirit 'makes it happen'—Paul refers to "the joy of the Holy Spirit" (1 Thes 1.6), and joy is included in the fruit produced by the Holy Spirit (Gal 5.22). This fruit is born, however, as the result (by-product) of "walking by the Spirit" of God (Gal 5.16). Furthermore, we are commanded to rejoice, implying that we 'make it happen' and that it is something we do or something we summon from within (1 Thes 5.16). Finally, Paul tells the Philippians that he is working for their "progress and joy in the faith" (Phil 1.25) and then asks them to "make my joy complete" (Phil 2.2). Apparently he depends on them to fill him with joy, and vice versa.

How are we to understand joy? Can all of these things be true?

Reminders of Eden

In C.S. Lewis' spiritual autobiography, *Surprised by Joy*, Lewis uses the word Joy to describe a particular recurring phenomenon that prodded him, over the course of many years, toward belief in God. To be clear, Lewis is not engaged in a word study of biblical joy; nevertheless, his reflections provide several important insights for our exploration.[4]

These moments that sparked what Lewis calls Joy were not experiences of contentment or fulfillment, but instead of "intense desire."[5] To say these moments were pleasurable would be to miss the point. "It was something quite different...from ordinary pleasure; something...'in another dimension.'"[6] The Joy which Lewis describes "must have the stab, the pang, the inconsolable longing."[7] It might have been sparked by a childhood memory, a poignant pas-

---

[4] In an attempt to differentiate, I capitalize Joy (as Lewis does) when referring to his use of the term.

[5] C.S. Lewis, *Surprised by Joy* (London: Harcourt Brace Jovanovich Publishers, 1956) 17.

[6] Ibid.

[7] Ibid 72.

sage of literature, or a piece of music, but once it was gone (which was usually instantly), "to 'have it again' was the supreme and only important object of desire."[8] Lewis was, from an early age, devoted to "the blue flower,"[9] captivated by the longing.

The mistake that Lewis made, however, was to pursue this Joy as the *object* of desire. As he says, "far more often I frightened it away by my greedy impatience to snare it."[10] He was left frustrated, because like other intense desires, Joy eludes the one who is focused on the feeling itself. Instead, "all Joy reminds. It is never a possession, always a desire for something longer ago or further back or still 'about to be.' "[11] A critical element of Lewis' spiritual journey was discovering what exactly Joy was a reminder of, and therefore what the ultimate object of the longing was. His conclusion was the same as that of Augustine of Hippo in the famous statement from his spiritual autobiography, "You stir man to take pleasure in praising You, because You have made us for Yourself, and our heart is restless until it rests in You."[12]

Biblical joy can be described in a similar way. Humans were made in the image of God, blessed, and charged to rule a world in which all was 'as it should be.' We walked with the God for Whom we were made, there was security and trust between man and woman, and humans worked together with creation to bring forth fruitfulness to the glory of God (Gen 1–2). Sin, of course, separated man from God, broke the trust between people, and brought a curse upon the ground which now frustrates man's purposes instead of aiding them (Gen 3–4).

We live in a broken world, and yet creation retains the memory of its former perfection (Rom 8.20–21) and we are still made in the image of God. For this reason, there are times when we experience some

---

[8] Ibid 73.

[9] Ibid 7.

[10] Ibid 169

[11] Ibid 78.

[12] Augustine, *Confessions.* Trans. Henry Chadwick (Oxford: Oxford University Press, 1991) 3.

of the goodness and beauty still woven into the world and are struck with a desire for 'something more.' It is as if we have a 'collective memory' of Eden, and are occasionally confronted with reminders of that lost perfection. When we are, we feel a deep longing for 'a world as it should be,' only intensified by the ever-present awareness that the world is not as it should be.

More than that, however, God has been working from the beginning to restore His connection to creation—to bring man back to Himself and set all things right again (Gen 3.14–15; Isa 65.17–25).[13] God's promise to Abram was that He would restore the original blessing to "all the families of the earth"—thus reversing the curse of sin (Gen 12.3). The prophets looked forward to the time of the Messiah in which "instead of your shame you will have a double portion, and instead of humiliation they will shout for joy over their portion. Therefore they will possess a double portion in their land, everlasting joy will be theirs" (Isa 61.7). When that Messiah was born into the world, He was announced with "good news of great joy which will be for all the people" (Luke 2.10). All people, therefore, who obey the good news of King Jesus enter a kingdom of "righteousness and peace and joy in the Holy Spirit" (Rom 14.17). In Christ, we have restoration of fellowship with God, reconciliation with our fellow man, and even a corrected understanding of what it means to be human in the world God made.

Joy and Grace

This connection between the saving work of God and the resulting joy is reflected in the word itself. Paul's typical word for joy

---

[13] This is one of many passages that describes the work of God in terms of restoration, reconciliation, and rectification. In this picture of new creation there is gladness and rejoicing between God and His people (65.17–19); sorrow, weeping, death, and futility are done away with as the blessing is brought back to God's people (65.19–23); there is even harmony between creatures who were formerly at odds (65.24–25). Finally, the serpent is made to eat dust and evil is forever removed (65.25), a promise which echoes the one made by God immediately after the fall.

("chara") is related to the word he uses for grace ("charis").[14] In a general sense, joy is the natural response to a gift (favor, grace) that one receives. In the biblical story, there is no greater gift than the favor of God which He offers to sinful people. This is the grace that David sought after his sin with Bathsheba. "Be gracious to me, O God, according to Your lovingkindness" (Psa 51.1). He longs "to hear joy and gladness" which he has lost in his separation from God (Psa 51.8). His ultimate desire, therefore, is to be reunited with God, for only in this restored relationship can there be joy. "Do not cast me away from your presence and do not take your Holy Spirit from me. Restore me to the joy of your salvation" (Psa 51.11–12). There is no joy without grace.

It is no surprise, then, that Paul is the "theologian of joy," because he is also the "theologian of grace."[15] Consider a passage that is typical of Paul's description of salvation and note how the concepts of grace and joy are linked (although the word "chara" is not used): "Therefore, having been justified by faith, we have peace with God through the Lord Jesus Christ, through whom also we have obtained our introduction by faith into this grace in which we stand; and we exult ["rejoice" ESV] in hope of the glory of God" (Rom 5.1–2). God's grace—given to us in Jesus—allows us to stand before God, to have peace with Him. We access that grace by faith, and the result is joyful exultation.

Joy as Resonance

With C.S. Lewis' personal reflections and the biblical story of joy set before us, consider a metaphor drawn from the natural world.[16]

---

[14] W.G. Morrice, "Joy" in G. Hawthorne & R. Martin, ed., *IVP Dictionary of Paul and His Letters* (Downers Grove: InterVarsity Press, 1993) 511–12.

[15] Ibid. Morrice points out that forty percent of the occurrences of joy in the New Testament are ascribed to Paul, along with almost sixty percent of the occurrences of *"charis"* (grace).

[16] Credit to my dad, Martin Broadwell Jr., former physics professor and life-long musician, for feeding me this idea.

In the physics of music, sympathetic resonance refers to "a harmonic phenomenon wherein a passive string or vibratory body responds to external vibrations to which it has a harmonic likeness."[17] For instance, take two tuning forks that are identical (tuned to the same note) and hold them in close proximity. If you strike one, the other will begin to sound without being struck, because it resonates with sympathetic vibrations.

We might say, then, that joy is sympathetic resonance with our Creator. We are made in God's image, with a nature that is inherently connected to His. Even though our lives are 'out of tune' because of sin, there are times when God's nature (His righteousness, His goodness, His beauty) resonates in us. This, again, is not mere pleasure. It's a deep sense that all is as it should be—or at least that it could be. Outside of Christ, these are only fleeting experiences that we don't understand, and like Lewis we may be tempted to chase the feeling instead of what (Who) is behind it. By God's grace in Jesus Christ, however, our brokenness is healed and we are regenerated and renewed as we receive the Holy Spirit of God (Tit 3.5–6). As a result, we are brought more and more 'in tune' with God, and our experience (resonance) of joy is deeper, richer, and more regular.

Joy in Suffering

This model of joy sheds light on the way Paul talks about joy in the Macedonian Epistles. First, consider the apparent contradiction in Philippians between Paul's situation and his joy. He sits in a Roman prison (where it was common practice not to feed prisoners[18]), unable to take the gospel to new places. He has opponents who seek to shame or discredit him, and he is uncertain of whether the outcome of his imprisonment will be release or execution. Even so, his words in Philippians 1, as he recounts all of this, are full of joy. How?

---

[17] "Sympathetic resonance," wikipedia.org/wiki/Sympathetic_resonance.

[18] N.T. Wright, *Philippians*, For Everyone Bible Study Guides (Downers Grove: InterVarsity Press, 2009) 8.

If joy is something like a deep sense of blessedness as God's Spirit brings us into closer fellowship with Him, then joy is not at all dependent on the 'pleasant-ness' of our circumstances. Instead, joy is the fruit of the Spirit's presence and the result of our alignment with the will of God. For Paul, it comes down to one thing: "Only that in every way…Christ is proclaimed; and in this I rejoice." (Phil 1.18). Paul has 'tuned' his heart—or his heart has been tuned—to desire the honoring of King Jesus above all else, and so as that happens his whole being resonates with joy.

Furthermore, Paul is not simply able to find joy in spite of his suffering, his suffering itself is a cause of joy because it is a way of being shaped into the image of Christ and furthering His kingdom. In the middle of the letter, Paul places Jesus front and center as the example of humility and obedience—even to death—and urges his readers to "have this mind" (Phil 2.5–11). For his part, Paul finds great joy in imitating the Savior by emptying himself for the sake of others. A few verses later, he says, "Even if I am being poured out as a drink offering upon the sacrifice and service of your faith, I rejoice and share my joy with you all" (Phil 2.17–18). As Jesus poured Himself out so that we could be pleasing to God, Paul envisions doing the same thing for the Philippians. In the next chapter, he says that he has "suffered the loss of all things" in order to "share [Christ's] sufferings, becoming like Him in His death, that by any means possible I may attain the resurrection from the dead" (Phil 3.8–11 ESV). Paul's intense desire is to conform to the image of Jesus of Nazareth—now and in the resurrection (Phil 3.21)—and so in his present suffering he experiences a joyful resonance.

Shared Joy

One of the interesting things about Paul's emphasis on joy in the Macedonian Epistles is how frequently he uses the word to describe what he feels toward the Christians in Thessalonica and Philippi. To return to the metaphor of sympathetic resonance, the phenomenon can also be observed at a piano. When a note is played, there are overtones (harmonics) which vibrate with sympathetic resonance to the single note that was struck. For example, playing middle C will cause the higher C (and the G above that, among other notes) to vibrate (assuming the damper has been lifted from those strings). The point is that one note causes multiple strings to vibrate together in sympathy.

As we have pointed out, God is the source of joy. True joy, therefore, is found in fellowship with Him in Jesus Christ and is produced by the Holy Spirit. Joy is a reminder of Eden, but man was never intended to experience union with God by himself (Gen 2.18). Man was made to relate to God and to relate to the other humans made in the image of God. When God acted to restore humanity's blessing in Jesus, it was not only to bring man back to God, but to restore human relationships (Isa 2.4; Mal 4.6). Therefore, as broken people are healed to find joy in their Creator, they resonate in sympathy with others who are being healed as well.

Paul describes this very thing in the opening of Philippians, saying that his joy and confidence in his readers are well-founded because they are "partakers with me of grace" (Phil 1.7). In Christ, we share God's grace with one another. Joy, like grace, is meant to be shared. According to the Swedish proverb, "Shared joy is a double joy, and sorrow shared is half a sorrow."[19] This is certainly true in God's kingdom—our joy multiplies as we experience God's grace together.

This 'multiplication of joy' is obvious in Paul's letters to the Macedonian churches. Both Philippians and 1 Thessalonians overflow with the gladness that Paul feels because of his fellowship with his readers. In fact, his joy depends on that shared union in Christ. "Therefore if there is any encouragement in Christ, if there is any

---

[19] Like many statements of "proverbial wisdom," this sentiment is expressed in various forms and attributed to various people. One version is "Happiness is only real when shared," and is attributed to Chris McCandless, an American adventurer who died of starvation in 1992 while (ironically) trying to survive alone in the Alaskan bush.

consolation of love, if there is any fellowship of the Spirit, if any affection and compassion, make my joy complete by being of the same mind, maintaining the same love, united in spirit, intent on one purpose" (Phil 2.1–2). Paul assumes that there is affection in Christ, and so pleads with his readers to share that with each other—and with him—in unity. This Christian fellowship results in a fullness of joy.

The joy which Paul expresses in these letters, however, goes beyond the joy that all believers share in Christ. It is the joy of someone who has invested everything in another, only to see that investment pay off and bear fruit. In 1 Thessalonians, Paul recounts his work among them, comparing himself to a "nursing mother" and "a father with his children" (1 Thes 2.7, 11). Any parent can understand the overwhelming joy that comes from seeing a son or daughter grow, mature, and stand firm on their own. In the words of the apostle John, there is "no greater joy" (3 John 4). Within the context of Paul describing himself as a spiritual parent, it is perhaps no surprise that Paul uses such strong language about the Thessalonians. "For who is our hope or joy or crown of exultation? Is it not even you, in the presence of our Lord Jesus at His coming? For you are our glory and joy" (1 Thes 2.19–20). As if that is not strong enough, Paul says later, "For now we live, if you are standing fast in the Lord. For what thanksgiving can we return to God for you, for all the joy that we feel for your sake?" (1 Thes 3.8–9). Paul does not have words to express the joy that he feels, because the spiritual well-being of the Thessalonians is everything to him.

Paul's relationship with the Philippians is much the same. Having invested so much in them already, he remains committed to them, determined to "remain and continue with you all for your progress and joy in the faith" (Phil 1.25). As we noted earlier, Paul says he is willing to be "poured out" as an offering for their sake, and in doing so would "rejoice and share my joy with you all" (Phil 2.17–18). Paul has given himself completely to the Lord and to these Christians in Philippi; when they grow in the Lord, Paul resonates sympathetically with joy.

His language is just as strong to them as to the Thessalonians: "Therefore, my beloved brethren whom I long to see, my joy and crown, in this way stand firm in the Lord, my beloved" (Phil 4.1).

Joy and Longing

In light of C.S. Lewis' description of Joy as a "pang" and a "stab," note how closely joy and longing are connected in the Macedonian Epistles. Because Paul has invested so much in these Christians, he feels tremendous joy at their progress in the faith. He also is dying to see them (so to speak). Notice the fuller context of Paul's surprising declaration that the Thessalonians are his joy:

But we, brethren, having been taken away from you for a short while—in person, not in spirit—were all the more eager with great desire to see your face. For we wanted to come to you—I, Paul, more than once—and yet Satan hindered us. For who is our hope or joy or crown of exultation? Is it not even you, in the presence of our Lord Jesus at His coming? For you are our glory and joy. (1 Thes 2.17–20)

It is painful for Paul to be separated from these Christians who were so dear to him. Twice in the next paragraph, Paul says that he sent Timothy to check on them because he "could endure it no longer" (1 Thes 3.1, 5). The Thessalonians, as it turns out, are also longing to see Paul (1 Thes 3.6). Even still, he is "night and day…praying most earnestly that we may see your face" (1 Thes 3.10). We understand Paul's emotions here; the people who bring us the most joy are those for whom we long so painfully when they are away from us. Paul is filled with joy because of the Thessalonians, so much that it hurts.

Paul anxiously awaits a reunion with these Christians, but he anticipates something much greater. The Thessalonians are his hope, joy, and crown "in the presence of our Lord Jesus at His coming" (1 Thes 2.19). The joy Paul experiences now and the joy he expects to experience upon Christ's return are both bound up in them.[20] He

---

[20] J. Stott, *The Message of 1 & 2 Thessalonians*. The Bible Speaks Today (Downers Grove: IVP, 1991) 43.

rejoices now as they stand firm in the Lord (1 Thes 2.8), and he will exult when they are standing with him when Jesus comes back.[21] The present joy anticipates the future joy, and the hope of future joy intensifies the present joy.

Working backward, we see this combination of joy and longing in our relationship with God. As we draw nearer to God, we experience more of the delight that comes from being in fellowship with Him—but even this joy is a reminder, a pointer, an anticipation. For all the blessings that we experience in Christ, we have not fully embraced the object of our desire. Our bodies and our world are still broken, waiting to be redeemed (Rom 8.18–24). We continue to wrestle against the forces of darkness, waiting for Jesus to come and abolish them, once and for all (Eph 6.12; 1 Cor 15.25). We still wait to hear the words, "Well done, good and faithful slave…Enter into the joy of your Master" (Matt 25.21), and to be fully reunited with the God for Whom we were made, in Whose presence there is "fullness of joy" (Psa 16.11). The joy which we experience now only heightens our awareness that we are not (fully) with Him. Not yet. We long for our Creator, because He is the object of all our desires. Our union with God fills us with joy, so much that it hurts.

Joy, I think we must say, is a feeling. Alternatively, we could say that joy is an "experience of gladness,"[22] or a "settled disposition,"[23] or a "positive attitude,"[24] but I am not sure there is a substantial

---

[21] Note that the similar plea in Philippians 4.1—that he longs to see them, that they are his "joy and crown," that he urges them to "stand firm in the Lord"—is based on his reminder that "we eagerly wait for a Savior, the Lord Jesus Christ" (Phil 3.20–21). When Paul thinks of the joy of Jesus' return, he thinks of those who will be his joy and crown on that day.

[22] "*Chara*" in F. Danker, ed., *A Greek-English Lexicon of the New Testament and Other Early Christian Literature*, Third Edition (Chicago: University of Chicago Press, 2000) 1077.

[23] Paul Earnhart, "Christian Joy," https://wordsfitlyspoken.org/audio/earnhart/index.html, December 31, 1989.

[24] "Joy" in R. Youngblood, F.F. Bruce, R.K. Harrison, ed., *Nelson's Student Bible Dictionary* (Nashville: Thomas Nelson, 2005) 135.

difference in the terms. Joy, of course, is not a fleeting emotion like others we might experience; it is a deep sense of wholeness, of rightness, of blessedness. It is produced in us by the Holy Spirit and is multiplied in our fellowship with each other. The more joy we experience, the more we long to be in the presence of the Source of all joy.

Given that joy is a feeling, what of Paul's command to "Rejoice Always" (1 Thes 5.16; Phil 3.1; 4.4)? Is God *commanding* us to have a feeling?

An Invitation to Worship

In John Stott's commentary on 1 Thessalonians, he says that Paul's command "can hardly be interpreted as a general call to Christians to 'be happy in your faith at all times,' for joy and happiness are not at our command, and cannot be turned on and off like a tap."[25] Instead, Stott points to the Philippians version of the command ("Rejoice in the Lord") and says,

> Then at once it reminds us of many Old Testament commands, like those which introduce the Venite, 'Come, Let us sing for Joy to the Lord,' and the Jubilate, 'Shout for Joy to the Lord.' In other words, Paul is not issuing an order to be happy, but an invitation to worship, and to Joyful worship at that.[26]

In similar fashion, N.T. Wright says of Philippians 4.4 that we tend to think of 'rejoicing' as "something that happens inside people, a sense of joy welling up and making them happy from within. All that is important, and is contained within Paul's command; but in his world and culture this 'Rejoice' would have meant what we call a public celebration."[27]

A Bible search for "joy" would reveal that the Book of Psalms is a hot-spot for the word. Over and over, the psalmists call us to "shout

---

[25] J. Stott, *The Message of 1 & 2 Thessalonians*. 100. "The Venite" is Psalm 95, and "The Jubilate" is Psalm 100, both titles derived the opening phrase in Latin.

[26] Ibid.

[27] Wright, *Philippians*. 46.

for joy" or "sing for joy." As someone whose mind was saturated with the language of the psalter, it is not hard to imagine that Paul is, in fact, inviting his readers to celebrate, to offer worship to the Lord in shouts of joy and songs of joy.

Consider, in particular, Paul's instruction to the Philippians to "join in following my example" (Phil 3.17). When Paul first came to Philippi, he and Silas were arrested for casting out an unclean spirit from a girl who had been making her masters quite a profit. Luke describes that the authorities "threw them into the inner prison and fastened their feet in the stocks," but goes on to say that "about midnight Paul and Silas were praying and singing hymns of praise to God" (Acts 16.24–25). We are not told what Paul and Silas were *feeling* as they sat there in the stocks. We assume that the prayerful hymns were associated with a sense of joy—but did a feeling spur them to sing, or did the singing stir up a feeling within them? Does it really make a difference? Either way, Paul invites his readers to imitate his example—to worship God with gladness regardless of the circumstances.

What happens when we worship God in song, in speech, or in prayer? We focus our attention on God; we proclaim Who He is and what He has done. In so doing, our perspective changes, and we begin to see our life (however pleasant or unpleasant it may be) in light of the nature and work of God. This shift in perspective reminds us of what (or Who) is most important; it rearranges our priorities and changes the object of our desire. Paul, for instance, was not concerned with the fact that he was suffering, starving, and stuck in a Roman prison, but only that the gospel of Christ was being advanced (Phil 1.12, 18).

Worship also reminds us of the reality of God's presence, which is (as we have seen) essential for joy. Paul's full command to the Philippians is, "Rejoice in the Lord always; again I will say, rejoice! Let your gentle spirit be known to all men. The Lord is near. Be anxious for nothing, but in everything by prayer and supplication with thanksgiving let your requests be made known to God" (Phil 4.4–6). Translations and commentators vary on where these sentences should be divided, but the ideas fit together regardless. Despite our circumstances, we can avoid anxiety and exude gentleness (or "reasonableness" in the ESV) before men. We are able to do that because the Lord is near; He is with us and He is coming back soon. Rejoicing in the Lord—worshipping Him— reminds us of both of those realities.

Furthermore, we should not ignore the communal aspect of the worship to which Paul invites us. Again, the backdrop of the Psalms is informative. The vast majority of the psalms of praise have a communal setting—the worship of God in the assembly of God's people. As one example (of many), Psalm 95 goes on to say, "Come, let us worship and bow down, let us kneel before the Lord our Maker. For He is our God, and we are the people of His pasture and the sheep of His hand" (Psa 95.6–7). The invitation to worship is made to the community, and the worship itself reminds the worshipper of his place within the community.

It may not be accidental that Paul's command to "Rejoice in the Lord" follows his urging for two women in the church to "live in harmony" (Phil 4.2–4). Paul makes this plea, reminding them of their common bond—they "share my struggle," they are "fellow workers, whose names are in the book of life" (Phil 4.3). When we rejoice in the Lord together, we are reminded of the identity, work, and joy that we share as the people of God. We become like those harmonic strings of a piano—our hearts resonating in sympathy as the song of joy sounds forth.

Worship is not a *therapeutic* practice (i.e. something we do to feel better) but a *formative* one. Worship shapes our hearts and minds. To return to our metaphor, worship is a mechanism for tuning ourselves to resonate with the character of God. As we sing for joy to the Lord, we think His thoughts, desire what He desires, and bring our will into alignment with His will. Whatever we may be feeling in the moment, we bow our heads in prayer and lift our voices in song—trusting that He is the One "who is at work in you, both to will and to work for His good pleasure" (Phil 2.13). With our hearts and minds so calibrated, God can (and will) work in us, even to cultivate the deep sense of gladness that is found in union with Him. So we pray, "Come, Thou Fount of every blessing, tune my heart to sing Thy grace."[28]

The Pursuit of Joy

How do we find and behold the "blue flower" of joy that we all so desperately seek? The answer is to stop looking for it. When we pursue joy for its own sake, we are really pursuing something in ourselves—we are looking for the feeling. In that case, our *desires* become the basis of our pursuit and the result is disastrous. We become like those whose "end is destruction, their god is their belly, and they glory in their shame, with minds set on earthly things" (Phil 3.19). Instead of finding healing, we repeat the pattern of the first humans and separate ourselves further from God and harm our fellow man (1 Thes 4.5–6).

Instead, fullness of joy is only obtained by the one who loses himself completely in the pursuit of God for Whom he was created. This man considers everything in his life to be "rubbish" (excrement!) "in view of the surpassing value of knowing Christ Jesus my Lord" (Phil 3.8). This woman imparts to others the gospel of God and her own life also (1 Thes 2.8) and is willing to be "poured out as a drink offering" so that others can be pleasing to God (Phil 2.17). This person sings and prays in hardship, gives thanks in all circumstances, and rejoices always as his or her life resonates with the character of God. Joy is among the greatest blessings given by God, and yet for this person joy is not the pursuit. God is.

On the last page of C.S. Lewis' *Surprised by Joy*, he describes how the experience of Joy changed once he came to believe in God.

---

[28] R. Robinson, "Come, Thou Fount of Every Blessing," 1758. https://hymnary.org/text/come_thou_fount_of_ every_blessing.

Interestingly, he says that he continued to experience the pangs of Joy just as often, but that it took on a lesser importance because he finally understood what (Whom) he was seeking. Joy is always a reminder, a pointer.

When we are lost in the woods the sight of a signpost is a great matter. He who first sees it cries "Look!" The whole party gathers round and stares. But when we have found the road and are passing signposts every few miles, we shall not stop and stare. They will encourage us and we shall be grateful to the authority that set them up. But we shall not stop and stare, or not much; not on this road, though their pillars are of silver and their lettering of gold. "We would be at Jerusalem."[29]

A life worthy of the gospel is a life full of joy—and, like Paul, we thank God for it—but we do not stop and stare, and we do not chase joy lest it elude us as well. Instead, we offer ourselves in devotion to God (for His glory) and others (for their salvation), and experience a blessedness which draws us to Him, binds us together, and spurs us toward our goal. So we sing, "Come, we that love the Lord, and let our joys be known! Join in the song with sweet accord and thus surround the throne. We are marching to Zion!"[30]

---

[29] Lewis, *Surprised by Joy* 238.

[30] I. Watts, "Come, ye that love the Lord," 1711. https://hymnary.org/text/come_we_that_love_the_lord_and_let_our.

The Peace of God that Surpasses Understanding

Contentment that is Worthy of the Gospel

Travis Walker

A contented mind is the greatest blessing that a man can enjoy in the world. (Joseph Addison)[1]

The quality of life in America, as well as in many places throughout the world, has changed considerably over the past century. Advancements in transportation allow people to travel farther and faster. In exploration, man has observed the majestic grandeur of some of the distant reaches of outer space and has also viewed the smallest elements that make up our physical universe. Developments in the field of communications have provided the ability for people to connect with others in greater numbers and with innovations, such as the internet, to be able to communicate more information than can be absorbed by any one individual. In the area of medicine, discoveries found cures for diseases that at one time debilitated and destroyed lives. In addition to these and many other advancements, the level of prosperity and access to material goods is greater than at any other time in human history. All these changes in our world can rightly be called improvements, and yet the sad reality is that while

---

[1] J. Addison, "No. 574," *The Spectator* 30 July 1714.

there is an increase in the quality of physical life, there has been a decrease in the quality of people's emotional and mental well-being. The personal happiness, satisfaction, and contentment of many find themselves lacking. An article in the Los Angeles Times stated, "Life in America keeps getting more miserable."[2] Maybe you do not feel that life is miserable, but sadly many around us, both those in Christ and those outside of Christ, live daily without joy, happiness, peace, and contentment. Here are some questions we have to ask ourselves: why are people unhappy? Why are people unsatisfied with life? In seeking to find the answers to these questions, it is discovered that there are pressures created by this world that convince people that their purpose in life, their significance in life, and their value and energies should be wrapped up in accumulation—increasing personal prosperity, prowess, popularity, and position. However, when people seek and pursue joy, happiness, peace, and contentment from what the world declares are fulfilling pursuits, they inevitably will find unhappiness, anxiousness, and emptiness. Worldly pursuits do not fulfill because worldly pursuits do not last. It is like a person who finds himself lost at sea, desperate, and dehydrated. He may think to himself that drinking sea water will quench his thirst, but what he discovers is that doing so only makes him thirstier.

A quote commonly attributed to Socrates says, "He who is not content with what he has, would not be contented with what he would like to have." The Preacher of Ecclesiastes, in his introductory remarks, arrives at a similar conclusion. He discovered that seeking to find satisfaction and purpose under the sun is both unfulfilling and unending. "…Vanity of vanities! All is vanity" (Eccl 1.2). As children of God, we are called to, and we have access to, a different kind of life, a better life, a life that is "worthy of the gospel" (Phil 1.27). When that kind of life becomes our goal, we will find that lasting joy and

---

[2] Christopher Ingraham; "Americans Are Becoming Less Happy And There Is Research To Prove It," March 23, 2019; *Los Angeles Times*; https://www.latimes.com/science/sciencenow/la-sci-sn-americans-less-happy-20190323-story.html.

peace are not found in the acquisition of things, nor in the change of a person's circumstances; they can only be found in the person of Jesus Christ and the perspective for living that He provides. Additionally, we understand that these traits of peace and contentment are identifying characteristics of the one who follows Christ. The actions and attitudes of an individual communicate their core beliefs. Do you find yourself anxious about daily needs? Remember Jesus said, "Seek first the Kingdom of God and his righteousness, and these things will be added to you" (Matt 6.33). Do you find yourself excessively focused and overwhelmed with daily living? Remember, "If then you have been raised with Christ, seek the things that are above, where Christ is, seated at the right hand of God. Set your minds on things that are above, not on things that are on earth" (Col 3.1,2).

Within scripture, Christians are encouraged to conduct themselves in a way that reflects a spirit of contentment. The Hebrew writer reminds us to "keep your life free from love of money and be content with what you have" (13.5). Paul tells the younger evangelist that, "…godliness with contentment is great gain, for we brought nothing into the world, and we cannot take anything out of the world. But with food and clothing, with these we shall be content" (1 Tim 6.6–8). Additionally, Paul admonishes the believers in Thessalonica to "aspire to live quietly, and to mind your own affairs, and to work with your hands, as we instructed you, so that you may walk properly before outsiders and be dependent on no one" (1 Thess 4.11,12) and to "work quietly" (2 Thess 3.12). These scriptures point followers of Christ to a manner of life that is characterized by contentment and peace. In Philippians 4, the apostle goes a step further than instructing his readers to possess a spirit of peace and contentment by also exemplifying these attitudes and encouraging them to follow his example. Notice what he says:

> What you have learned and received and heard and seen in me—
> practice these things, and the God of peace will be with you. I re-

joiced in the Lord greatly that now at length you have revived your concern for me. You were indeed concerned for me, but you had no opportunity. Not that I am speaking of being in need, for I have learned in whatever situation I am to be content. I know how to be brought low, and I know how to abound. In any and every circumstance, I have learned the secret of facing plenty and hunger, abundance and need. I can do all things through him who strengthens me. (Phil 4.9–12)

These words that Paul wrote by inspiration give insight into the peace that he possessed. What makes them even more impactful is understanding the context of his current situation. For more than two years he had been imprisoned because of his love and faith in Christ and his dedication to the gospel of Christ. Despite the difficulties of his situation, there was joy in his heart and peace and contentment in his thinking. He lived "worthy of the gospel."

How can we adopt and practice these same attitudes exemplified in the life and words of Paul? There are two words Paul uses that we need to understand better. The first is the word "content." What does Paul mean and what does he not mean, by this word found in v. 11? Second is the word "learned." What is it that Paul intends to communicate by using this word? Let's begin with discussing the word content. There is a common term found in nearly every definition of contentment. It is satisfaction. "Desiring no more than what one has; satisfied."[3] "To be free from care because of satisfaction with what is already one's own."[4] It is being satisfied with who you are, with what you have, and with your circumstances in life. While these definitions are accurate, for the child of God contentment is more than just personal satisfaction. Christian contentment is a peace that comes from knowing God's person. God is always good, and He al-

---

[3] The American Heritage Dictionary of the English Language, Fifth Edition by HarperCollins Publishers.

[4] (James Orr et al., eds., "Content, Contentment," *The International Standard Bible Encyclopedia* (Chicago: The Howard-Severance Company, 1915), 705.

ways does good. James writes that "every good gift and every perfect gift is from above, coming down from the Father of lights, with whom there is no variation or shadow due to change" (Jam 1.17). Contentment is also recognizing God's power and position as sovereign. The psalmist says, "our God is in the heavens; he does all that he pleases" (Psa 115.3). And contentment is the peace that comes from knowing God's promises are unfailing and immutable because He "never lies" (Tit 1.2). In defining contentment, we must also exercise some caution lest we make some inaccurate conclusions. While contentment is satisfaction, it is not the absence of desire. One could draw the conclusion that if I am to be content in my life then I should not desire something more or something different. This would be incorrect. Contentment is an understanding that while I may have hopes and desires, and while I may make plans to achieve those goals, "it is the purpose of the Lord that will stand" (Pro 19.21) and I am at peace with God with what happens. The apostle Paul demonstrates this as he reveals his wants and desires. In the second chapter of Philippians, he expresses his wish to send Timothy to Philippi (vv. 22,23) and also how he wanted to go there himself (v. 24). Contentment is not the absence of desire, nor is contentment the same thing as complacency. What does it mean to become complacent? Complacency is self-satisfaction to the point of inactivity. Notice Paul prayed that the love of his readers would not become stagnant, but rather, that it would "abound more and more, with knowledge and all discernment" (Phil 1.9). He wanted his readers to continue to put forth the effort to grow in love one for another. Paul also speaks that while he desired to "depart and be with Christ" (Phil 1.23), remaining in this life would be for their "progress" (Phil 1.25) and growth in the faith. Later Paul writes, "…work out your own salvation with fear and trembling" (Phil 2.12). Keep going and keep growing.

The second thing we need to appreciate is that contentment is a secret that can be learned. Notice what Paul says in Philippians 4.11,12: "Not that I am speaking of being in need, for I have learned in whatever situation I am to be content... In any and every circumstance, I have learned the secret...." Contentment is not a default attitude of humanity. Mankind constantly seeks more. This is evidenced by Adam and Eve, who could eat from any tree within the garden with only one exception. Satan took advantage of their desire and tempted them by speaking to their discontentment concerning the blessings of food God had provided, and their dissatisfaction with their position as humanity. In fact, could we not say that all temptation to sin is based on some form of discontentment? That is why contentment is a challenging mindset to possess. It is the battle between pursuing my will or the will of God. As difficult as it may be to have and maintain a spirit of contentment, Paul reminds us that it can and must be learned. So, what is the secret that Paul learned? The secret to a contentment that is worthy of the gospel can be discovered in the expressions of joy made by the jailed apostle within the book of Philippians.

Contentment is Found in a Focused Life

Consider the statement Paul makes about the joy he possessed in Philippians 1.18. He writes, "What then? Only that in every way, whether in pretense or in truth, Christ is proclaimed, and in that I rejoice." What did Paul believe that enabled him to possess this perspective of joy while imprisoned for the cause of Christ? What did he understand that gave him a sense of satisfaction? He recognized that God had a purpose, and that aim was Paul's priority in living. It was his focus. Earlier, Paul had acknowledged that the things which happened to him, namely his imprisonment, had served to accomplish a purpose (Phil 1.12).

The first purpose of God that Paul identifies is that God was working to advance the gospel. Paul said, "I want you to know, brothers, that what has happened to me has really served to advance the gospel" (Phil 1.12). The message of God's love, mercy, and grace in Jesus Christ was being extended through Paul to individuals who had not previously heard the good news. Paul took his obstacle and used it as an opportunity to glorify God. Typically, people respond to adversity by focusing on self, personal pain, and personal frustrations. As believers, rather than turning inward, should we not seek to use our obstacles as opportunities to communicate to others that our faith, love, and hope are not in this world, but in Jesus Christ? This focus on the spreading of the gospel can also be seen in the acknowledgment that his obstacles emboldened most of the saints to "become confident… and are much more bold to speak the word without fear" (Phil 1.14). How was it that Christians had found the courage to share the message of Jesus Christ through Paul's imprisonment? As fear can be contagious, courage can also be contagious. The manner Paul approached his relationship with Christ and his relationship to his circumstance had a tremendous impact on the saints. They fed off his confidence and became confident themselves. They saw his willingness to share the gospel and became more willing to share the gospel. Consider the many letters Paul sent to congregations; they were written not only to enrich their understanding of Christ, but also to encourage greater faithfulness in practical living. Were his words disconnected from his practice or perspective? No. His words were extensions of his actions and attitudes. For example, notice what he writes in 1 Corinthians 15.57,58: "Therefore, my beloved brothers, be steadfast, immovable, always abounding in the work of the Lord, knowing that in the Lord your labor is not in vain." These words are not just an exhortation, they were a reflection of his reality. As Paul approached the end of his life, it is evident that what he taught and what he practiced were consistent with each other. He testified to his unwavering faith, his diligent work for the Lord, and his confidence that the result at the end of his life would be a "crown of righteousness, which the Lord, the righteous judge, will award to me on that day" (2 Tim 4.7,8). The conduct of life in Christ and for Christ can either encourage or discourage others to live in Christ and for Christ. Paul's boldness became an inspiration for the boldness of others. Paul's priority concerning the spreading of the gospel can also be seen in his reaction as he recognized that some preached from goodwill and sincerity, and some preached from rivalry and selfish ambition. However, the apostle did not respond in bitterness, anger, or resentment. His response was to assert that "…whether in pretense or in truth, Christ is preached, and in that I rejoice" (Phil 1.18). When God's purpose becomes my priority, then no matter the circumstances, whether it be positive or negative, good or bad, I can rejoice and be at peace.

The second purpose of God that Paul identifies as his priority is the unity and fellowship of the saints. Once again, Paul conveys that the joy, peace, and contentment he had was the result of making God's purpose his focus. His ability to find joy was connected to his appreciation for the prayers of the brethren and the help of the Spirit of Jesus Christ (Phil 1.18,19). The prayers made on his behalf were not solely expressions of a desire for the apostle to continue his labor for the Lord, but they were also expressions of deep love that resided in the hearts of the Philippian brethren for Paul. It was this relationship of mutual love and harmony that brought Paul such joy and a spirit of contentment. Is this not one of the blessings of prayer? In our supplications, not only do we ask for God to grant peace and provision in the life of the individual we are praying for, but through the prayer itself, there is an inherent provision of strength and support. When faced with difficulties, have you found encouragement, strength, and peace through the prayers offered by others on your behalf? Paul again identifies a connection between contentment and God's purpose of unity and fellowship of the saints when he admonishes Euodia and Syntyche to settle their differences (Phil 4.2,3) because the conflict that is not resolved inevitably results in a lack of peace and joy. It affects our relationship with God, it affects our relationship with each other, and it affects our relationship with ourselves. If we struggle to have godly relationships with others, how can we seek God's forgiveness and have a relationship with Him?

Jesus said, "but if you do not forgive others their trespasses, neither will your Father forgive your trespasses" (Matthew 6.15). The result, unless we harden our hearts, is a lack of peace. When we struggle with forgiving others it is very easy to start reading people's actions as ill motives. Every action of the offender is perceived through the lens of "they did me wrong." Ironically, that individual may not even realize that there is a problem and the only one living without peace is you. One of the saddest results of unresolved conflict is when we take our frustrations out on a person who has absolutely nothing to do with the situation. This should not be. So, why do we do that? It's the effect of discontentment caused by unresolved conflict.

Paul again reveals that in making God's purpose his priority and his focus he was able to discover joy, peace, and contentment. What is the third purpose of God in Philippians that brought peace and contentment? It is knowing Christ. Paul begins the third chapter by exhorting Christians to "rejoice in the Lord" (v.1). While some may, and Paul could, put confidence for salvation in the flesh, whatever Paul could have counted as gain, he "counted as loss for the sake of Christ" (v.7) and "as loss because of the surpassing worth of knowing Christ Jesus my Lord" (v.8). Paul declared that his heritage, his position, and his zealous work were all things to be thrown away. They were nothing to Paul; Jesus was everything. The apostle of Christ desired to know Christ (Phil 3.10). He longed for a deeper and more devoted relationship with his Savior. He desired to share the sufferings of Christ (Phil 3.10) to be identified as a follower of Christ, to suffer as Jesus suffered. Paul knew that the disciple who follows his Master will receive much of the same responses that his Master received. Recall what Jesus told his apostles, "Remember the word that I said to you: 'A servant is not greater than his master.' If they persecuted Me, they will also persecute you. If they kept my word, they will also keep yours" (John 15.20). Lastly, Paul longed to be received by Christ (Phil 3.11). It is ironic that the result of the child of God who learns to be content in this life because he has made God's purposes (the advancement of the gospel, the unity and fellowship of the saints and knowing Christ) his priority, will certainly become discontent with remaining in this life. Paul expresses this discontent when he writes, "For to me to live is Christ, and to die is gain. If I am to live in the flesh, that means fruitful labor for me. Yet which I shall choose I cannot tell. I am hard pressed between the two. My desire is to depart and be with Christ, for that is far better" (Phil 1.21–23). Later he says, "Not that I have already obtained this or am already perfect, but I press on to make it my own…one thing I do: forgetting what lies behind and straining forward to what lies ahead, I press on toward the goal for the prize of the upward call of God in Christ Jesus" (Phil 3.12–14). In Paul's second epistle to the Corinthians, he revealed his deep desire in the words, "For in this tent we groan, longing to put on our heavenly dwelling…For while we are still in this tent, we groan, being burdened…" (5.2,4). How is it that discontentment with remaining in this life is the byproduct of contentment in this life? One's circumstances in life are fluid. They change and then change again. Periods of prosperity can be followed by scarcity. Moments that bring laughter give way to those that bring tears. While we can and should have peace in all of our extremes, do we not long for something better? Do we not long to be with Christ?

Contentment is found in a Maturing Life

The apostle Paul's desire to know Christ, to be identified with Christ, and to be found in Christ (Phil 3.8–10) stands in contrast to those who sought confidence in the flesh. They lived to please themselves, they were proud of their shameful behavior, and they lived only for today (Phil 3.19). This disparity between the aspirations of Paul and those of whom he wrote reminds us that many desire and pursue things other than Jesus to find joy and happiness, peace and contentment. What do people seek, and what is the result of their search? These are the same questions that the Preacher asked in the book of Ecclesiastes. Consider his journey to find purpose and happiness. He began by applying his heart "to know wisdom and to know madness and folly" (Eccl 1.17). He concluded that it was "striving after wind" and rather than finding happiness, he found sorrow. The Preacher then continues his quest by having a good time and accumulating a lot of things (Eccl 2.1–11). The result? He said, "…all was vanity and striving after the wind" (v.11). He then focuses his energy on finding happiness and purpose in the pursuit of power (Eccl 4.13–16). Once again, he discovers that it held no lasting benefit (v.16). Not giving up, he turns his attention to prosperity (Eccl 5.10–17), and he concludes that there is no satisfaction in loving or pursuing money. Three thousand years later and people seek the same things to discover happiness and purpose. Are their results any different than the Preacher's? Not at all. The paths that many have convinced themselves will lead to happiness, lead only to restlessness, emptiness, and craving for more. Why is that? It is impossible to find lasting happiness in something that, by its nature, does not last. As the Preacher of Ecclesiastes aged and matured, he discovered that the only pursuit that provided purpose, and perspective, the only one that was enduring and satisfying, was seeking the Lord (Eccl 12.13,14). All that Paul had as a source of confidence before Christ, he was willing to throw away. To him those things were nothing and Christ was everything. May we grow to see Christ as our everything.

Contentment is found in a Thankful Life

In Philippians 4.10, Paul once again expresses the joy found in his heart while he found himself imprisoned in Rome. He writes, "I rejoiced in the Lord greatly…." What was the source of Paul's joy? His heart of joy was the result of his heart of gratitude. Having learned and practiced the secret of contentment, he was able to face the extremes of want and plenty in peacefulness (Phil 4.12,13). It is useful for us to notice the location of his remarks in their context about the secret of contentment. They find themselves in the middle of Paul expressing his gratitude for the brethren (Phil 4.10,14–19). They had been concerned about Paul's well-being, they had sent Epaphroditus to minister to his need (Phil 2.25), and they also provided financial support (Phil 4.14–18). For these gifts, Paul says, "Thank you." Gratitude changes attitudes. Sadly, many fail to appreciate where they are and instead live with a "when then" mentality. "When I get what I desire, then I will be happy." "When I get to a specific position at work, then I will be happy." "When I have a certain amount in my bank account, then I will be happy." "When my kids leave home and go to college, then I will be happy." And on and on it goes. Here is the problem--there will always be another "when then." Stop and be thankful for where you are now. It is God's blessing. "Give thanks in all circumstances, for this is the will of God in Christ Jesus for you" (1 Thess 5.18). To fail to express thanks is an expression of dissatisfaction in the provision of God and disbelief in the power of God to provide. Take some time every day to think about the blessings in your life and express appreciation to the One who provided them. When we do so, we will find that the things we do not possess become less significant.

Contentment is found in a Hopeful Life

As Paul had encouraged his readers previously to "rejoice in the Lord" (Phil 3.1), he does so again in Philippians 4.4. "Rejoice in the Lord always; again I will say, rejoice." What is it about the Lord that Paul emphatically states is the source of our joy? While the answers to that question are without end, let me provide you with a couple of thoughts to consider. First, rejoice that Jesus is your Lord. While lost in sin and without hope, God in His wonderful grace and mercy paid the price for my transgressions by the sacrifice of His Son so that I could have hope. "He himself bore our sins in his body on the tree, that we might die to sin and live to righteousness. By his wounds you have been healed" (1 Pet 2.24). He is my Lord, my Savior, my King. Second, rejoice that He walks with you. "...The Lord is at hand; do not be anxious about anything" (Phil 4.5b,6). "Keep your life free from the love of money and be content with what you have, for He has said, 'I will never leave you nor forsake you'" (Hebrews 13.5). Notice the connection between the call to be content and the continual presence of the Lord. Seeing that Jesus is with me, what do I have to fear? Since Jesus is with me all day and every day, what do I have to worry about? Whatever the situation may be, plenty or hunger, abundance or need, I can find peace. Third, rejoice in God's promise. "But in everything by prayer and supplication with thanksgiving let your requests be made known to God. And the peace of God, which surpasses all understanding, will guard your hearts and your minds in Christ Jesus" (Phil 4.6b,7). Rejoice in the promise that God loves and provides for you. As a loving Father, He provides for our physical needs. "Therefore I tell you, do not be anxious about your life... Look at the birds of the air: they neither sow nor reap nor gather into barns, and yet your heavenly Father feeds them. Are you not of more value than they?" (Matt 6.25–34). Also, rejoice that He provides for our emotional needs. "I can do all things through him who strengthens me" (Phil 4.13). As a prisoner in Rome, Paul's ability to have peace and contentment in his circumstances was not because of his strength or ability. The peace that guarded his heart and mind, the peace that rises above all human understanding (Phil 4.8), was a peace that did not have its source from within himself, but from the Lord. Rejoice that He meets our spiritual needs. "And through him to reconcile to himself all things, whether on earth or in heaven, making peace by the blood of his cross" (Col 1.20). You can have peace, and you can have contentment, and you can have joy today. Why? Because by the blood of Jesus Christ, whenever this life comes to an end you can have peace.

"What you have learned and received and heard and seen in me—practice these things, and the God of peace will be with you" (Phil 4.9).

Relief to You Who Are Afflicted

Comfort that is Worthy of the Gospel

Jared Hagan

Christians in America have long experienced a time of relative peace. We have not been widely persecuted. This blessing sometimes makes it difficult for us to appreciate the plight of the first century Christians. Nevertheless, there is a widespread sense among us that days of persecution are headed our direction. How will we endure the coming affliction? We need to learn from those early Christians and equip ourselves with the comfort and relief that can only come from the gospel.

Affliction (*thlipsis*) means to be pressed together.[1] It is a term that reflects the inner turmoil caused by external forces. The early Christians were being squeezed. They not only faced persecution; they felt its effects deep in their souls.

The Macedonian churches were no strangers to affliction. Paul described their situation as "a great ordeal of affliction" and "deep poverty" (2 Cor 8.1–2).[2] Their tribulation began while they were babes in Christ, forcing them to decide—would they remain faithful to God, or would they reject the gospel?

The Philippian church was the first church to be established in Macedonia and also the first to witness the tribulation that would

---

[1] K, Wuest, *Hebrews in the Greek New Testament.* Wuest Word Studies From the Greek New Testament 2 (Grand Rapids: Eerdmans, 1979) 188.

[2] All quotes from Scripture are from the New American Standard (1995 edition).

accompany the faith. It was Philippi where the Christian movement was accused of "throwing our city into confusion" and being unlawful for Romans to participate in (Acts 16.20–21). These accusations resonated, as "the crowd rose up together against them" and the governing authorities took Paul, stripped him, delivered "many blows" with rods, and threw him into prison (Acts 16.22–23). What chance would a new church have when they lived in such a hostile community as this? It would seem, though, that they had it easy in comparison to the Thessalonians.

The persecution at Thessalonica began in a similar fashion to what had happened in Philippi. Paul began preaching and made new converts to the faith (Acts 17.4). Then opposition arose along with similar accusations. "These men who have upset the whole world have come here also," they said, and also added that this new faith was "contrary to the decrees of Caesar" (Acts 17.6–7). Once again, the message resonated, a mob formed, and the city authorities got involved.

However, it was not Paul who endured persecution in Thessalonica. The mob searched for him, but not finding him, they instead dragged "Jason and some brethren before the city authorities" (Acts 17.6). In Philippi, the persecutors, terrified of their own actions, begged Paul to leave the city. They preferred to sweep the whole incident under the rug (Acts 16.35–39).[3] Not so in Thessalonica. The Thessalonian oppressors were more zealous to eliminate Christianity. Their obsession extended beyond the borders of their own city and into the surrounding region. When they discovered that Paul had proclaimed the word of God in Berea, they took it upon themselves to march nearly fifty miles[4] to stir up the crowds there (Acts 17.13). The Berean brethren sent Paul even farther away to escape the rising

---

[3] Despite this, the Christians in Philippi would eventually be persecuted. By the time the Philippian epistle is written the Christians there had opponents (Phil 1.28), suffered for Christ's sake (Phil 1.29) and experienced the same conflict they saw in Paul (Phil 1.30).

[4] J, Stringer, *The Book of Acts*. Truth Commentaries. (Bowling Green: Guardian of Truth Foundation, 1999) 351.

problems in the region, but what about those new Christians living in Thessalonica? At some point, the zealous oppressors would return home. It's hard to believe that the persecutors would let this upstart religion thrive in their city just because Paul had escaped their grasp. The Christians would have to live side by side with those who remained determined to stamp out Christianity.

In the Thessalonian epistles, Paul calls attention to the Christians' affliction. They had "received the word in much tribulation" (1 Thes 1.6), had "endured the same sufferings" as the churches in Judea (1 Thes 2.14), and were themselves the afflicted ones (2 Thes 1.6–7). Despite their "persecutions and afflictions," the Christians grew in their love, faith, and perseverance (2 Thes 1.3–4).

Paul does not address them with secret strategies on how to outsmart their persecutors and bring an end to the opposition, nor does he fill the epistles with the cold advice, "It is what it is, so deal with it." Instead, he offers two things to those squeezed by affliction: comfort and relief.

Comfort in 1 Thessalonians 4.18 comes from the Greek word *parakaleo*. It may not be obvious in the English texts, but *parakaleo* is a theme of the epistle. Paul uses the word eight times in five short chapters (1 Thes 2.11; 3.2,7; 4.1,10,18; 5.11,14). If not for 2 Corinthians, this would be the highest concentration of that word in the New Testament epistles. *Parakaleo* means to call to one's side[5] and is also translated as encourage or urge. Paul sets the example of how he wants the Christians to comfort one another by the way he exhorted and urged them to greater righteousness. Like a father, he begged them (1 Thes 2.11). He strengthened them (1 Thes 3.2). He reminded them (1 Thes 4.1,9–10). He focused them (1 Thes 4.1,10). This was their example to follow when he called on them to "comfort one another" (1 Thes 4.18; 5.10). He wanted the Christians to respond to affliction by pulling together, holding each other up, and

---

[5] W, Vines, *Vine's Expository Dictionary of New Testament Words* (McClean: MacDonald Publishing Company) 209.

strengthening each other to face their troubles. Their strength would come from reminding each other of the gospel of God the way he had reminded them of God's message and their commitment to it.

In 2 Thessalonians, Paul states that God will give relief to the afflicted (2 Thes 1.6–7). Relief "signifies rest...from endurance and suffering."[6] Paul did not promise an immediate end to suffering but a relief that would come "when the Lord Jesus will be revealed from heaven" (2 Thes 1.7). Until that day, the Thessalonians were not left to despair. Instead, Paul blessed them, saying, "may the Lord of peace Himself continually grant you peace in every circumstance" (2 Thes 3.16). While they faced outer tribulation, they could enjoy inner peace until the day that God brought an ultimate end to the oppression and affliction.

What Comfort and Hope is There for the Afflicted?

When thinking about relief and comfort for the afflicted, we naturally turn to the hope-filled message of the gospel. "One day we will be in heaven," we say to each other. When a loved one is taken from us, we add, "They've gone to a better place." This is, of course, a proper source of comfort. Paul began with those same thoughts in 1 Thessalonians 4.13–18 which led to the instruction, "Comfort one another with these words." This reassuring source of comfort is worthy of its own article and receives such treatment in this collection. A reader has not properly examined the subject of Christian comfort without digging into and digesting the strength that comes from our salvation and the promise of eternal life. However, one has also not fully examined the subject of godly comfort if they stop there. After all, Paul didn't. He expanded on other sources of comfort for the Thessalonians (primarily in 1 Thes 5.1–11 and 2 Thes 2.3–10). What comfort does God offer the afflicted aside from the assurance of our salvation? The answers might not be what we typically think of, but they are there for our edification nonetheless.

---

[6] Ibid. 354.

First, there is comfort to be had in the purpose of our suffering. It is one thing to suffer senselessly and another thing entirely to suffer for a good cause. The pain is the same, but the latter produces an unwavering resolve. Soldiers who fight for a war they neither understand nor agree with will have low morale and will easily surrender. On the other hand, soldiers who believe in the cause will endure tremendous hardships, courageously fighting against impossible odds, because the fight itself is worth it. Paul stated that it was the kingdom of God "for which indeed you are suffering" (2 Thes 1.5). It meant everything to the Christians. Their efforts to exalt their king, to expand His influence, to maintain their citizenship had brought them affliction, but the purpose made the pain worth it.

Second, comfort comes to the afflicted when they find their value in suffering. Paul states that the Thessalonians endured persecution and affliction "so that you will be considered worthy of the kingdom of God" (2 Thes 1.4–5). What greater task can we set our hands to than to live in a manner worthy of the kingdom (1 Thes 2.12)? Such worth is not found by declarations of our faith in times of peace and prosperity. It would be excusable if someone, thinking about the greatness of heaven and the weakness of men, came to the conclusion that we can never come close to being worthy of the kingdom. That sounds good. It seems reasonable. But it contradicts what Paul stated about these Thessalonian Christians. Through their faith and endurance of tribulation, they had achieved greatness in God's eyes. They were worthy. Put another way, they belonged in God's kingdom.

Observe how these first two points combine in the example of the apostles. "So they went on their way from the presence of the Council, rejoicing that they had been considered worthy to suffer shame for His name" (Acts 5.41). Fortified by their proven worth and the purpose of the kingdom, the apostles rejoiced even while pain coursed through their battered bodies.

Third, comfort comes from appreciation. Paul always gave thanks for the Thessalonians (2 Thes 1.3), and he spoke proudly of them to the other churches of God because of their "perseverance and faith in the midst of all your persecutions and afflictions which you endure" (2 Thes 1.4). Paul meant a great deal to the Thessalonians (1 Thes 3.6), so naturally it meant a great deal to them when he was proud of them and boasting about them to other churches. In the same way, can there be anything greater for Christians than to hear Jesus say, "Well done, good and faithful servant" (Matt 25.21,23)? Certainly, we look forward to the promise of reward that immediately follows that pronouncement, but isn't there joy and comfort to be found simply in the words of appreciation from the Master whom we love and serve? Patiently enduring mistreatment when we have done what is right finds favor with God (1 Pet 2.20). What more do we need? If by suffering for our faith our God is pleased with us, then does that not fill us with comfort and a strength to persevere until the very end?

Fourth, comfort comes from our destiny. "For God has not destined us for wrath, but for obtaining salvation through our Lord Jesus Christ" (1 Thes 5.9). It would be easy to skip the first half of that sentence and focus instead on the salvation, but not being destined for wrath deserves attention. In our journey to the Promised Land, we do not want to be like the Israelites who questioned God's plan for them. The journey wasn't always easy, and this led them to say things like, "You have brought us out into this wilderness to kill this whole assembly with hunger" (Exod 16.3). Those who doubted their destiny did not finish their journey. They perished on the way. Wouldn't the Thessalonians have sounded the same if they complained and doubted God because of their suffering as though God had forgotten them or didn't care about them or was delighted to see their destruction? Paul assures the Thessalonians that they have a better destination. They had been chosen by God (1 Thes. 1.4; 2 Thes. 2.14), and God is faithful (1 Thes 5.24). If we have faith in God's destined plan for His saints, then we have strength to endure persecution and affliction. Our perspective changes, seeing such things as merely part of the journey rather than the destination.

Fifth, and perhaps most shockingly, we find comfort in the judgment of God on the wicked. This is a key point in 1 Thessalonians 5.1–10 and is revisited in 2 Thessalonians 1.3–9. 1 Thessalonians 5.1–10 is focused on the destructive nature of Jesus' return. It will catch the wicked unprepared, but not us. No, the Christians are ready for it and will avoid what those of the darkness will not be able to escape. After saying this, Paul returns to the same instruction that he gave in 1 Thessalonians 4.18. The wording may be a little different in the English translations, but it's the same in the Greek--"Comfort one another" or "encourage one another" (1 Thes 4.18; 5.11). 2 Thessalonians adds to the comfort of judgment. Judgment from God is both "just" and also "relief to you who are afflicted" (2 Thes 1.6–7).

The Thessalonian letters emphasize that the oppressors of Christians and those rejecting God are in extreme danger. "They are not pleasing to God" (1 Thes 2.15). "Wrath has come upon them to the utmost" (1 Thes 2.16). "God is the avenger in all these things" (1 Thes 4.6). "Destruction will come upon them suddenly like labor pains" (1 Thes 5.3). "They will not escape" (1 Thes 5.3). The Lord will deal "out retribution to those who do not know God" (2 Thes 1.6–8). "These will pay the penalty of eternal destruction away from the presence of the Lord and from the glory of His power" (2 Thes 1.9).

God's enemies and the persecutors of Christians are clearly doomed. They don't expect what is coming, but it will come. When they aren't looking and when they think that all is well, the judgment of God will overtake them and there will be no escape. Most Christians readily accept this to be true, but where is the comfort?

For many, the notion of finding comfort in others being judged is positively unchristian. However, the Scriptures reveal multiple reasons why judgment is both comfort and relief. First, judgment means that the persecution will come to an end. Persecutors, even at their worst, are limited. Eventually we escape their grip. They can seize our belongings, harm our bodies, and take our lives, but after that, they are powerless (Luke 12.4). One way or another, we will gain relief from their persecution. Second, the certainty of judgment means that those who have done heinous things against God and His saints will get what they deserve. The punishment is not excessive. It is just (2 Thes 1.6). God's judgment is righteous (2 Thes 1.5).

Somewhere along the line, modern day Christians seem to have lost sight of justice in favor of mercy. Maybe it is because we have been worn down by the worldly arguments that a loving God would not send people to hell. Maybe it is because we are blessed with easy living and lack firsthand knowledge of what it is like to suffer persecution. Regardless, we must learn to love justice again. Somehow, a balance must be struck between mercy and judgment. Mercy is essential (Luke 6.36–37; Jam 2.13), but it does not exclude justice. Jesus combines the two and marks their importance when dealing with the misfocused Pharisees. They had "neglected the weightier provisions of the law; justice and mercy and faithfulness" (Matt 23.23). Disciples of Christ must not lose a proper sense of justice.

This is not a small matter. One cannot fully know God without also embracing justice. God wants to be known as a punisher of the wicked. That is, after all, how He described Himself when giving the Ten Commandments (Exod 20.5), and when He revealed Himself to Moses, He said, "He will by no means leave the guilty unpunished" (Exod 34.7). Should God be ashamed of this aspect of His character? Is He somehow wrong, not only for being this way but for unabashedly declaring it about Himself?

Jesus, the loving and merciful Savior, announced the judgment to come. More than that, He yearned for it. "I have come to cast fire upon the earth; and how I wish it were already kindled" (Luke 12.49). He desired judgment! Yet in the very next breath, He describes the distress of His coming immersion into pain and death (Luke 12.50). He would follow through with that course of suffering on behalf of all men. Somehow, He found a way to love all of humanity while at the same time earnestly desiring for judgment to begin. Can we truly be disciples of Jesus if we refuse any attempt to find the same balance in our lives?

However, recognizing the godly and just nature of judgment is not the same thing as deriving comfort from it. Where is the comfort in hell's existence? What is this comfort that is worthy of the gospel?

The affliction that Christians face may be unique in that it comes from faith in the gospel, but affliction itself is not a unique experience. The people of the world are oppressed and afflicted. One only needs to watch the news or listen to a conversation for confirmation. Non-believers are vexed. They are squeezed by a constant barrage of senseless violence and evil. For example, no place is immune from mass shootings. Every city, large or small, is vulnerable. Malls aren't safe. Concerts are dangerous. Not even schools are safe havens from this horrendous evil. And the world—lacking faith in God's upcoming judgment—is completely without comfort.

When evil men take the lives of our children, then, having accomplished the wickedness they crave, they choose to end their own life, where will the world find comfort? The victims died for no purpose. Their suffering is not appreciated. They have gained no worth, only a grave. Their journey has ended horribly; what destiny do they have left? The same goes for the mourners who are left behind. Only pain and woeful emptiness remains. No purpose. No appreciation. No worth. No destiny. Therefore, no comfort. Just pain and injustice.

Worse, the depraved, cowardly killer got what he wanted. He is dead and untouchable. We can't make him answer for his crimes. The unbelieving world is filled with grief, befuddled by the unstoppable onslaught of violence, and wholly without comfort. Not so for Christians.

Christians believe in the Day of the Lord (1 Thes 5.2). That is the day when everyone will answer for their deeds and all wrongs will be made right. That day will accomplish what no movement, no march, and no law can—that day will bring an end to wickedness. No more violence. That day will accomplish what no human court can—total, inescapable justice. The suicidal killers may escape the grip of the law, but they rush headlong into the hands of an Almighty God. Vengeance is His (Heb 10.30–31). The criminal's foolish glee will be turned into utter terror. They will not get away with what they've done because their deeds will go before them to judgment (1 Tim. 5.24) and they will give an answer (2 Cor 5.10). On that day, God will triumph, and so also will all those who love righteousness, justice, and peace.

The ultimate judgment of God will occur whether people believe in it or not, but for believers, it is a source of tremendous comfort that all will be made right even though we are surrounded by unrighteousness now. We do not wait with eagerness to see the unimaginable suffering of hell's eternal flames engulfing our enemies, nor will we derive great pleasure in their wails of agony. That's not what brings us joy and comfort. It's that we love when good triumphs over evil.

I regret that men have been deceived and have embraced wickedness. I regret that they have not come to their senses and repented. Paul wept about this (Phil 3.18), so should we. On the Day of the Lord evil will come to an ultimate end—it will meet an Almighty Foe who cannot be fooled or conquered.

That evil will be utterly destroyed, never to rear its ugly head again; that mass shootings will be no more; that child and spousal abuse will be abolished; that lies and thefts will no longer be known; that the lingering pain of betrayal, adultery, and divorce will be annihilated; in this I greatly rejoice. In this the afflicted find their comfort—comfort that can only come from the gospel of God.

Let the day of the Lord come. Let it come! For on that day the righteous will have their wounds mended, and their enemies will not be able to touch them anymore. How long, O Lord? How long?

Until then, let us walk as children of day, shining light in the darkness, calling out to the lost. Warn them of the landslide of judgment barreling their direction. In mercy, save as many as we can. All the while, let us patiently endure affliction and comfort one another with the words of the gospel. For when the world wants to stamp us out, we stand strong, strengthened by our purpose, worth, and appreciation. We know our destination, and in the end, we will witness the complete and final triumph of good over evil. That is a comfort worthy of the gospel.

Not Grieve As Others
Hope That Is Worthy of the Gospel

Shane Scott

Hope is fundamental to the gospel. When Paul reminds the Colossians of the initial gospel preaching they received, he says that they heard about "the hope laid up" in heaven (Col 1.4–5). And in 1.23, Paul summarizes the message the Colossians heard as "the hope of the gospel." Yes, the gospel looks back to the past work of Jesus' death and resurrection (1 Cor 15.1–8). And yes, the gospel also applies that work in the present through faith and in baptism (Rom 6.3–4; Col 2.11–12). But the gospel, as preached by the apostles and their associates, also includes a future dimension and the hope of glory with God forever.

Gospel preaching that does not include this hope is incomplete at best and heretical at worst. This is because the nature of Christian hope is inextricably connected to the lordship of Jesus Christ, which is the centerpiece of the gospel. Christ was exalted as Lord through his decisive victory over sin and death through the cross and resurrection (Acts 2.22–36). His final victory as Lord will occur when He subdues all enemies, and every tongue confesses that he is Lord (1 Cor 15.22–26; Phil 2.9–11). The confident expectation that characterizes Christian hope draws its confidence from what the Lord Jesus has already done and its expectation from what he will eventually do.

This forward-looking perspective of the gospel is a key theme in the letters addressed to the churches of Macedonia, First and Second Thessalonians, and Philippians. When Paul commends the Thessalonians for the great reputation they have in Macedonia and Achaia, he says: "For they themselves report concerning us the kind of reception we had among you, and how you turned to God from idols to serve the living and true God, and to wait for his Son from heaven, whom he raised from the dead, Jesus who delivers us from the wrath to come" (1 Thess 1.9–10). There is a "turning from" and also a "waiting for" that is supposed to happen when the gospel is received. Similarly, after thanking the Philippians for their concern for him, Paul expresses his confidence that "he who began a good work in you will bring it to completion at the day of Jesus Christ" (Phil 1.6).

The focus of hope in these three letters revolves around the resurrection of the dead and the second coming of Christ, events that Paul links in both epistles. Additionally, in 2 Thessalonians Paul addresses a misconception about the second coming that created alarm among some of the Christians there. Those three subjects—the resurrection, the second coming, and the misconception—will serve as the guideposts for this lecture.

The Resurrection

In the first century, there were three basic views regarding the issue of life after death. Some pagans believed that the physical body is all that exists, and that at death, we cease to be.[1] The Sadducees also held this view. Other pagans believed we are souls trapped in bodies and that at death our souls are liberated. A third view, embraced by the Pharisees, held that we are made to be body and soul, and that while death ruptures this unity, it will be restored through the resurrection of the body. Jesus and Paul took the same view as the

---

[1] Both Greek and Latin inscriptions have been found that read, "I was not, I was, I am not, I care not" (cited by Gene L. Green, *The Letters to the Thessalonians* [Grand Rapids, MI: Eerdmans, 2002], 218).

Pharisees (Luke 20.27–40; Acts 23.6–8). This view reflects the fundamentally good nature of how God created us as embodied souls.[2]

The notion of a resurrection involves much more than a vague experience of life after death. When we die, and our souls are disembodied, we will live in the presence of Christ (Phil 1.23). But beyond that, there is another chapter in the story to tell, and that is the resurrection of the body. We will not remain disembodied. That condition will be temporary and intermediate. To use Paul's language in 2 Corinthians 5.1–5, at death, we are "unclothed" from this body, and in the resurrection, we will be "further clothed" with a new body. We will not remain "naked."

In the Macedonian letters, Paul addresses the future hope of the resurrection primarily in two chapters, 1 Thessalonians 4 and Philippians 3.

"The Dead in Christ Will Rise First" (1 Thessalonians 4)

As Paul begins his treatment of the resurrection in 1 Thessalonians 4, the issue of hope is central. "But we do not want you to be uninformed, brothers, about those who are asleep, that you may not grieve as others do who have no hope" (1 Thess 4.13). Unlike pagans, Christians have hope regarding those who "sleep," a common metaphor in pagan, Jewish, and Christian writings for death (cf. John 11.12–13). Given the fact that the Thessalonians were primarily a Gentile group of Christians (see 1 Thess 2.14), it is understandable that these new Christians were not clear about the nature of this "sleep." Paul assures them that since the sleep of death is not permanent, Christians grieve, but not hopelessly (cf. Phil. 2.27).

This assurance is predicated on the resurrection of Jesus. "For since we believe that Jesus died and rose again, even so, through Jesus, God will bring with him those who have fallen asleep"

---

[2] For more on these views, see my "The Hope of the Resurrection" in *Studies in Church History: Essays in Honor of Daniel W. Petty*, ed. David McClister (Florida College Press, 2020). For a detailed treatment, see N.T. Wright, *The Resurrection of the Son of God* (Minneapolis: Fortress, 2003).

(1 Thess 4.14). It is also founded on the word of Jesus. "For this we declare to you by a word from the Lord" (1 Thess 4.15a), the teaching Jesus gave during his personal ministry (as in John 5.28–29). In deed and word, Jesus guarantees our resurrection, which will occur when he returns.

We who are alive, who are left until the coming of the Lord, will not precede those who have fallen asleep. For the Lord himself will descend from heaven, with a cry of command, with the voice of an archangel, and with the sound of the trumpet of God. And the dead in Christ will rise first. Then we who are alive, who are left, will be caught up together with them in the clouds to meet the Lord in the air, and so we will always be with the Lord (1 Thess 4.15b-17).

To relieve the anxieties of the Thessalonians over their departed brethren, Paul assures them that those who have already died are not at any disadvantage. In the first place, they are with Christ in death, and he will bring them with him when he returns (see v. 14 again). In the second place, "the dead in Christ will rise first," meaning that they will receive their new bodies before Christ transforms those who are alive when he returns. At that point, those who are left will be "caught up together with them." The language of being "caught up" was typically used in pagan writings for being snatched away in death, but to Paul, the "snatching away" for Christians is the gathering up to be with Christ. Christ transforms the language of death into the language of life.

"Therefore encourage one another with these words" (1 Thess 4.18). Here Paul uses a key term in this letter, (*parakaleō*), translated variously as "encourage," "exhort, "urge." This "comfort" (NASB) on the one hand comes from the Lord himself, whose own resurrection and promises are the catalyst for our hope. It also comes from Paul's instructions in this letter. Paul, though, wants the Thessalonians to extend this cycle of comfort/encouragement/exhortation by encouraging "one another." Encouragement on the basis of the hope of the resurrection is a mutual responsibility of God's people.

"Who Will Transform Our Lowly Body" (Philippians 3)

Paul's discussion of the resurrection in Philippians adds more detail as to the nature of the resurrection body. He begins by expressing his single-minded desire to know Christ Jesus, including "the power of his resurrection" (Phil 3.8, 10a). He is willing to "share his sufferings, becoming like him in his death, that by any means possible I may attain the resurrection from the dead" (3.10b-11).[3] Paul exhorts the Philippians to seek the same goal, especially in light of the "enemies of the cross of Christ" that oppose the gospel (3.19; cf. 1.28). In contrast to these opponents whose "end is destruction" because their minds are "set on earthly things" (3.19), the people of Christ have a different mission and end: "But our citizenship is in heaven" (3.20a).

Paul began the letter by reminding these disciples of their heavenly citizenship, though most English translations obscure this. In 1.27, Paul urges the Philippians, "Only let your manner of life be worthy of the gospel of Christ." The primary definition of the term translated as "manner of life" (*politeuomai*) has to do with one's citizenship (see the ESV footnote). The *New Living Translation* says, "Above all, you must live as citizens of heaven, conducting yourselves in a manner worthy of the Good News about Christ." It is possible that Paul stresses the heavenly citizenship of these disciples because they lived in a city that was proud of its status as a Roman colony. Roman citizenship was a tool Paul used for the sake of the gospel, including in his initial work at Philippi (Acts 16.37–39). However, Roman citizenship was not his primary identity, and it was not to be that of the Philippians.

Their identity and their destiny are in heaven. "But our citizenship is in heaven, and from it we await a Savior, the Lord Jesus

---

[3] In the Thessalonian and Philippian texts, Paul does not address the issue of the resurrection of those outside of Christ. This does not mean that Paul did not believe in the general resurrection—he clearly did (cf. Acts 24.15). The better explanation is that what was at issue in both letters (explicitly in 1 Thessalonians and implicitly in Philippians) was the fate of the dead in Christ specifically, and Paul's comments were confined to the relevant issue.

Christ, who will transform our lowly body to be like his glorious body, by the power that enables him even to subject all things to himself" (3.20–21). The terms Paul uses here for Christ—"savior" and "lord"—were often used of Roman emperors, but the true Savior and Lord will conquer the enemy that no earthly ruler ever could. He will raise his people from the dead, just as he himself conquered death. This will not simply be a resuscitation. It will be a transformation. Christ will transform "our lowly body to be like his glorious body."

One of the reasons the Sadducees questioned the truth of the resurrection is because they assumed that the state of affairs after the resurrection would be exactly the same as the state of affairs before the resurrection (see Luke 20.27–33). This is why Jesus rebukes their failure to understand the power of God, as well as their failure to understand the Scriptures (Matt 22.29). Those who are raised from the dead "cannot die any more because they are equal to angels and are sons of God," according to Jesus (Luke 20.36). This new state of affairs is made possible by the power of God. A similar objection seems to have been behind the denials of the resurrection among those in Corinth who asked questions like, "How are the dead raised?" (1 Cor 15.35). Paul points to God's power as the reply to this question (1 Cor 15.38).

In Philippians 3.21, Paul says Christ will transform us to be like him in the resurrection "by the power that enables him even to subject all things to himself." In this text, Paul does not give us much information about the precise nature of this transformed bodily existence other than to say that it will be "glorious" rather than "lowly." There are philosophical and cultural factors present in our own time that downplay the value of our embodied existence, just as there were in Paul's day. Because of this, I want to stress that whatever the nature of this transformation, it will be a *bodily* transformation. Christ rose from the grave bodily, and so will we. His body was transformed, but it was still a body. The same will be true of us (1 Cor. 15.42–44).

Death is not the end of the story, and neither is life after death. There is a glorious existence that unites all of those in Christ with Christ—a bodily resurrection like his. "When, blessed and glorified,/ the flesh is robed about us once again, / we shall be lovelier for being whole" (Dante, *Paradise*, 14.43–45). That loveliness "for being whole," for once again dwelling body plus soul as God intended, is a crucial component to the comfort the doctrine of the resurrection affords. We will be with those we love once more, and they will not be mere phantasms or ghosts. They will be whole. After describing the glory of the resurrection body, the poet Dante says this about the response of those awaiting the resurrection in God's presence:

> So prompt and ready was the loud "Amen!"
> both choirs responded, it was clear to me
> how much they yearned to see their flesh again,
> Maybe less for themselves than for their mamas,
> their fathers, and the others they held dear
> before they had become eternal flames (*Paradise* 14.61–66).

Those who die, according to Paul, depart to be with Christ and await this final act in the drama of redemption. We will now turn to the moment when Paul says this will occur—the second coming.

The Second Coming

Although I am treating the resurrection and the second coming separately, the two events are part of the same package of hope. This is clear in both texts I just examined. 1 Thessalonians 4.15b identifies the timing of the resurrection as taking place at the "coming of the Lord." Likewise, in Philippians 3.20–21 Paul says that we "await a Savior" who will raise and transform our bodies. The return of Jesus will usher in the transformation of death into life.

"For the Lord Himself Will Descend" (1 Thessalonians 4)
In the Thessalonian letters, the term Paul most frequently uses to describe the second coming is *parousia* (1 Thess 2.19; 3.13; 4.15;

5.23; 2 Thess 2.1, 8, 9). It can refer to the sudden manifestation of the power of a deity, and it can also refer to the visit of a person of high rank, such as a king. The combination of these images made *parousia* the perfect term for Paul to describe the second coming. In 1 Thessalonians 4.13–18, Paul extends this imagery in his depiction of the second coming. Just as a delegation of dignitaries would go out to meet the official retinue of a king and welcome him into the city (cf. Acts 28.15), Paul says that when the Lord comes, he will be greeted by those he raises from the dead.

For the Lord himself will descend from heaven with a cry of command, with the voice of an archangel, and with the sound of the trumpet of God. And the dead in Christ will rise first. Then we who are alive, who are left, will be caught up together with them in the clouds to meet the Lord in the air, and so we will always be with the Lord (1 Thess 4.16–17).

Some interpreters contend that this passage assumes two separate events will take place in connection with the second coming. The first event is an invisible coming of Jesus to carry Christians (living and dead) away to heaven, called the "rapture." This event will signal the beginning of a period of intense tribulation lasting seven years, at the end of which Jesus will return visibly and rule the world from Jerusalem for a thousand years.[4] Rapture theorists hold that the first/invisible coming will be "for the saints," and the second/invisible coming with be "with the saints."[5]

It is ironic that 1 Thessalonians 4 is the chief proof text of a theory that says Christ will return secretly and invisibly, given that this is one of the "noisiest" passages in the New Testament.[6] "For the Lord himself will descend from heaven with a cry of command, with the

---

[4] This is part of a larger eschatological system known as *dispensational premillennialism*. There are some writers who do not hold to this system who use the term *rapture* to describe the second coming.

[5] For a more recent defense of this view, see Craig A. Blaising, "The Day of the Lord and the Rapture," *Bibliotheca Sacra* 169 (July-September 2012): 259–270.

[6] This point is not original to me, but I cannot recall its source.

voice of an archangel, and with the sound of the trumpet of God" (v. 16). While Paul does distinguish those that Jesus "will bring with him" from those "who are left," it is clear in the text that Paul is not describing two separate events. At one time, Jesus will come *with* those who have already died and come *for* those who remain.[7]

Paul's first-person language in 1 Thessalonians 4.15 ("*we* who are alive") has also been misinterpreted by some to mean that Paul believed that the *parousia* would occur in his lifetime. Others take this a step further and argue that the *parousia* did, in fact, occur while Paul was alive, identifying it with the destruction of the temple in Jerusalem in AD 70. Those who hold this position deny that there will be a future second coming of Jesus.[8]

While it is certainly the case that Paul thought it was possible that he would be alive at the return of Christ, he also acknowledges in 1 Thessalonians 5.10 that he may be dead at the Lord's return ("so that whether we are awake or asleep we might live with him"). In other passages, such as 1 Corinthians 6.14, Paul uses similar first-person language as he contemplates being raised from the dead rather than remaining alive until the return of Christ. Since Paul believed that Christ would return but did not know the exact moment of that return, he uses language in his letters about the second coming (and resurrection) that is inclusive but not decisive regarding his own status. On one point, however, Paul is dogmatic. Because the *parousia* is also the time of the resurrection, if the dead have not been raised, the *parousia* has not taken place.

"The Day of the Lord Will Come Like a Thief" (1 Thessalonians 5)

The uncertain timing of the second coming is the focus of 1 Thessalonians 5.1–11. Paul begins with a simple analogy: "Now concerning

---

[7] The lack of textual support for the rapture theory explains why it emerged so late in church history. See https://www.thegospelcoalition.org/article/will-christians-be-left-behind/.

[8] This view is called full preterism (from the Latin term for the *past, praeter*). It is also commonly called the "AD 70 doctrine."

the times and the seasons, brothers, you have no need to have anything written to you. For you yourselves are fully aware that the day of the Lord will come like a thief in the night" (1 Thess 5.1–2). Just as a homeowner cannot predict when a thief will break into their home, we cannot predict when Jesus will return. We do not know the "times and seasons" ("times and dates," NIV) of the *parousia*. This is not a new truth for the Thessalonians ("you have no need to have anything written to you"). Paul had already taught them about the uncertain timing of the Lord's return.

Jesus (Matt 24.43–44) and Peter (2 Pet 3.10) use the same illustration of the coming of a thief to express the surprising timing of the "day of the Lord." In the case of Jesus' use of this simile, it is possible that he was describing the judgment on the temple in Jerusalem. This is because the expression, "the day of the Lord," may refer to God's judgments in history (such as the judgment on Babylon in Isaiah 13.6) as well as to the ultimate "day of the Lord" at the end of history. Since all judgments have certain features in common—including catastrophic suddenness—it stands to reason that the same kind of language and illustrations may be used for temporal "days of the Lord" as well as the final "day of the Lord."[9]

In verse three, Paul shifts to a different word picture. "While people are saying, 'There is peace and security,' then sudden destruction will come upon them as labor pains come upon a pregnant woman, and they will not escape." Just as an expectant mother may have a due date but may also go into labor at any time, history has a "due date." That date is unknown to us but known to God. When his Son returns, "sudden destruction" will come upon those who have not obeyed the gospel.

Those who love the Lord and long for his return will not be taken by surprise, though. "But you are not in darkness, brothers, for that day to surprise you like a thief. For you are all children of light, chil-

---

[9] My great teacher Phil Roberts liked to say that the "day of the Lord" is more of a *what* than a *when*.

dren of the day. We are not of the night or of the darkness. So then let us not sleep, as others do, but let us keep awake and be sober" (1 Thess 5.4–5). On the one hand, the day of the Lord will be a surprise for believers in the sense that none of us knows precisely when it will occur. But it will be a pleasant surprise, not a traumatic surprise like the larceny of a home or the emergency delivery of a child. Since the Thessalonians love the Lord and listen to him, they are in neither moral nor intellectual darkness. They will not be caught unaware of the Lord's return should it happen in their lifetime, so long as they remain vigilant (1 Thess 5.6–10).

As Paul brings this discussion of the second coming to a close, he stresses that the *parousia* is not simply about an event, but about a person. "Whether we are awake or asleep we might live *with him*" (v. 10). Just as the significance of a wedding is about the relationship of the wedded rather than the date of the event, the hope of the second coming is centered on the one who is coming, the Lord Jesus. This prospect, eternal union in Christ, should encourage and fortify us (5.11), just as the hope of the resurrection does (cf. 4.18).

Times of suffering accentuate the need for such hope, similar to the times facing the Thessalonians. In his first letter to them, Paul reflects on the opposition the fledgling Christians faced from their pagan community (1 Thess 2.14). At the start of the second letter, Paul again commends them for their endurance. "Therefore we ourselves boast about you in the churches of God for your steadfastness and faith in all your persecutions and in the afflictions that you are enduring" (2 Thess 1.4). Here, he speaks of persecution in the present tense, which may indicate a new outbreak of hostility.

Persecution will not last indefinitely, however. When the Lord comes for his people, he will punish those who have done harm to those he loves.

God considers it just to repay with affliction those who afflict you, and to grant relief to you who are afflicted as well as to us, when the Lord Jesus is revealed from heaven with his mighty angels in flaming fire, inflicting vengeance on those who do not know God and on those who do not obey the gospel of our Lord Jesus. They will suffer the punishment of eternal destruction, away from the presence of the Lord and from the glory of his might, when he comes on that day to be glorified in his saints, and to be marveled at among all who have believed, because our testimony to you was believed (2 Thess 1.6–10).

Judgment in the Bible is both punitive and redemptive. The deliverance of the people of Israel and the destruction of the armies of Pharaoh were two sides of the same coin of salvation. Similarly, the second coming will mean redemption for some, and it will mean retribution for others. Those who "marvel" at the return of Christ because they believe the apostolic testimony will be delivered, and those who do not will be destroyed.

"He... Will Bring It to Completion at the Day of Jesus Christ" (Philippians 1)

Paul also mentions active opposition to the gospel in his letter to the Philippians (Phil 1.28). Since the Philippian letter was written several years after the Thessalonian correspondence, it is unclear whether the conflict Paul mentions in it is the continuation of long-lasting antagonism toward the gospel in Macedonia, or whether it reflects a more recent flare-up of hostility. Regardless, he sees the faithfulness of the Philippians in the midst of suffering in the same light as that of the Thessalonians—a "clear sign" of salvation for them and destruction for their enemies (Phil 1.28; cf. 2 Thess 1.5).

This salvation will be revealed at the second coming, which in Philippians Paul calls the "day of Christ" (1.10; 2.16) or the "day of Jesus Christ" (1.6). Paul's language draws upon the "day of the LORD" phraseology of the Old Testament and applies it to Jesus Christ, implicitly identifying Jesus with the LORD of the Old Testament (cf. Phil 2.9–11). As Lord, Christ is sovereign, and his sovereignty over history means that what he has initiated in history, he will also bring to completion at the end of history in his own time (Phil 1.6).

There were those among the Thessalonians, however, who were unsettled by the question of the timing of the end. If the day of the Lord could occur at any time, some of the brethren there wondered if it was possible that it had already occurred. Paul addresses this matter in 2 Thessalonians 2 with reference to one of the most enigmatic figures in all of Scripture, the "man of lawlessness."

2 Thessalonians 2 and the Man of Lawlessness

The consternation among the disciples was created "by a spirit or a spoken word, or a letter seeming to be from us" (2.2). "A spirit" refers to an alleged prophetic message ("prophecy," NIV; see 1 Thess. 5.19–21; cf. 1 John 4.1–3). "A spoken word" is either a message from another teacher or someone's misconstrual of Paul's own message. "A letter seeming to be from us" could refer to a forgery or to a distortion of a letter Paul actually wrote. Whatever the source of this misinformation, if indeed the day of the Lord had dawned, nothing would remain for God to do. And if God's purposes were indeed consummated, then there was no further hope for the Thessalonians to find relief from the Lord in the midst of their affliction. No wonder they were shaken and alarmed!

"Unless the Rebellion and the Man of Lawlessness Is Revealed"

To reassure them that this is not, in fact, the case, Paul reminds the Thessalonians of two events he had previously told them would occur (cf. 2.5). Since neither had taken place at the time of Paul's writing, it simply was not possible that the day of the Lord had come. The two events are the "rebellion" and the revelation of the "man of lawlessness" (2.3). The basic point of this passage is that these two events, which were to take place within history, had not yet occurred and, consequently, the day of the Lord at the end of history could not have occurred, either.

What is much more complicated is identifying the "rebellion" and the "man of lawlessness," as well as their relationship to the second coming. Is Paul saying that the rebellion and revelation of the man of lawlessness will occur far from the time of the Thessalonians into the future and shortly before the Lord's return? Or is Paul saying that the rebellion and man of lawlessness will appear in the time of the Thessalonians, before the coming of the Lord? I believe the latter is the case. Paul's teaching here must be connected to events that the Thessalonians were themselves experiencing. This chapter was not about something remotely future to the Thessalonians, but something they were already experiencing. Notice the reference to what they know is happening "now" (2.6, 7) and to what is "already at work" (2.7). If this is the case, to what does the "rebellion" refer, and to whom does the "man of lawlessness" refer?

The term Paul uses for "rebellion" (*apostasia*) can refer to a political rebellion or a religious apostasy. Neither were in short supply in the time frame of the first century. In view of the many imminent warnings in the New Testament about a falling away from the faith (such as Matt 24.10–12 and Acts 20.28–32), I will assume that Paul has spiritual rebellion in mind.

Far more difficult to identify is the "man of lawlessness," whom Paul also calls the "son of destruction." Those who believe that Paul has a figure in mind, far distant from the time of the Thessalonians, often connect the "man of lawlessness" with two other sinister personalities in the New Testament, the "Antichrist" in the letters of John (1 John 2.18, 22; 4.3; 2 John 1.7) and the "Beast" of Revelation 13. According to this interpretation, the Antichrist will be a world leader who epitomizes evil, unleashing persecution on the church shortly before the coming of the Lord.[10] Since the time of the Reformation, another common interpretation among Protestants has been to identify the "man of lawlessness" with the papacy.[11] Paul's description of this diabolical figure points in a different direction.

---

[10] This is the view of dispensational premillennialists as well as many amillennialists, such as Anthony Hoekema. See his *The Bible and the Future* (Grand Rapids: Eerdmans, 1979), 154–162.

[11] Martin Luther was fascinated by the topic of the Antichrist, whom he identified as the Pope. This has been a common position among Lutherans historically. See

According to Paul, the man of lawlessness "opposes and exalts himself against every so-called god or object of worship, so that he takes his seat in the temple of God, proclaiming himself to be God" (2.4). This language is derived from Daniel 11.31–36, a prophecy about a king in the intertestamental period named Antiochus IV, infamous in Jewish history for desecrating the temple and exalting himself as a god. He took the name Antiochus *Epiphanes*, "God Manifest" (the Jews called him *Epimanes*, "The Mad Man"). Just as Jesus drew from another related section of Daniel to warn about the desecration of the temple by the Romans (using Daniel 9.27 in Matthew 24.15), Paul is taking descriptions of one pagan persecutor of God's people in the past to describe a pagan persecutor in the future—Rome. In other words, what Paul is describing in 2 Thessalonians 2 is the same thing John pictured in Revelation 13.

John (using another passage from Daniel, Daniel 7.15–22) sees Rome, in general, and Nero, in particular, as a beastly enemy, doing the bidding of Satan in deceiving the world into idolatry and persecuting God's people. Paul anticipates the same development here.[12]

The seeds of this sort of exaltation and persecution by the emperors had already been sown. In the generation before the birth of

---

Charles A. Gieschen, "Antichrist in the Scriptures and the Lutheran Confessions: The Relevance of Reformation Exegesis of 2 Thessalonians 2.1–12 for the Church Today, *Concordia Theological Quarterly* 81 (2017), esp. 263–268. The identification of the Pope has also been a popular interpretation in the Restoration Movement. For instance, it was the view of Alexander Campbell. See John Davis Jones, "Stone, Campbell, and the Man of Sin," *Restoration Quarterly* 61 (2019): 160–166. In their commentary on 2 Thessalonians, J.W. McGarvey and Philip Y. Pendleton conclude, "In short, while we will not attempt to say that the final form of antichrist, Papal or otherwise, may not exceed in wickedness all that we have yet seen (for prophecies are certainly iterative), yet we are constrained to contend that if no other form appears, the Papacy has already fulfilled the prophecy" (*Thessalonians, Corinthians, Galatians and Romans* [Cincinnati: Standard Publishing Company, 1916]), 41.

[12] For a survey of the historical data connecting the "man of lawlessness" with the imperial cult, see D. Clint Burnett, "'Seated in God's Temple': Explicating 2 Thess 2.4 from Epigraphic and Archaeological Sources Connected to Roman Imperial Divine Honors," *Lexington Theological Quarterly* 48 (2018): 69–94.

Christ, the Roman general Pompey dared to enter the holy of holies after his successful siege of Jerusalem (see Josephus, *Antiquities of the Jews* 14.70–71). And just a few years before Paul wrote the Thessalonians, the mad emperor Gaius (better known as "Caligula") announced plans to erect a statue of himself in the Jewish temple, plans which were thwarted when he was assassinated by his own guard.[13] More broadly, the pagan reaction to Paul's ministry in Thessalonica foreshadowed the collision course on which Christianity was set with imperial Rome, when instigators characterized Paul's message as "acting against the decrees of Caesar, saying that there is another king, Jesus" (Acts 17.7). Within this political and religious milieu, the rise of a ruler who would exalt himself as a god and oppose God's people was possible, if not inevitable.[14]

"You Know What Is Restraining Him"

But his time has not yet come. Paul goes on to say, "And you know what is restraining him now so that he may be revealed in his time" (2.6). This presents us with another puzzle—what is the "restraining" power?[15] While this is a puzzle for us, it was not a puzzle for the Thessalonians, since Paul says they knew what it was ("and you know"). If the man of lawlessness is to be identified as Nero and other rulers like him, perhaps the restraining influence is the rule of law that, before his time, maintained a degree of restraint on the persecution

---

[13] For an excellent survey of the biblical and historical context of Paul's language here, see J. Julius Scott, Jr., "Paul and Late-Jewish Eschatology—A Case Study I Thessalonians 4.13–18 and II Thessalonians 2.1–12," *Journal of the Evangelical Theological Society* 15 (Summer 1972): 133–143. On Caligula's scheme and its relevance to 2 Thessalonians 2, see Nicholas H. Taylor, "Caligula, the Church of Antioch, and the Gentile Mission," *Religion and Theology* 7 (2000), 1–23.

[14] An alternative interpretation of the "man of lawlessness" as a first century figure is the view that he is a Jewish opponent of the gospel, such as one of the high priests. For this view, see Gary DeMar, *Last Days Madness* (Atlanta: American Vision, 1994), 311–350.

[15] For a survey of interpretations, see Paul S. Dixon, "The Evil Restraint in 2 Thess 2.6," *Journal of the Evangelical Theological Society* 33 (December 1990): 445–449. Dixon takes the view that the "restrainer" is Satan.

of God's people. This would be consistent with Paul's experiences in the Book of Acts in which Roman law (the "what" of verse 6) and its representatives (the "he" of verse 7) offered some protection for the gospel mission (see Acts 16.36–39; 18.12–17; 19.35–41; 21.31–36; 22.22–29; 23.16–35; 25.11).[16]

At some point, though, there will no longer be such a restraint, and the trends of idolatry and persecution that already exist will converge in the man of lawlessness. "For the mystery of lawlessness is already at work. Only he who now restrains it will do so until he is out of the way. And then the lawless one will be revealed" (2.7–8a). In verses 9–11, Paul says that the man of lawlessness' coming is "by the activity of Satan," by whom he deceives the nations with false signs (again, language strongly reminiscent of John's description of the beasts of Revelation 13). The divinely intended purpose of civil government is to serve God (Rom 13.1–8), but when it assumes for itself the worship of a god, it degenerates into a tool of Satan.

There is one more piece of data we must take into account in this text. In verse 8, Paul explains that the fate of the "man of lawlessness" is destruction by Jesus Christ when he returns: "whom the Lord Jesus will kill with the breath of his mouth and bring to nothing by the appearance of his coming." If I am correct in identifying the "man of lawlessness" as a reference to imperial Rome and its rulers, what are we to make of Paul's reference to his destruction at the Lord's return? Rome has long ceased to be a political power,

---

[16] The term translated "restrains" can also mean "prevails." See Jason Longstreth's very helpful comments in "Paul's View of the End" in *From the Pen of Paul*, 2nd ed., edited by Nathan Ward (Temple Terrace FL: Florida College Press, 2022), 178–179. For a detailed discussion of the options, see Charles H. Giblin, *The Threat to Faith: An Exegetical and Theological Re-Examination of 2 Thessalonians 2*, Vol. 31 (Analecta Biblica. Rome: Pontifical Biblical Institute, 1967); Jon A. Weatherly, *1 & 2 Thessalonians*, The College Press NIV Commentary (Joplin, MO: College Press Pub. Co., 1996); Charles A. Wanamaker, *The Epistles to the Thessalonians: A Commentary on the Greek Text*, New International Greek Testament Commentary (Grand Rapids, MI: W.B. Eerdmans, 1990); Ernest Best, *The First and Second Epistles to the Thessalonians*, Black's New Testament Commentary (London: Continuum, 1986).

yet Christ has not returned.[17] This is a primary reason many interpreters object to an identification of the "man of lawlessness" as a contemporary figure of the Thessalonians.

However, this objection assumes that the revelation of the man of lawlessness and the appearance of Jesus Christ must be in close chronological proximity. The text does not say this. Paul does list the two events in close sequential order, but he does not give any time indicators addressing the relationship between the two. Indeed, it is common in prophetic passages in Scripture to bundle together several events in close sequential order that occur in distant chronological order. For instance, Jeremiah packages together the return from Babylonian exile and the establishment of the new covenant in the same message in Jeremiah 31.[18] It is the *sequence* of events that Paul is emphasizing in 2 Thessalonians. The day of the Lord could not have come yet because certain events that Paul had previously mentioned to the Thessalonians have yet to take place. But once those events occur, the only chronological information about the Lord's appearance that Paul shares with the Thessalonians is that which he previously detailed in 1 Thessalonians 5.1–11. No one knows the "times and seasons."

The fact that the "man of lawlessness" was a figure proximate to the time of the Thessalonians does not preclude the possibility of the rise of a malevolent world leader in the future. Remember, Paul's description of the "man of lawlessness" in 2 Thessalonians 2 draws from a wide array of biblical and historical precedents. But whatever forces may yet be revealed against God and his people, their fate will be the same.

---

[17] Some interpreters argue that the "coming" in 2 Thessalonians 2 is a coming in judgment in history rather than the second coming at the end of history. See Kenneth Gentry, *Perilous Times: A Study of Eschatological Evil* (Covenant Media Press, 1999), 137–138. I do not believe this is correct since Paul's reference to the coming in judgment in 2 Thessalonians 2 is in the same immediate context as the second coming in 2 Thessalonians 1.

[18] Hoekema refers to this as "prophetic perspective" (*The Bible and the Future* 9, 11, 148–149).

God will judge, during history and finally at the end of history itself, the imperial systems that put themselves in his place. There have been enough of these in our own recent past for us to see something of the way they operate, the deceits they weave, and the way in which people get caught up in the web of their lies. What Paul would have us urgently grasp is the fact that God remains sovereign over all, and will one day put all wrongs to rights, and bring all human empires under the rule and judgment of his own saving kingdom.[19]

Just as his teaching regarding the resurrection and the second coming was designed to elicit hope for his readers, Paul follows his description of the rise and destruction of these dark forces with a word of encouragement. "Now may our Lord Jesus Christ himself, and God our Father, who loved us and gave us eternal comfort and good hope through grace, comfort your hearts and establish them in every good work and word" (2 Thess 2.16–17).

The challenges facing the Thessalonians and Philippians were the same kinds of challenges facing us: evil, hostility, and suffering. Our experience of these realities at the moment may differ in degree, but not in kind. Many of us have a gnawing sense that darker times lie ahead for God's people, but this is no reason for resignation or despair. History is going somewhere, and its destination is Jesus. In the meantime, our path from here to eternity—from here to Him—is hope that is worthy of the gospel.

---

[19] Tom Wright, *Paul for Everyone: Galatians and Thessalonians* (London: Society for Promoting Christian Knowledge, 2004), 149.

Contributors

Trevor Brailey ('94) has been married to Sharon (Pratte, '93) for twenty-five years. He graduated from Florida College with an A.A. degree before obtaining a B.S.E.E. degree at the University of South Florida. He was an engineer for seven years before preaching full-time. He has worked with the Hillcrest Church of Christ in Utica, Ohio, for eighteen years. He and Sharon have four children; Brian is a graduate of Florida College ('22), Joy is a current student, and Grace and Melody may be headed there in the next few years. Trevor also works as a substitute teacher, which has helped him write a Bible workbook called *Growing Up in the 2020s*. His other interests include understanding the Bible's use of logic in interpretation, learning Biblical languages, and preaching in India. His email address is trevor.brailey.17@gmail.com.

Daniel Broadwell ('12) lives in Houston, Texas with his wife, Elizabeth, and son, Asher. Originally from Atlanta, Georgia, he graduated from Florida College in 2012 with a bachelor's degree in Liberal Studies. After teaching elementary school in Tulsa, Oklahoma for two years, he moved to the Houston area for a training program at the Kleinwood church of Christ. He currently works as an evangelist and Bible teacher with the Bellaire church of Christ in southwest Houston. In 2019, Daniel earned a Master of Liberal Arts degree from Houston Baptist University, which he has used to do some adjunct teaching in the humanities. If you would like to contact Daniel, he can be reached at danieljady@gmail.com.

Jonathan Brown ('97) was born and raised in Columbus, Mississippi. He graduated from Florida College in 1997 with a B.A. in Biblical Studies. He has been married to his wife, Alena (Beltz, class of '97), for 25 years. The Lord has blessed him with 8 children and one grandson. Jonathan has worked with churches in Lincoln, NE, and Zanesville, OH, and is currently preaching and serving as an elder in Owensboro, KY.

Andy Cantrell lives in Champlin, Minnesota with his wife Claire and two sons, Cade and Chay. A native of San Diego, California, he has worked alongside Christians in Fayetteville, Arkansas (1996–1997), North Hills, California (1998–2006), and New Hope, Minnesota (2006–present).

Todd Chandler ('93) and his wife Jeannie (Payne, '92) have been married 29 years and are blessed with four children and two daughters in law: Timothy and Beth (McKee), Daniel and Farley (Wood), Micah, and Kayla. Currently, Todd teaches biology courses as a full-time faculty member at Florida College and previously served as the Mathematics and Science Department Chair, the Pre-Professional Health Science Coordinator, and the Associate Academic Dean for Student Affairs. Todd graduated from Florida College (A.A., 1993), the University of Florida (B.S. 1996; M.Ed. 1997), and Western Kentucky University (M.S. 2006). He worked in a preaching training program at the Glen Springs Road congregation in Gainesville, FL, preached full-time for ten years for the West End congregation in Bowling Green, KY and part-time for five years at the Livingston Ave. congregation in Lutz, FL and continues to preach meetings. Todd has spoken on the FC lectureship twice before and is published in the 2013 lecture book *He was Raised and Appeared*. He has one academic publication in the *Journal of Plant Physiology and Biochemistry* (2014). Todd has a special interest in the evolution and creation discussion and has presented on that topic on the campus of USF and UF and in various congregations.

Terry Francis ('95) was born January 7, 1975 in Murfreesboro, TN. He and his wife, DewAnn (FC class of 1992), have four children: Peyton (23, FC 2018–20), Jillian (18, current freshman at FC), and Jamison (15). Terry attended Florida College (A.A. 1995) and Western Kentucky University. He trained under Wilson Adams at the Riverside Drive Church of Christ in the summer of 1997. He has worked with the New Hope Church of Christ in Fairview, TN (1998–2004); the Hillview Church of Christ in Nashville, TN (2004–2007); the East Shelby Church of Christ in Collierville, TN (2004–2018); and now currently works with the Chelsea Church of Christ in Chelsea, AL. His address is 300 Emerald Lane, Chelsea, AL 35043.

Jared Hagan ('97) met his wife, Bonnie (McCowan), at a Gospel Meeting in Denver when they were in high school. He received a Bachelor of Arts in Biblical Studies from Florida College in 1997, graduating in the first accredited class to receive this degree. He preached at Northside church of Christ in Colorado Springs, Colorado for twenty-five years and has recently accepted a position with the Brookhill church of Christ in Killen, Alabama.

Benjamin Lee has been preaching the gospel since 2001. After working for eight years for Pfizer Pharmaceuticals and preaching part time, Benjamin decided to devote his life to preaching the gospel in 2009. Benjamin began working with the West Main Church of Christ in Lewisville Texas (www.westmaincoc.com) on March 1, 2018. He and his wife Nikki have been married for 18 years. They have an 11-year-old son named Joshua. Benjamin is passionate about faith, family, fitness, and food. He has had the opportunity to preach and teach in Africa, Mexico, and throughout the U.S. You can find his sermons, blogs, books, and I Can Do Podcast at www.benjaminlee.blog.

Phillip Martin was born and raised in Northern California. Since 1998 he has worked with local churches in Louisiana, Oregon, Tennessee, and Georgia, and has aided in Evangelistic Work in St. Croix, Barbados, and the Philippines. In 2017, he began working with the Eastside church in Sharpsburg, Georgia. Alongside his work as a minister, he has consulted with a number of churches as they developed their in-house digital media teams and support. He expects to complete an M.A. in Bible: Old Testament at Amridge University in May of 2023. Phillip and his wife Jill have three children: Jesse, Halle, and James. He can be contacted at: pwmartin@gospeldefender.com.

Mark Reeves ('84) was born in San Antonio, Texas, on May 25, 1964. He married Carmen (Rivadeneira) in 1998. The Reeves have two children, Luke (2022 graduate of Florida College) and Sabrina (currently enrolled at Florida College). After receiving the A.A. at Florida College (1984), Mark studied at FC for an additional year in the upper division Bible program (1984–85). His preaching has been with churches in Duff, Indiana (1986–89), New Braunfels, Texas (1989–97), and Studebaker Road in Long Beach, California (1997–present). Since 2015 he has also been serving as one of the Studebaker Road elders. He has travelled frequently to preach in Mexico, Central and South America, and Spain. He can be reached at markhreeves@gmail.com.

Shane Scott ('89) was born and raised in Winchester, KY. He attended Florida College from 1985–1989, earning the four-year Bible diploma. After graduating, he began preaching in central Kentucky, and since then his local work has taken him to Chicagoland and to Nashville. Currently, he preaches in our area for the Valrico congregation. Shane served on the Biblical Studies faculty in 1998–2001 and is excited to return to the classroom this year. In his spare time, Shane is an avid Kentucky Wildcats fan, and also enjoys singing barbershop.

Adam Shanks serves as the evangelist for the Edwards Lake Church of Christ in Birmingham, AL, having served there for three years. He has previously worked with congregations in Florida, Tennessee, and Alabama. He and his wife Tiffany are both four-year graduates of Florida College and they are raising five wonderful children. He and his wife have recently been appointed the directors of the FCAL summer camp and they spend most of their free time making plans for this upcoming "best week of the year." He has written several workbooks and books, including *In God We Trust* and *Laying the Tracks*. You can find out more about his writing or contact information on his website (edenhollow.com).

Collin Stringer ('85) was born on November 8, 1964 in Nashville Tennessee. He and his wife, Jori (Sasser), also an FC Alumnus, have three daughters: Rachel, Anna, and Naomi. Collin received an AA Degree from Florida College in 1985 and a Bachelor of Arts Degree from the University of North Alabama in Secondary Education in 1988. He has preached for churches in Florence, Alabama; Anderson, Alabama; Brno, Czech Republic; Fort Collins, Colorado; Lawrenceburg, Tennessee; Columbia, Missouri; and presently Tustin, California. He has written articles published in *Christianity Magazine* and currently lives at 9025 N. Valleyview Street, Orange, CA 92865.

Travis Walker ('92) was born in Portland, Oregon, and grew up on the west coast. He attended Florida College earning his A.A. degree in 1992 and his Advanced Diploma in Religious Studies in 1994. He has been married to Elizabeth (Hatcher) Walker of Indianapolis, Indiana for 26 years. They have three children: Andrew Walker and his wife Rachel reside in Knoxville, Tennessee, Sara (Walker) McClendon (FC 2018–2021) and her husband Nicolas reside in Dawsonville, Georgia, and Jordan Walker (FC 2020-present). Travis has been preaching for 28 years having worked with congregations in Butler, Missouri (1994–1996), Dallas, Oregon (1996–2002), Brea, California (2002–2010), and Clovis, California (2011–2020). Currently, he resides in Midland, Texas, and preaches for the congregation on Billy Hext Rd. in Odessa.

Joseph Ryan Works and his wife Beth have six children: Hannah Jinks (FC, 2012); Miriam Broadwell (FC, 2012); Micah (FC, 2017); Naomi (FC, 2020), Noah (FC, Current student); and Lydia. They also have eight grandchildren. Brother Works has worked with churches in Fairfax, OH; Embu Guaçu, São Paulo, Brazil; Ellisville, MO; Indiatuba, São Paulo, Brazil; Fair Lawn, NJ; Newark, NJ (Portuguese-speaking congregation). Currently he is working with the church in Elmira, NY. He makes regular preaching trips to Lisbon, Portugal and Beira, Mozambique. He has worked with the Northeast FC Camp since 2008. Joe is co-director of the Sons Of Light Bible Camp. He and his family live at the School of Good Works, a former monastery which has been converted into a facility for having Bible camps and weekend Bible lectureships. His address is 1310 West Church St, Elmira, NY 14905.